Cultural Influences on Strategic Planning

Contributions to Economics

Albrecht Ritschl
Prices and Production
- Elements of a System - Theoretic
Perspective -
1989. 159pp. Softcover DM 59,-
ISBN 3-7908-0429-0

Arnulf Grübler
The Rise and Fall of Infrastructures
- Dynamics of Evolution and
Technological Change in Transport -
1990. 305pp. Softcover DM 85,-
ISBN 3-7908-0479-7

Peter R. Haiss

Cultural Influences on Strategic Planning

Empirical Findings in the Banking Industry

With 22 Figures

Springer-Verlag Berlin Heidelberg GmbH

Series Editor
Werner A. Müller

Author
Dr. Peter R. Haiss
Rauscherstraße 21/9
A-1200 Wien/Austria

CIP-Titelaufnahme der Deutschen Bibliothek

Haiss, Peter R.:
Cultural influences on strategic planning: empirical findings in the banking industry / Peter R. Haiss. - Heidelberg: Physica-Verl.; New York; Berlin; Heidelberg; London; Paris; Tokyo; Hong Kong: Springer, 1990
(Contributions to economics)
ISBN 978-3-7908-0481-2 ISBN 978-3-642-49993-7 (eBook)
DOI 10.1007/978-3-642-49993-7

Originally published by Physica-Verlag Heidelberg in 1990.

7100/7130-543210

PREFACE

This book challenges the universal applicability of strategic management concepts. It argues that it is necessary to pay attention to contextual facets of the environment, in particular to societal culture. It also depicts the current planning situation in the banking industry. The culture-boundness of strategy formulation and implementation is challenged and advocated trough discussing planning systems, processes, and heuristics, and contextual influences both on a theoretical basis and with empirical research.

The book is based on my doctoral dissertation, which was completed at the Marketing and Banking Departments of the Vienna University of Economics under the auspices of Fritz Scheuch and Gustav Raab. Their teaching, constructive criticism, and encouragement provided the intellectual stimulation for bringing this dissertation to completion. This applies equally to several professors at the University of Illinois at Urbana-Champaign. Harry Triandis and Anant Negandhi introduced me to cross-cultural research and international management. Howard Thomas, Marjorie Lyles, and Irene Duhaime helped me to crystallize thoughts. Hanns-Martin Schönfeld, Seymour Sudman and Gerald Salancik challenged my thoughts about organizational behavior and methodology. Richard Watson, University of Georgia, and Louis Flores of Northern Illinois University were very helpful in providing address material for Australia and Latin America, as well as through assistance with translations. Norihiro Suzuki of Int'l Christian University, Tokyo, and Hiro Matsusaki of Tokyo University helped with Japanese translations.

I wish to express my sincere appreciation to those who made this study possible. A special acknowledgement is due to the 28 American bank executives who were interviewed during the field research for this study and to the over 500 bank managers who completed the questionnaire. Their enthusiastic cooperation made this phase of the study very rewarding and enjoyable. Special thanks are addressed to the Österreichische Länderbank Aktiengesellschaft, Vienna, which was very helpful in establishing contact with several US banks, and for general support with regard to this book. Of equal importance was the support by David Hubbard, MS, of Harris Bank, Chicago.

I am indebted to the Austrian-American Educational (Fulbright) Commission and the Austrian Federal Chamber of Commerce for Awarding Doctoral Research and Study Grants, as well as the Austria-Illinois Exchange Program for participation, and the Austrian Savings Banks' Research Institute for granting the 1989 Research Award.

Finally, I wish to express my deepest appreciation to my parents, whose tender care, faith, understanding and support has always served as a motivating force in the difficult situation of being a doctoral student and practicing bank planner at the same time. And, to my girlfriend Ulli and several special friends, whose faith, encouragement and patient understanding at critical periods contributed immensely to this research project.

ABSTRACT

This research develops a framework for the investigation of the impact of societal culture on strategic planning processes. It consists of a theoretical and an empirical part.

In the theoretical part, functions of planning are explained and both normative and empirical findings with regard to planning approaches, contextual influences, industry influences, cultural influences, and planning heuristics are reviewed. Amongst the contributions is the development of a conceptual model of planning approaches, a model of cultural influences on the strategic planning process, and a model of non-rational heuristical influences on the process of strategy formulation and implementation. Findings from the streams of Strategic Management, Comparative Management, Organizational Behavior, Psychology, and Banking were integrated in these models.

The empirical part consists of field research undertaken in the banking industry. Interviews were held with 28 American bank executives. More than 500 responses to a self-developed questionnaire were obtained from thirty-three countries on five continents. The responses cover more than one third of the world's largest 550 banks. The goal was to increase the knowledge on bank planning, to investigate industrial and cultural influences on planning practices and to empirically test the Culture-Planning Model and its facets developed in the theoretical part.

From the empirical research undertaken the conclusion is drawn that if industry, company size, and level of the economic development and volatility of the respective countries are held constant, there still remain differences in strategic planning systems (time frames, reasons), heuristics, and processes (characteristics, activities), attributable to cultural influences.

ABOUT THE AUTHOR

Peter R. Haiss holds a doctoral degree with honors in Business Administration (Marketing and Banking) from the Vienna University of Economics, Vienna, Austria (Wirtschaftsuniversität Wien), and an MBA (Marketing and Int'l Business) from the University of Illinois at Urbana-Champaign, IL, U.S.A. He published several articles in marketing and banking journals.

Currently, Peter R. Haiss is with the Strategic Planning Department of Länderbank Vienna, Austria. He also is a lecturer at the Vienna Institute of European Studies, and a freelance writer for the Austrian business magazine Gewinn. He also was with the Marketing and Controlling Departments of Mercedes Benz, Stuttgart, FRG, and New York, U.S.A., as well as with several other companies.

CONTENTS

TABLES

FIGURES

APPENDICES

1 INTRODUCTION

This chapter will briefly describe the research question, its theoretical rationale and the methodological framework that was applied. It pictures the model of basic relationships between groups of variables that were examined and thereby serves as an outline of the whole book. The goal of this chapter is to guide the reader through the following chapters and to explain the links within the three parts of the thesis: planning theory (process, systems, heuristics, context, and culture); method of field research (data collection and analysis), and results (conclusions and recommendations). Basic terms are defined and the importance of the research is put in perspective.

1.1 Theoretical Framework

This section describes the object scope and basic assumptions of the research that was undertaken. It was decided that, in order to characterize the process of the research, it is necessary to describe the content partly. This lays the ground for understanding the way in which operationalizations were developed over time. Units of analysis, the action-context of the investigated managerial tasks, as well as theoretical constructs utilized are delineated.

1.11 Linking Strategy and Comparative Management

It has frequently been proposed that there exists a link between the features of a firm's strategic decision process and its environment (Anderson/Paine 1975; Miller/Friesen 1980; Mintzberg 1978; Mintzberg/Waters 1985). Several studies related the content of strategies to environments (Hambrick/Lei 1985; Jauch/Osborn 1981). Others tied the process of strategy-making to structure and environment. See Huff/Reger (1987) for a recent literature review. Of central concern in the strategy literature is the link between planning and organizational performance. Excellent reviews of this stream of literature can be found in Armstrong (1982), Lorange (1979), and Shrader/Taylor/Dalton (1984). Technology (Woodward 1958; Lawrence/Lorsch 1967), task environment, structure (Chandler 1962), size, organizational culture (Deal/Kennedy 1982) among other factors were investigated with regard to their relation to strategy formulation and implementation.

In yet another stream of literature, the seminal works by Hofstede (1980), Negandhi (1975a; 1987), Negandhi/Prasad (1971), Triandis (1972; 1977) and others brought insight into similarities and differences in managerial behavior and their respective effects. For an overview on the comparative management literature, see Adler (1986) or Adler et al (1986). Again, the impact of environmental facets ranging from technology to national culture were examined. Many of these studies, however, were concerned with differences and similarities in marketing practices (Sheth/Prakash 1981), employee relations and other administrative differences between multinational companies (Negandhi 1975; Negandhi/Welge

1984), control issues (Horovitz 1980) and organizational behavior in a broad sense, not with specific managerial functions.

While the study of values and culture is not new (see, e.g. Parsons 1951; Kluckhohn/Strodtbeck 1961), the impact of the environmental facet "national culture" has only recently been introduced to models of strategic management (Jaeger/Baliga 1985; Tosi/Slocum 1984; Sekaran/Snodgrass 1986a, 1987; Schneider 1989). If there are differences in managerial behavior attributable to culture, these should be observable in any of Fayol's (1972:3) managerial activities, which are planning, organizing, control, and execution (Horovitz 1980:41). Strategic planning, introducing high levels of uncertainty, complexity, and exchange of information to organizations, should specifically be suited to observe these cultural impacts (Hofstede 1980:383; Snodgrass/ Grant 1986; Triandis 1983:156).

We still do not have knowledge of a systematic relationship between specific dimensions of culture and the specific managerial task of strategy development and planning, as only a few empirical studies were completed in this emerging field (Kagona et al 1985; Horovitz 1980; Negandhi 1987; Rieger/Wong-Rieger 1984). The current model development and empirical research was undertaken to fill this void. It covers the planning practices of 372 banks in five continents, including one third of the worlds' biggest 550 banks.[1] Given that senior executives of most firms have to do business in multi-cultural environments, cultural influences on the critical managerial function "planning" should be of vital interest to both practitioners and theoreticians in order to increase the effectiveness of the planning process.

1.12 Purpose and Clarification of the Subject

The purpose of this thesis is to provide information on the influence of national culture on strategic planning practices.[2] The study argues that national culture can influence the strategic planning process of firms in a given industry, with a given size, technology and level of development, as it impacts planning systems, processes, and heuristics.[3] It addresses the question,

[1] Why the banking industry was chosen for this research is explained in section 1.31 Referent.

[2] The terms "strategic planning" and "planning" will be used synonymously. In case references are made to other forms of planning, this will be shown by depicting terms, e.g. operational planning or tactical planning.

[3] The terms country, nation, and culture are not always synonumous. And, there are cultural differences within countries (Seeger et al 1987). As in most comparative management studies, national boundaries are accepted as surrogate definitions for culture. See Adler (1984:48) for further discussion of this methodological problem.

whether or not strategic planning frameworks are culture bound.[4]

The basic assumption here is, that in spite of size, technology, industry and other contextual factors of strategy formulation, firms in different cultural settings will approach the managerial function "planning" in ways which mirror underlying cultural values, cognitions, perceptions, and behaviors (Snodgrass/Grant 1986:207; Triandis 1984). Preferred modes of action, for example in information selection, interpretation and priorization approaches, as well as decision making, are influenced by culture (Child 1981).

Culture, consequently has two effects on the planning process: it influences the planning framework and it affects the measures managers use to evaluate it. "Although the end result, the strategic decision, may be the same, the process by which it is arrived at will be different (Schneider 1988:5). This will be further explained in the chapter on culture.

1.13 Object Scope and Approach

The focus of this study is on one domain of managerial activities, that of the strategic planning process, i.e. the procedures, formal and informal interactions for formulating and implementing business and corporate strategies during the whole input-through-put-output-cycle (Katz/Kahn 1966).

To study processes, merely by looking at "results" or "events" is not appropriate as it neglects the flow of choices and their implementation that lead to the outcome (Burgelman 1985:85). One should also include the structure that forms the processes and heuristics that "happen" during the planning processes as major influencing factors (Bettinger 1986; Ramunajam et al 1986a, 1986b). In a similar context Bettinger (1986:18) finds that "It is not the strategic planning process itself that makes the difference, but the way in which the process is conceptualized, implemented and managed."

Structure, process and heuristics themselves are influenced by cultural factors (Adler 1986:134; Adler/ Selnicek 1986; Miller 1984:70; Redding 1980; Quinn/McGrath 1985; Schein 1985:82; Sekaran 1986:20; Sheth/Sethi 1981:381; Triandis 1984:305; Wright/Phillips 1980:239).

To overcome these problems, the environment-organization-effectiveness paradigm (Downey/Ireland 1979:630) was applied here. Regarding the organization as an open system (e.g. Lawrence 1981), it was found possible (Negandhi 1986:3) to describe planning frameworks [F] as a function of environmental constraints [C]:

---

[4] Putting the emphasis on the cultural element in planning is no attempt to reduce all dissimilarities across companies to culture. However, it questions the position of universal rationality of planning systems and processes assumed by many authors.

F = f(C1 ...Cn), following Farmer/Richman (1964:58), with managers as intervening variables (Weigele 1983:82). Industry, political, economic, cultural, technological and legal context influence the structure of planning systems, and the heuristics that are part of it (Hambrick/Lei 1985; Litschert/Nicholson 1974; Robinson 1983; Negandhi 1987:228: Scott 1981:165). In this contingency view of strategy (Hambrick/Lei 1985:764;), both systems and heuristics influence managerial processes. Hirsch (1975) in his "industry system model" and Negandhi (1983b) used similar perspectives including both open and closed system variables (contextual, environmental and sociocultural factors) in his "integrating model" (Negandhi 1983:21).

Therefore, several indicators for strategic planning frameworks have been explored empirically: strategic planning systems were defined through their time horizon, structure, and reasons (goals). Heuristics were represented by schemas, assumptions and behavioral aspects. The planning process was depicted by its characteristics and activities. As the focus here is on the impact of culture on planning, Hofstedes' (1980) empirically derived dimensions that "provide a good framework" (Hunt 1981:56), "make sense" (Triandis 1982:90) and are widely used in the literature (Adler 1986:35; Birnbaum/Wong 1985; Bosland 1985; England 1983; Jaeger 1986; Jackofsky et al 1988; Miner 1984; Sekaran/Snodgrass 1987; Triandis 1984; Westwood/Everett 1987) were the starting point for conceptualizations of terms, and for linking systems, heuristics, process, industry and culture.[5]

These dimensions, however, were not just applied in their pure sense. The value-cognition model of Kluckhohn/Strodtbeck (1961), and the findings of Glenn (1981) and Sullivan/Nonaka (1986, 1988) about information processing perceptions and behaviors were integrated to form the "Culture-Planning Model." It is briefly depicted below. For an in-depth explanation, see the chapter on culture.

1.14 Integrated Concepts

The approach described in the last section seeks to integrate relevant concepts from organization theory, comparative management, systems and contingency theory. They were chosen, because they are empirically based, provide comprehensive frameworks, are consistent with several analytical paradigms, and provide measurement tools for managerial tasks (Kagona et al 1985:11). For clarification, they are briefly reviewed below and will be explained and used further throughout the following chapters.

---

[5] Hofstedes (1980) dimensions here are used in a very broad sense. Their application here is not restricted to distinguishing between the managerial approaches taken in different countries. They are used to distinguish between managerial approaches in general.

In general, organizations are seen here as open, stochastic, non stationary, discrete, cybernetic, multistable and complex systems (Scheuch/Hasenauer 1981:31).

In systems theory, the whole organization can be seen as a conglomerate of a number of elements that act interdependently (Ackoff 1971; Scholz 1987:10). The transactions (e.g. planning) an organizational unit performs depend not only on the available inputs, but also on the relations between the system's elements (Zutshi 1981:85). Important are not only the relationships among the system's parts, but also the relationships of the system to contextual factors (Amey 1986:240). Thus, effectiveness criteria have to mirror the entire input-throughput-output cycle (Gibson et al 1985:33). The big advantage of this view is that it stresses the process rather than the products (i.e. the plan itself) per se as the distinctive element (Hage 1980:11).

Following the cognitive model of environmental analysis, a top management's collective understanding of its environment is thought to be anchored in a cognitive structure and fashioned out of experience (Lenz/Engledow 1986). It therefore draws attention to cognitive limitations, for example during information processing (Bazerman 1986). As strategy making is a social learning process (Burgelmann 1985:94), this notion was integrated into the Culture-Planning Model through the dimension Organizational Learning. This view will be further explored in the chapters on planning systems and heuristics.

Firms do not act anonymously. They can be classified as open systems (Weigele 1983:31). One of the main features of this approach to studying organizations is the proposition that there is no clear boundary between the organization and the broader environment. Therefore, firms have cultural, economic, legal etc. properties in common, for example, with their competitors, suppliers and clients (Katz/Kahn 1966:28). The ecological orientation underscores the importance of external environmental factors on management practices and effectiveness and the relevance of cultural components (Pondy/Mitroff 1981; Negandhi 1983b:17).

Lawrence/Lorsch (1967) state that the best way of organization is dependent on the nature of the environment to which the organization relates. The contingency theory indicates that there is no one best way to plan, and that any way of planning is not equally effective (Scott 1981:113). Planning, hence, is the future-oriented process of creating a pattern in the stream of important, complex actions and decisions (Mintzberg/Waters 1985).

Comparative management attempts to identify aspects of managerial processes which are similar and aspects which are different in cultures around the world (Adler 1983:20). Emerging similarities are seen as universality. Emergent differences are seen as cultural specific (Adler 1986:42). Culture, in short, is defined as the "collective mental programming of the mind which distinguishes the members of one human group from another" (Hofstede 1980:25).

1.2 Conceptual Framework

This section describes the derivation of hypotheses from the research questions. Both research questions and the hypothesis are given. Next, the Culture-Planning model is outlined. To introduce the reader to the Culture-Planning Model, it is portrayed in three stages, going from general to specific. Sets of dimensions and variables and their interactions are described. A graphic representation of the model is given.

1.21 Research Questions and Hypothesis

The heart of the study is a worldwide survey covering 372 banks, including one third of the world's largest, concerning their planning frameworks and practices.[6] The survey is designed to provide answers to the following questions:

Are variations in planning approaches among companies situated in different cultural settings larger than within-culture differences (Bazzaz/Grinyer 1981:155; Weigele 1983:13)? Are there cultural based differences in functional managerial practices (i.e. planning), not only in general terms (Redding 1980:143)? The impact of the external culture (the societal subsystem), seen as an independent variable, on the internal strategic planning framework (managerial subsystem) of the planning processes (dependent variable) is studied.

The second purpose and aim of this research is to establish a model of the interaction between societal culture and planning frameworks. What factors are of influence? Why is "planning" performed differently? Specifically,

- What planning <u>systems</u> (structures, reasons) do companies in specific cultures have?
- What planning <u>processes</u> (characteristics, activities) do companies in specific cultures have?
- What behavioral <u>heuristics</u> take place during planning in specific cultures?

As a null hypothesis on cultural influence, it is assumed that

H1: no significant variation in planning <u>systems</u> will be associated with the firm's cultural environment.

H1/1: no significant variation in planning <u>structures</u> will be associated with the firm's cultural environment.

H1/2: no significant variation in planning <u>time horizons</u> will be associated with the firm's cultural environment.

---

[6] Why the banking industry was chosen for this research is explained in section 1.31 Referent.

H1/3: no significant variation in the reasons for planning will be associated with the firm's cultural environment.

H2: no significant variation in planning processes will be associated with the firm's cultural environment.

H2/1: no significant variation in characteristics of the planning process will be associated with the firm's cultural environment.

H2/2: no significant variation in activities performed during the planning process will be associated with the firm's cultural environment.

H3: no significant variation in behavioral aspects (heuristics) during the planning process will be associated with the firm's cultural environment.

1.22 The Culture-Planning Model

Figure 1.1 depicts the conceptual framework of the culture-planning model. It shows important components for organizational comparisons as applied here. The purpose is to provide a sound theoretical framework for the investigation of the interaction between culture and planning. Its development and application will be shown throughout the following chapters.

The model consists of independent, exogenous variables and dependent, endogenous variables, following the tradition of theory building often utilized (Friedrichs 1980:86; Scheuch 1982:22; Sheth/Sethi 1981:371). Following Lazarsfeld (1967), it flows from theoretical constructs to a partition in dimensions, to the choice of indicators and their integration, and is explained in two stages.[7]

The first stage argues that the context influences strategic planning frameworks, which in turn influence the planning outcomes. The second stage takes out culture as one contextual, exogenous variable, which - among others - influences strategic planning frameworks. These are depicted by systems and heuristics, which in turn influence planning processes. These stages are designed to capture the distinct aspects of culture and planning frameworks.

Culture is operationalized by the dimensions of power distance, uncertainty avoidance, individualism/ collectivism, and organizational learning (Hofstede 1980; Ginter/White 1982; Sullivan/Nonaka 1986). Exogenous variables are treated as given in within-country comparisons.

---

[7] The model is largely conceptual. In practice, the dynamics of interaction are, of course, much more complex. Such a conceptual model, however, provides a good overview of major interactions and allows for the detection of patterns (Miles/ Huberman 1984:34; Mintzberg 1979:584).

Independent **Dependent** **Dependent**

CONTEXT ------> STRATEGIC PLANNING ---> OUTCOMES

Consists of:

INDUSTRY
POLITICAL
ECONOMICAL
CULTURAL ---> SYSTEMS & HEURISTICS ---> PROCESS
TECHNOLOGICAL
LEGAL

Preferred Modes of Action

Explained by:

-Power Distance	Structure	Schemas	Characteristics
-Uncertainty Avoidance	Goals & Reasons	Assumptions	Acts
-Organizational Learning		Behavior	
-Individualism/ Collectivism			

Dimensions   Questionnaire & Interview Indicators

Figure 1.1: Graphic Representation of the Culture-Planning Model.

In this stepwise refinement of the model, each group of factors has to be read column wise from top to bottom, e.g. context-culture-PDI, UAI, OL, IDV.[8] For further details not covered here in the introduction, see the chapter on culture.

---

[8] To ease reading, the following abbreviations will be used for these variables: PD for power distance, UA for uncertainty avoidance, IDV for individualism-collectivism, and OL for organizational learning (Hofstede 1980: Sullivan/Nonaka 1986).

However, in the cross-cultural model depicted here, these dimensions differ from one culture to another in their interactive effect on planning frameworks (Sheth/Sethi 1981:371). Planning system refers to the time frame, structure, and reasons (goals) of planning frameworks. Schemas, assumptions, and non-rational behavior form what was termed "heuristics."[9] Planning processes are depicted in terms of characteristics and activities performed. The theoretical reasoning for the variables chosen here and their interaction are explained in the following chapters.

1.23 The Cultural Dimensions

As explained earlier, the following dimensions were used to represent the cultural context of planning systems.[10] They are briefly reviewed here and will be explained in greater depth with regard to their relation to planning systems (time frame, reasons, structure), heuristics (behavior) and planning processes (characteristics, activities) in the subsequent chapters.

Individualism versus collectivism (IDV) relates to peoples self-concept, their orientation and commitment towards the 'I' or the 'we' in organizations (Hofstede 1984a:390). Human relations can be individualistic, lateral, or hierarchical (Kluckhohn/ Strodtbeck 1961). In individualistic contexts, people put emphasis on individual initiative and the task to be performed. Openness and directness are the way problems get solved. (Hofstede 1984b:87). In collectivist organizations, the company is regarded as an in-group. Policies and practices based on loyalty and a sense of duty, trust and faith are preferred to openness and directness of task completion (Hofstede 1984b:88).

For planning processes, this dimension refers to the participativeness of decision making (Hofstede 1980:226), the value of individual initiatives (Hofstede 1980:229), emphasis on

---

[9] This concept is used to avoid value judgments with regard to the rationality of planning frameworks. Due to the wide differences in values among cultures, the question of rationality is less meaningful in a cross-cultural context. (Sheth/Sethi 1981:371). For further details, see the chapter on planning systems and on heuristics.

[10] Hofstede (1980) introduced yet another dimension, termed masculinity vs. femininity, which was not used here because its content overlaps with other dimensions and does not directly refer to differences in planning practices (Hofstede 1980; 1984b). Masculinity vs. Femininity relates to the degree people prefer achievement, heroism and assertiveness or relationships, modesty and caring for others (Hofstede 1984b:84). In organizations with masculine orientation, competition between managers is encouraged, whereas solidarity is encouraged in feminine organizations. This dimension however, did not find widespread acceptance. Instead, Organizational learning is used as a fourth dimension, based on the findings of Sullivan/Nonaka (1986).

orderliness or variety (Hofstede 1980:230), and security versus autonomy (Hofstede 1980:235), as reflected in the strategy literature for example in Hax/Majluf (1984) or Lorange (1986).

Power Distance (**PD**) refers to concentration of authority and task specialization (Hofstede 1980:384). It is the degree to which people accept a hierarchical order or strive for equality (Hofstede 1984b:83). Status differences and centralization are more common in high-PD contexts (Hofstede 1984b:88). For planning, these contrary positions are reflected in political vs. strategic thinking, in the value of more or less centralization, and in taller or flatter planning hierarchies (Hofstede 1980:135;384). For example, bottom up, top-down or a combination of the two extremes are widely discussed planning process elements (e.g. Steiner et al 1982).

Uncertainty Avoidance (**UA**), depicts the way people handle the fact that the future is unknown (Hofstede 1980). As introduced by Cyert/March (1963), it refers to the absorption of ambiguity (March/Simon 1958) and reduction of anxiety (Schein 1985:82). One possible reaction is formalization and the structuring of activities, e.g. separation of strategy formulation and implementation (Hofstede 1980:384; 387). Uncertainty avoidance, as used here, is the degree to which managers think that the environment is under their control (dominance vs. subjugation), the degree of their future orientation (past/present/future), and how they value activity to overcome the perceived uncertainty (doing/ being; Kluckhohn/Strodtbeck 1961). Strong UA refers to a high concern with stability and security. Emphasis is on activity, as time is a scarce resource.

For planning, this clearly relates to the structuring of planning activities either through explicit formalization, standardization, and specialization or through implicit rules and rituals (Hofstede 1980:187). The appropriateness of broad planning guidelines versus rigidly specified procedures is equally widely discussed in the strategy literature (e.g. Kühn 1985).

Organizational Learning (**OL**) refers to how organizations create, acquire, communicate, share and interpret information, knowledge and cause-effect relationships (Fiol/Lyles 1985; Hedberg 1981; Shrivastava 1983:9; Shrivastava/Grant 1985:109; Sullivan/Nonaka 1986:129). For example, it refers to whether associative or abstract information is used (empirical, analytical vs. qualitative, personal intuition and experience; Hofstede 1980:187; Rhyne 1987), and whether broad ideologies or narrow, pragmatical facts are the starting point for information search (Glenn 1981). The latter can be active search or passive monitoring (Burgelman 1983; Ginter/White 1982; Horvath/McMillan 1979; Schneider 1989: 151; Shrivastava/Grant 1985), based on issue diagnoses or issue solution (Drucker 1971; King/Cleland 1978:275).

These cultural dimensions will be explained further and used throughout the following chapters. For theoretical rationale and empirical evidence see the chapter on culture.

1.3 Methodology

This section is a brief overview, of how the research questions explained in the previous section were tested. The rationale for choosing the banking industry as a referent population is given. Also an introduction into the research instruments used is given.

1.31 Referent

To test the hypotheses stated above, a suitable sample population had to be defined. At first, the criteria for the choice were established. As the simple fact of doing research across national, cultural and language boundaries already introduces quite a bit of complexity, a major concern was to hold as many other factors constant as possible (Adler 1984, 1986; Hofstede 1980).

- The size of the enterprises in the sample should be held constant within a certain range, as this factor heavily influences the strategic planning process (Gup/Whitehead 1983:26; Lindsay/Rue 1980:401; Negandhi 1987; Robinson 1983; Robinson/Pearce 1983:198).

- The use of a multi-industry sample introduces problems of sample homogeneity/heterogeneity, i.e. comparability. The strategy making process is an interplay between external influences and internal properties of the firm and is therefore difficult to compare across industries (Jauch 1983:167). Planning practices differ to some extent across industries (Chinta et al 1987:545). Hence, strategic decision processes have to be investigated in their specific context (Horvath/McMillan 1979:93). Performance comparisons across industries raise methodological concerns (Birnbaum/Wong 1985:268; Chakravarthy 1986:439; Hirsch 1975; Hofstede 1980:38; Price/Mueller 1986:132). Thus, contingency perspectives of strategy should be examined in single industry contexts (Tushman/Romanelli 1985).

- It should be an industry that can be found world-wide and that fulfills the same function in different societies (Hofstede 1980:348).

The limitation ot one industry only naturally has a negative impact on the generalizability of this study (Ginsberg/ Venkantraman 1985:429). However, it might provide the basis for future research in other industries or an extension to further countries.

- It should be an industry where strategic planning efforts are not too rigidly fixed, where they are ongoing processes. It will be easier to observe differences in the early stages of creation and implementation of the process (Harper 1986; Hasperslagh 1982:62; Javidan 1984; Weigele 1983:6).

Evaluating these criteria, the banking industry was taken as referent population within a multi-country sample (Hofstede 1977:39; Miner 1984:89). It can be found worldwide, within certain size ranges, has industry similarities and fulfills roughly the same functions in different societies (Davis 1985:128; Graddy et al. 1985:62; Revell 1985a, 1988:3). In addition, planning is often in the introductory phase at banks, compared to other industries (Holmberg/Baker 1982:219; Giroux/Rose 1984:137; Litschert/Nicholson 1973:47; Metzger/Rau 1982:62; Prasad 1984; Rule/Sedgwick 1986:46; Sapp 1980:34). Given the increasingly interdependent competitive setting and the world-wide move towards deregulation of financial services (Donnelly et al 1985:7), banking appears to be an excellent industry for the purpose of examining strategy processes (Fombrun/Zajac 1987:33).

1.32 Research Design

According to Downey/Ireland (1979:630), methodological issues must always be answered within the context of a particular research setting. In this study, field research methods were chosen as the major tool for carrying out this research. Based on participative observation, a case study and semi-structured interviews with a total of 28 senior planning managers at 14 banks, a questionnaire was developed and pretested. The questionnaire was sent in seven language versions to about 1,000 banks in Europe, Australia, Japan, North- and Latin America.

Given the fact that Latin America and Japan were in the sample, the over all response rate of about 25%, with a total of 501 usable questionnaires is quite successful. The 501 responses cover 372 banks worldwide, with assets of $b 8,732. This includes one third of the worlds' 550 biggest banks as measured by assets less contra accounts (Banker 1988a) which responded to this survey. Further details on research method selection, the instrument development, sample populations, and characteristics of each of the five continents surveyed can be found in the chapter on research design and data collection.

1.33 Data Set

To investigate the impact of culture on strategic planning frameworks in comparison to other influences, data from the questionnaires, and secondary bank-specific and culture-specific data was combined.

Questionnaire	Bank-Specific	Country-Specific
* Structure * Reasons (Goals) * Time frame	* size measured in total assets	* Hofstedes (1980) dimensions
* Activities * Characteristics	* country/state	* economic stability indicators (GDP/capita, inflation rate)
* Heuristics	* world-ranking	* ranking withn country

Table 1.1 Data Set Construction.

Data from the questionnaire was already explained earlier. Bank size and rankings were measured in total assets (less contra accounts). Country-specific data includes Hofstede's (1980) dimensions, within-rankings and economic stability indicators. For the latter, the gross domestic product per capita, and the annual inflation rate, both figures for 1988, were used. The chapter on research design and methodology includes a more elaborate discussion of the country and bank data variables included.

This data set will not only allow for the investigation of cultural influences on strategic planning frameworks. The influences of bank size, volatility of the economy and other factors can be investigated with the underlying database in further research.[11]

1.4. Relevance

For practing managers this study could provide a detailed summary of current corporate planning practices in banks around the globe. Executives will be able to compare their planning practices with those in the sample and hence gain insights into possible improvements of their planning frameworks.

The value for management theory lies in the attempt to deepen the knowledge of the culture-strategy-linkage. A further contribution to management theory is the development of a conceptual model of planning approaches, a model of cultural influences on the strategy development process, and a model of non-rational heuristical influences on the strategy development process. Moreover, a model was developed that links Hofstede's (1980) dimensions with general management theory. In doing so, it represents an integration of many of the foregoing theoretical perspectives. Its value lies in producing an integrated and empirically testable framework for the analysis of strategic planning frameworks and practices.

1.5 Subsequent Chapters

Before outlining the remainder of the book, it is critical to clarify its philosophy. Putting the emphasis on the cultural element in planning is no attempt to attribute all dissimilarities across companies to culture. However, the study questions the position of universal rationality of planning systems and processes assumed by many authors.

---

[11] In the outset, several additional indicators were planned for inclusion: bank type (retail, wholesale etc. bank), a legal indicator to show the extent of legal entry/exit barriers, e.g. restrictions to branch banking, accessibility to domestic financial markets for foreign banks etc; profitability and performance indicators, e.g. pre-tax ROA etc. for planning effectiveness comparisons; position of the respondent, for organizational influences.

In the development of the Culture-Planning Model, terms are defined, theoretical and empirical work is reviewed, and cultural influences are discussed for the concepts touched. Therefore, the topics covered in the following advance from the company-internal (process, systems, heuristics) to the company-external (environment, industry, and culture).

Chapter two explores functions of planning as decision making. The development and interrelation of the concepts of strategy and planning are reviewed. Normative and empirical views of the planning process are explained. A planning process conceptualization is presented to clarify the terminology. The phase theorem of decision making is critically reviewed to set the stage for the following chapter on approaches to planning systems.

In chapter three, a model is proposed to categorize planning process approaches. The goal is to further develop the Culture-Planning Model and to see if it can be used to discriminate between approaches to planning. The rational of this model is described. The distinction is drawn between rational-analytical, avoidance-emergent, incremental-adaptive, political-power and action-vision approaches to strategic planning. Emphasis is put on specifying and comparing the underlying assumptions of what is suggested to be the major planning models.

Chapter four examines heuristics and biases in strategic decisions from several perspectives. Relevant heuristical influences on strategic decision processes and their sources are identified. Heuristics are explained in their interaction with planning phases. The Culture-Planning Model is proposed to specify underlying characteristics and the influence of societal culture. Heuristics and their interaction with corporate culture are reviewed.

Chapter five sets the company-internal planning process in perspective to the company-external environment. The specific goal of the chapter is to give room to environmental influences on planning other than culture. Possible influences of industry, economic volatility, technology, and the legal environment are discussed. Environmental constructs are reviewed. The banking industry is depicted by the characteristics of its services. A literature review about industry influences on planning is presented, with specific attention to bank planning. The outcomes of these influences on planning are discussed.

The goal of chapter six is to develop a framework for the examination of the impact of culture on the planning process.
The notion of societal culture is explained. Cultural dimensions and constructs that are frequently used in the literature to describe cultural influences on managerial practices are reviewed. Conceptual models that link planning and culture are discussed. The Culture-Planning Model as developed throughout the chapters is summarized and explained. Empirical evidence from comparative planning studies is reviewed.

Chapter seven discusses research design and methodology. Research method selection and instrument development is described. The survey instruments are commented on. Sample issues with regard to population, selection, and sample characteristics are given. For the questionnaires, data handling and chosen statistical procedures and tools are explained. Methodological problems are discussed.

Chapter eight reports the findings from the empirical study. A comparison of questionnaire responses from US and German banks, holding constant bank size and economic and legal facets, constitutes the first part. Secondly, questionnaire responses from ten groups of countries are compared. Thereby, the Culture-Planning model is critically reviewed. Potential contributions to theory and practice are explored. Recommendations for the design of planning systems and processes are developed as well as recommendations for further research.

1.6 Summary

The preceding sections have presented an overview of the rationale of this study. Specific goals of the project were discussed and the methodology was developed. Key terms were briefly explained.

2 THE STRATEGIC PLANNING PROCESS

This chapter explores functions of planning as decision making. In order to compare and evaluate strategic planning frameworks, it is necessary to define the domains explicitly (Zutshi 1981: 18). Therefore, the following sections explain the development and interrelation of the terms strategy, planning, and process. The evolution of strategic planning is discussed. The planning process is depicted to set the stage for the next chapter on approaches to planning systems.

2.1 Strategy

Significant contributions on the concept of policy and strategy have been developed in a number of fields, based on business, game, military, or futures' metaphors (Evered 1983:57; Mintzberg 1978:935; Scholz 1987:5). The following sections explain the usage and development of the term in these fields and its application in the current research.

2.11 The Military Concept of Strategy

2.111 The Source of the Concept

The word strategy itself comes from the combination of the Greek words for army (stratos) and leader (agos). In its narrow sense of "strategos " it stands for a general in command of an army (Bracker 1980:219; Higgins 1980:1; Eckardt 1979:37). In the Western hemisphere, the usage of the term evolved from its initial reference to a <u>role</u> (the general in command of the army) to encompass the <u>skills</u> necessary to occupy such a position, to overthrow opposition and to create a powerful governmental system (Evered 1983:58). As the Greek terms refer back as far as 550 BC, Sun Tzu wrote on military strategy in China around 360 BC (Tzu 1936). In Europe, the military definition of strategy by Clausewitz (1918:77) as

> "the art of the employment of battles to gain the object of war. In other words strategy forms the plan of the war, makes out the proposed course of the different campaigns which compose the war, and regulates the battles to be fought in each"

became very popular. For Clausewitz and his followers, the aim of a strategy is to destroy the competitor (Kotler 1983:68). Strategy in that sense deals with large movements of troops over wide spaces, long times, and prior to contact with the competitor, whereas tactics deal with clashes directly on the battlefield (Evered 1983:63). Liddell-Hall (1967) distinguishes between pure or 'military strategy' in its literal meaning of generalship, and 'grand strategy,' the policy of combining it with other weapons.

The military usage of the term is still prominent to day, but as will be shown, not unquestioned. Henderson (1981:8), for example draws upon a military metaphor in describing marketing strategies:

> Successful market strategies in effect segment the total market in a way that minimizes competitors' strengths while maximizing yours. The parallel in military strategy is 'isolating the battlefield.'

Managers often use military metaphors to describe their competitive situations. Expressions like price wars, market invasion, guerilla warfare, advertising as propaganda arm, and strategies of attack (frontal, flanking, encirclement, bypass, and guerilla) are clearly derived from warfare language (Kotler 1983:68).

2.112 The Applicability to Management Strategy

"Strategies are plans for acquiring power" (Mason/Mitroff 1983:33). However, although military principles and statements aid in providing insight for survival on the marketplace, they are not the whole answer to competitive strategy (Kotler 1983:80).

First, the application of military analogies pretends that someone clearly loses and someone clearly wins, which is not necessarily true in business (Weick 1979b:47). Second, military analogies limit managements' choice to a restricted set of solutions (Peters/Waterman 1982:101). Third, it is culture bound (Faucheux 1977:135; Ohmae 1982:221; Weick 1979b:50) and therefore not acceptable for comparative research.

Aron's (1976:240) critique of the American military strategy literature pinpoints two major shortcomings of that analogy in the Western understanding of management strategy:

> ".. they limit themselves to strategic analysis (as in the use of force), whereas strategy today contains a much larger component of policy (in all senses of the word) than in the past. ... What results is the risk of a misunderstood formalism, abstract controversies, and unlikely conclusions. ... Yet nothing proves that American rationality is the same as chinese rationality. (Rationality, whether American or Chinese, assumes an order of preference and an approximate evaluation of what is at risk and what is at stake, both based on a world view)."[12]

Similarly, Ohmae (1982) argues that the conception of strategy derived from military, which is often used in the Western management literature, "separates thinkers from doers, and information collectors from strategists" (Ohmae 1982:221), which is, for example, not the case in Japan. And, it has been shown that the analogies and metaphors of Japanese organizations are different (Kagona et al 1985:110).

---

[12] Quoted in translation from Faucheux (1977:135).

2.12 The Management Concept of Strategy

In management literature, strategy is an inherently open systems concept (Bigler 1986:4). Its definitions, therefore, depend on the level of analysis (business vs. corporate (induced vs. autonomous; Burgelman 1983); the breath (situation specific, universal, or contingent; Hambrick/Lei 1985:763), the static or dynamic view towards the construct, e.g. as "Strategies are both plans for the future and patterns from the past" (Mintzberg 1987:67). Underlying is the notion that strategies themselves are not goals, but rather means to pursue ends (Giroux 1981:34). For a review of conceptualizations of strategy, see Hofer/Schendel (1978) and Venkatraman/Grant (1986).

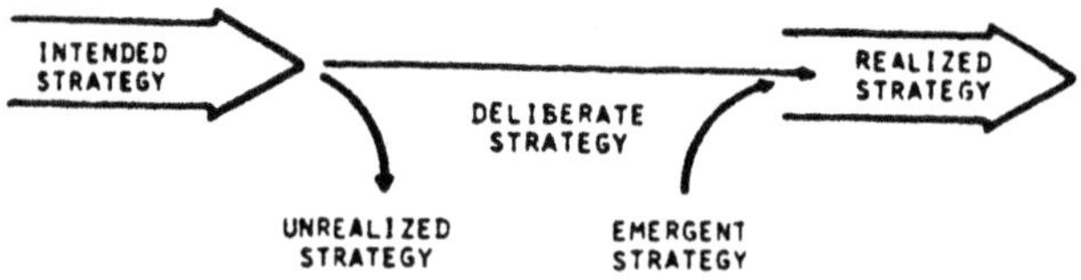

Figure 2.1 Types of Strategies.

Source: Mintzberg, Henry / Waters, James (1985:258): Of Strategies, Deliberate and Emergent. In: Strategic Management Journal, 6, pp. 257-272.

2.121 Deliberate Strategy

Chaffee (1985) reviewed research on the strategy construct and categorized the findings into three models: linear, adaptive, and interpretive strategy. Some of the underlying assumptions are explained and used in the chapter on strategic planning systems.

In the linear model, strategy is composed of decisions, actions and plans in order to achieve goals, for example competitive advantage (Porter 1980) or success potentials (Gälweiler 1987:28;110). Whereas Andrews (1970) puts more emphasis on the pattern of decisions to reach goals, Chandler (1962:13), as quoted below, puts more emphasis on the content.

> Strategy is the determination of the basic long-term goals of an enterprise and the adoption of courses of actions and the allocation of resources necessary to carry out these goals.

In the adaptive model, the firm's actions are seen as responses to the nature and size of environmental changes (Chaffee 1985:91). Not the goals, but the definition of the competitive domain of the firm, and the match between the firm and its environment are important. According to Hofer/Schendel (1978),

> a strategy describes the development of a match an organization achieves between the opportunities and risks present in the external environment and the

organizations capabilities and resources for exploiting these opportunities.

The interpretative model puts the emphasis on the processes that take place within an organizations' culture. Here, strategy is a integrative, coherent, holistic and unifying representation of the organization. As defined by Chaffee (1985:83),

Strategy is the orienting metaphors to motivate behavior expected to produce favorable organizational results.

2.122 Emergent Strategy

The above stated definitions treat strategy as explicitly, consciously and purposefully developed, formulated in advance of implementation decisions, which are called 'intended strategies by Mintzberg (1977:30; 1978:935). However, strategy can also emerge from a series of single, unconnected decisions and actions (Mintzberg/ Waters 1982:466). Strategies "can form as well as be formulated (Mintzberg 1987:68). 'Intended strategy is an ex-ante concept, whereas realized strategy is an ex-post result (Fiegenbaum et al 1986:6). Strategy formulation and implementation are seen as complementary, not necessarily sequential.

This consistency in the behavior of an organization was termed 'gestalt strategy,' (Mintzberg 1976:57) or 'emergent strategy' (Mintzberg/Waters 1982:466). Similarly, Porter (Thomas 1984:140) puts emphasis on the process aspect of strategy in defining strategy as "the process of managerial translation and implementation of these policy guidelines in organizational terms to that a coherent strategic pattern emerges." Then, strategy can be defined as 'patterns in the streams of actions and decisions,' following (Mintzberg 1987:934 and Mintzberg/Waters 1985:257).

2.123 Strategy as Pattern

The definition of strategy as a pattern delineated above was chosen for several reasons for this comparative research, following Evered (1983:59;71):

(1) 'Patterns in the stream of actions and decisions' include both deliberate and emergent strategies, as patterns can be set and can develop.
(2) It focuses on the company as a whole, on decisions that influence its identity, character, purpose. And, it puts emphasis on integration and synthesis rather than analysis.
(3) It introduces a consistent statement. It includes both deliberate and emerging strategy concepts. It allows for different interpretations of contingency-based rationality in strategic decision making. And, it is a widely recognized, dynamic definition, which was derived empirically.
(4) It introduces a balanced picture of the strategy concept, which has gradually evolved from Andrews (1970) 'patterns of decisions' to Mintzbergs (1987) 'patterns of actions.' It encompasses both corporate-level strategy (referring to the type

encompasses both corporate-level strategy (referring to the type of business a company should be in) and business-level strategy (how to compete in a particular industry or product/market segment; Hofer/Schendel 1978:27), although it is used with the former notion throughout the following chapters.
(5) It is not culture-bound, and therefore can be applied to the cultural dimensions of uncertainty avoidance (risk), power distance (e.g. centralization), individualism (e.g. type of commitment), and organizational learning that are inherent in the strategic planning process (Hax/Majluf 1988; Mintzberg 1976, 1987; Mintzberg/Waters 1982, 1985; Thomas 1984).

2.13 Summary

This and the former section explained the development of the term strategy with emphasis on military and managerial strategy. Relevant literature was identified and reviewed. The military metaphor was rejected, because it is culture-loaden. The conclusion was drawn that strategy should be seen as pattern in the stream of actions and decisions, following Mintzberg (1987). The next section will explore the term 'planning.'

2.2 Planning

The meaning of the word "plan" may be descriptive or prescriptive (Rutland 1985:50). The plan can be seen as a picture of perceived reality, picking out the features that are regarded to be relevant to be accepted as objective circumstances. And, it can be seen as intention, as a means for reducing uncertainty, as a vehicle for purposive activity, depending on its reasons, which may be mind-stretching, the development of corporate and short-term strategies, the development of a framework in the minds of senior management, management development, control, and internal communication and co-ordination etc. (Camillus 1975:34; Greenly 1986:105; Köhler/Uebele 1986:140). These reasons reflect different conceptions of planning.

2.21 Conceptions of Planning

As was the case for the term strategy, there is an equally wide range of meanings for the term 'planning' (Lilienthal 1944:96; Mintzberg 1981:319; Morgan/Martin 1986:219; Planning has its origins in the structural design arts of engineering and architecture (Daneke/Steiss 1979:98). The word 'planning' itself is derived from latin, where 'planum' in a narrow sense means plain, even surface; in the broader sense, something that can be overlooked and surveyed (Gälweiler 1986:27). Applying the systems approach to organizations, planning (as well as organizing, motivation and controlling) is intrinsic to management (Steiner

1979:3;).[13] It is a dynamic, open systems model (Cauwenberg/ Cool 1982:246; Grant 1987:92). Several conceptions of planning were derived from these notions.

Gamm (1976:71) distinguishes between planning as design (structural aspect), as social action (problem solving and policy formulation), as invention (innovative aspect), and as monitoring and analysis (analytical and implementation aspects). Similarly, Taylor/Hussey (1982:43), quoted from Hare (1985:65), discriminate between planning as a central control system, a framework for innovation, a social learning process, a political process, and as a conflict of values.

Mintzberg (1981:320) classifies planning into future thinking (resource allocation, building liaison contacts, monitoring the environment, handling disturbances), into planning as integrated decision making (joint decision making across different areas), into planning as formalized procedure and articulated result (systematic, explicit, formalized analysis), and into planning as programming (the articulation, justification, and elaboration of the intended strategy the firm already has). For further conceptional definitions of corporate planning in empirical research, see Pearce et al (1987).

2.22 Planning as Frame of Action and Decision Making

The above conceptions of planning can be described in terms of the futurity of current decisions, processes, philosophies, and structures (Steiner 1979). Strategic planning deals with assessing the future outcomes of current decisions (Steiner 1979:13) and the mental anticipation of future activities (Hahn/Taylor 1980:17). It provides a structure for handling risk and uncertainty (Sapp/Smith 1984:9). It is the process of developing strategies and 'maintaining a viable fit between the organization's objectives and resources and its environmental opportunities' (Kotler 1984:44). Strategic planning is a philosophy, a pattern of thinking in looking at a problem (Kumar 1978:31) with special attention to facets external to the company (Ramanujam et al 1986:351). Planning is evolutionary in nature (Hussey 1985:10; Litschert/Nicholson 1973:52) and provides slack resources (Gibson

[13] This collection of managerial tasks, as was referred to in the introductory chapter, dates back to Fayol (1916) and is one of the most used schemes in the Western management literature. Recently, this view has been challenged by Mintzberg (e.g. 1975, 1976), who distinguishes between the managers interpersonal roles (figurehead, leader, liaison), the managers informational roles (monitor, disseminator, spokesman), and the managers decisional roles (entrepreneur, disturbance handler, resource allocator, negotiator). Similar arguments against Fayol (1916) can be found in Kotter (1982:156). Although this empirically derived distinction is both meaningful and appropriate, the author went along with most of the strategy and comparative management literature in using the term 'planning' in Fayols' understanding.

et al 1985:506). The task environment of strategic planning includes all elements, groups and stakeholders that are affected by the planning efforts (Buchholz 1986:457; Howe 1986:33; Scott 1981:188).[14]

2.23 What Strategic Planning is not

Here, planning will be seen as <u>frame of action and decision making</u>. Therefore, it is important to specify what strategic planning is not. For clarification, the following distinctions are given.

(1) It does not deal with future decisions. It deals with todays decisions and actions that will affect the firms future position (Sawyer 1983:1; Gup/Whitehead 1983:24).
(2) There is a pattern, but not a strict sequence of ends (mission, corporate objectives), ways (strategies), and means (implement using resources) in planning (Hayes 1985:112).
(3) The value of planning is in the process and not in the plans themselves. Plans are dynamic, not static (Kudla 1981:2; Tull 1979:39).[15]
(4) It is not a prescribed set of processes, procedures, structures, or the application of quantitative techniques and models to business decisions. It may incorporate these tools, but its conceptual base is analytical thinking about the commitment of resources to action (Gup/Whitehead 1983:24).
(5) Strategic planning cannot eliminate uncertainty. However, it allows management to evaluate the risk that must be faced in transforming uncertainties into risk (Gup/Whitehead 1983).
(6) Strategic planning is not synonymous with forecasting. In fact, planning is necessary because we cannot forecast the future with certainty (Gup/Whitehead 1983:24).
(7) Strategic planning (where the domain of the company is open to question) is not the same as long-range planning (where the domain of the organization was considered given; Prasad 1984:77; Rhyne 1986:429).

---

[14] As will be referred to in a later chapter, the task environment for strategic planning includes both the societal environment (social, cultural, political, legal, technical, economical forces), the internal environment (e.g. structure, corporate culture, size, resources, and the core task environment (e.g. stockholders, governments, customers, creditors, competitors, employees, and communities (Negandhi 1983a:21; Wheelen/Hunger 1984:9). For task analysis, see Campbell (1988), or Haiss (1983). For planning tasks, see Szyperski/Müller (1986:306) or Freeman/Lorange (1985:18).

[15] This distinction is important, because the wrongful application of planning as a managerial technique makes it understandable, if researchers like Tull (1979:37) find that "The greatest value of static written plans is that they make excellent bookends (last year's plan on the left and this year's plan on the right, in chronological order.)"

2.24 Risk Reduction Through Planning

For Naylor/Schauland (1976), strategic planning is a management system for transferring uncertainty into risk. Uncertainty pertains to situations, where problem structure, consequences, and the probability of an event are not fully known; risk describes situations where the consequences of a decision and the probability of consequences are known[16] (Diller 1980:22; Guttentag/Herring 1986:9; Mason/Mitroff 1981; Raffée 1974:101). Sources of uncertainty are environmental conditions, such as diversity, volatility and turbulence of the environment, and disagreement about cause-effect relationships (Leblebici/Salancik 1981:580; Baird/Thomas 1985:233).

Research findings indicate an inconsistent impact of uncertainty on strategic planning (Boulten et al 1982a; Jauch/Kraft 1986; Javidan 1984). However, as planning makes priorities, assumptions, required changes, timing, and expected rate of change better known, Channon (1986:8), Kudla (1981:1) and Boulton et al (1982a) argue, that firms adopted planning systems to cope with the increasing volatility of the firm's internal and external environment, and to absorb uncertainty by reducing information overload. This 'knowledge' can be acquired through explicit standardization and formalization, or through implicit rules and rituals. The uncertainty avoidance perspective pertains especially to banks, which essentially make money on accepting risk (Revell 1980).

2.25 Planning Dimensions

The concept of planning is not culture-free (Hofstede 1980:383). Managers' perceptions about time, risk, appropriate decision structure and process, type of commitment, reasoning, information handling etc. are different. Western planning theory symbolized the techno-scientific culture (Zutshi 1981:14) and postulates that the strategy-maker 'formulates,' while subordinates 'implement' (Mintzberg 1978:946),[17] which does not hold true in non-Western cultures.

Planning intrinsicly entails the idea that the future can, to some extent, be altered by design. "Not all cultures accept this Faustian concept, and it is difficult to get .. managers deeply

---

[16] Eilon (1985:374) distinguishes further between decision making under uncertainty (with goals well defined) and decision making under ambiguity (with goals unclear). As will be explained later, both situations can pertain to strategic decision making and planning. Therefore, this distinction is not applied here.

[17] A nice example for that view gives Lilienthal (1944:99): 'The idea that planning and responsibility for action may and should be divorced - the maker of plans having little or nothing to do with their execution - follows the analogy of the planning of a house, an office building, any fixed structure. But the analogy is a mistaken one.'

involved in planning if they believe that the future lies solely in the hands of Fate" (Garland/Farmer 1986:34). "For instance, in Japan the culture directly influences organizational planning at all levels ... This welding together of organizational and societal goals is the result of a practicing philosophy of planning" (King/Clelland 1978:278). The typical American goal of corporate planning centers normally on shareholder wealth maximization (e.g. Graddy et al 1985). In other countries, there usually is more emphasis on additional factors, for example the optimal allocation of scarce resources (e.g. Jacob 1986:14).

The issues discussed above under the notion of planning clearly refer to planning as a way of handling the unknown future (uncertainty avoidance), power distance through involvement of managers on different levels, participation and initiative (individualism) and organizational learning, for example through the need of reformulation during implementation (Mintzberg 1978:946). Moreover, planning requires systems, i.e. specific reasons, an appropriate time horizon, structures for preparation, review, decision and implementation of the plan (Golvan 1986). It also requires a process with certain characteristics (e.g. attention to external facets) and activities. Heuristics take place both in systems' construction and during the planning process. And, there are fields of cultural impact on planning. A closer look at these issues will be provided in the following chapters.

2.26 Summary

In this section, conceptions of planning were discussed. Strategic planning was defined as 'frame of action and decision making.' It was explained what strategic planning is and what it cannot be. The concept of planning was put in perspective with the concept of culture. As the two sections above both put much emphasis on strategic decision processes' in the definition of strategy and planning, the next section will explain the underlying concept of "decision making."

2.3 Decision Processes

2.31 Attributes of Strategic Decisions

Decisions are commitments of resources to action (Mazzolini 1981:85; Mintzberg et al 1976:246). Decisions are purposive processes of choice between alternative future activities (Gzuk 1975:17). Processes are the sequence of activities incorporated in a particular decision system (Dutton/Ottensmeyer 1987:358). The term 'decision' itself is derived from the latin word 'incision,' which stands for cutting off further consideration (Pascale/Athos 1981:172).

Decisions can be classified by the stimuli that evoked them (opportunity, crisis, or problem), by solution (given, ready-made, custom-made, or modified, or the decision process used to arrive at them (Mintzberg et al 1976:251). Anthony (1965) and Bauer/Gergen (1968) distinguish between three types of decisions:

routine, tactical and strategic. Complexity, width of effects, length of the time horizon, level of management involved, and breadth of political complications cover the main differences in the continuum from routine to strategic decisions.[18]

By definition, strategic decisions are important, complex, novel, open-ended, (Mintzberg et al. 1976:246), "messy" (Ackoff:1974), mostly ill-structured (Mitroff/Emshoff (1979), "wicked," (Mason/Mitroff 1981:12), and lead to heuristics (Schwenk 1984:112; 1985a:75).

Therefore, strategic decisions are about non-routine matters (Hage 1980). Each decision is somewhat unique and cannot be solved by simple decision rules. Strategic decisions involve a somewhat irrevocable commitment of major resources and require risk-taking (Mintzberg et al 1976; Thomas 1984:140). They are on important issues, with restriction to the core issues, and proactive, in that they are geared towards early responses (Scholz 1987:6; Schwenk 1988:6). Most of the issues are ill-structured, indicating that there is no consensus as to the definition of the problem. Some strategic problems, however, are well structured, for example problems that have been imposed on the company, as is the case for governmental regulations (Lyles/Mitroff 1980).

Strategic decisions are future-oriented, environmentally related activities that directly affect the over-all organizational purpose (King/Clelland 1978:8). They are organizational phenomena of high leverage that are built on interdependent elements (Quinn 1978:8; Dutton et al. 1983). The main focus is on long-term factors (Gälweiler 1987:36). As strategic decisions are an interplay between external influences and the internal strategic facets of the firm, the strategic decision process must be analyzed in its context (Horváth/ McMillan 1979:93; Mintzberg 1979b).

2.32 Decision and Planning Processes

The last section explained, what strategic decisions are about. This section will explain normative views and empirical findings with regard to strategic decision and planning processes.

2.321 Normative Views

2.321.1 Normative Views of Decision Processes

Normative descriptions of decision processes typically consist of

---

[18] In using the word 'strategic,' we need to apply some caution. As Leontiades (1986:140) noted, 'The word strategic became a ubiquitous prefix attached to every aspect of every plan, and many subjects with no connection to planning. Would any planner admit to an unimportant or nonstrategic approach to planning?' This clearly indicates the importance of emphasizing appropriate definitions of the terms 'strategy' and 'strategic.'

a set of sequential steps, as given below (Adler 1986:135; Gibson et al 1985:570; Raffée 1974:96), mostly based on Dewey (1933:107).[19] These decision steps are often applied to describe regular, routine, problem-based decision making by both individuals, groups and organizations:

> Establishing of objectives and problem recognition; information search and development of alternatives; evaluating and choosing an alternative; implementing the decision; and control and evaluation.

Problems are situations where alternative courses of action are available which differ significantly in their consequences and introduce uncertainty as they require guesses about future outcomes of current actions and guesses concerning future preferences for these outcomes (Ackoff 1981:354; March 1978:589, 1979:9). Choices are selections among at least two alternatives (Brunsson 1982:29). Problem-setting processes differ from problem-solving processes in their focus, the required analytical skills, and levels of understanding (Dunbar/Dutton 1986). Solutions begin with the detection of stimuli for actions and end with a commitment to act (Mintzberg et al. 1976:246; Daft/Steers 1986:438).

2.321.2 Normative Views of Planning Processes

Normative descriptions of strategic planning processes follow the pattern of sequential steps in general decision making as outlined above quite closely (Cowan 1986; Ginter et al 1985:582; Glueck, 1980:280; Graddy et al 1985:118; Gup 1980; Higgins 1984:192; Hofer et al 1980:8; Thompson/ Strickland 1983:21,41; Steiner et al 1982:18; Weigele 1983:53; Zapotocky/Malzer 1984:308), in general based on Cohen/Cyert (1973):

> Establishing mission, purpose and goals; infor- mation search with regard to SWOT (strengths, weaknesses, opportunities, threats) and resulting gaps; development of scenarios; formulation of strategy and action-plans; implementation; review and control.

Such phase models aid in the systematic description of processes, provide guidance in the delineation of general suggestions, and clarify the constituting elements (Clement/Lukesch 1981:13). However, such phase models may lead to simplifying interpretations. Within a step, processes seem to be much more similar than they are in reality. Phase models suggest uniformity, where there is broad variety. They are often solely descriptive, deal with single activities out of the respective context, and lead to

---

[19] For reviews of other decision making perspectives that will be applied to strategic planning in the next chapter, see Hutt et al (1988:5), or Szyperski (1974):26). Here the emphasis is on providing the normative, rational-analytical perspective of the decision process, on which much of the strategic planning literature is based.

the impression of aboslute truth of purely rational-analytical-deductive models (Heckhausen 1981; Zutshi 1981:67).

2.321.3 Culture and Normative Processes

Due to the close resemblance of normative views on general decision making and on normative views of planning processes, it is helpful to review cultural influences on general decision making in a normative framework as depicted below.

Normative Steps	**Cultural Variations**	
Problem Recognition (Mission etc.)	Problem solving; Situation should be changed.	Situation accepting some situations should be accepted, not changed.
Information search (SWOT)	Gather "facts"	Gather ideas and possibilities.
Constructing Alternatives (Development Scenarios)	New, future oriented activities. People can learn and change.	Focus includes past present, and future alternatives. Adults can't change substantially
Choice (Formulation)	Individuals decide. Decision making responsibility delegated Decisions made quickly Decision rule: is it true or false?	Groups decide. Only senior management makes decisions Decisions are slow Decision rule: is it good or bad?
Implementation (Implementation)	Fast; managed from the top. Responsibility of one person.	Slow; involves participation of all levels. Responsibility of the group.

Table 2.1: Cultural Contingencies in Normative Steps of Decision Making and Planning.

Adapted from: Adler, Nancy (1986): Int'l Dimensions of Organizational Behavior. Kent Publ., Boston, MA 1986.

Some of the above shown distinctions refer to "typical Japanese" decision making, based on such structural features as the 'newwamashi' and 'ringi-systems' (Doktor 1983; Misumi 1984:526; Pascale 1978) and industry structures of 'zaibatsus' and 'keiretsus' (Wright/Pauli 1988:51).

In a similar vein, Ansoff (1984:426) normatively distinguishes between the <u>Western</u> decision making model (optimization of choice, decisiveness, serial sequence), resulting in quick decisions, long action cycle, resistance to planning, and implementation delays/frustration), and the Japanese decision making model (acceptance of choice, implementability, optimization, parallel sequence, resulting in longer decisions, shorter action cycle, cooperative planning, and supportive implementation). However, as will be shown below, the reality of decision making does not always stick to these normative descriptions of a truly rational flow of decisions.

2.322 Empirical Views

In empirical research, the decision process is seen a set of actions and dynamic factors (Mintzberg et al. 1976:246) which include streams of choices, streams of problems, the flow of solutions, and streams of energy from participants (Cohen et al. 1972:3). Streams of energy are used in thinking backward to understand the past and in looking forward to predict the future (Einhorn/Hogarth 1987:66).

Strategic decision processes are seen to vary in their initiation, the role of goals, the means/ends link, relationship, the interpretation of strategic action, and it's comprehensiveness (Fredrickson 1986b:283).

The variety and complexity of factors influencing the strategic decision lead to considerable latitude in understanding a specific issue (Dutton et al 1983:308). It is a continuous, complex process that reaches across functional boundaries and hierarchical levels. Lines of communication, content, way of gathering and probability of accuracy of information are not strictly prescribed or even predictable (Spekman/Stern 1979:56). The process deals with issues with an undefined range of alternatives that are multidimensional in nature. To overcome information overload and assure for relevant outcomes, restrictions of target and action scopes are necessary (Scholz 1987:33).

The process affects various stakeholder groups and multiple actors whose involvement is temporally and functionally divided and who have different risk levels (Jemison/Sitkin 1986:16). It sets of 'waves' of lesser decisions, which result in organization-wide consequences (Mintzberg et al 1976).

Ginter et al (1985:581), while trying to conform the normative model of strategic management, found that the phases were all included, but the relative importance of the steps varied significantly. Fredrickson (1984:455) could only prove the appropriateness for firms in industries with stable environments.

Witte (1972) addressed the issue of the phase theorem. He tried to discover whether such distinct phases as described above do actually exist, and whether they follow any sequence. He found that there is a high level of activity at the beginning and at the end of strategic decision process, and a lower level in the middle (Witte 1972:178). However, he found that the activities that are subscribed to the specific steps in the normative literature are performed simultaneously (Witte 1972:180). Similarly, Mintzberg et al (1976:252) found logic in 'delineating distinct phases of the strategic decision process, but not in postulating a simple sequential relationship between them.'

Their widely recognized model of strategic decision making seems to come much closer to the reality of strategic planning than the normative models described before. The intertwined steps they identified were: identification (recognition; diagnosis), development (memory, passive, trap, or active search; design) and selection (screening; evaluation-choice through judgment, bargaining, or analysis; authorization.

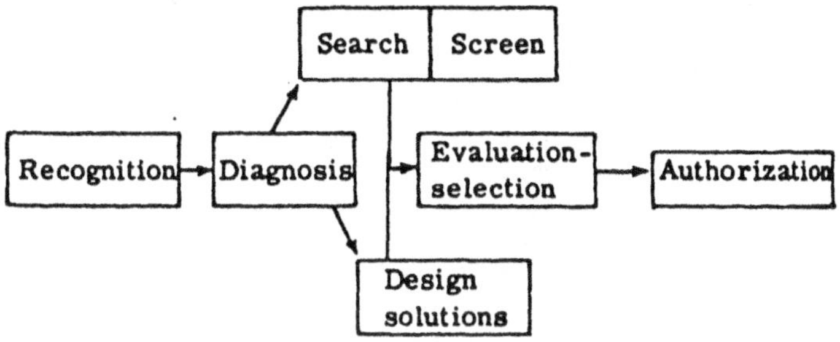

Figure 2.2 General Model of the Strategic Decison Process

Source for this simplified model: Butler, Richard / Astley, Graham / Hickson, David / Mallory, Geoffrey / Wilson, David (1979:11): Strategic Decison-Making: Concepts of Content and Process. In: Int'l Studies of Management & Organization, 9, 4, pp. 5-36.

Their analysis showed that 'there is not a steady, undisturbed progression from one routine to another; rather, the process is dynamic, operating in an open system where it is subjected to interferences, feedback loops, dead ends, and other factor' (Mintzberg et al 1976:263). Similar findings with regard to the phase theorem were reported by Nutt (1984b) and Shrivastava/Grant (1985).

Again, the emphasis here is to show the contextual impact on strategic planning. While there may be phases, their content and degree of overlap may be culture-bound, eg. through the difference in convergent and divergent thinking (Mintzberg et al 1976:255),[20] the attention to and the use of information (Schneider 1989), continuous versus discrete flow of decisions (Pascale/Athos 1981:173), the serial or parallel sequence of formulation and implementation (Ansoff 1984:4260), or decision making in general

---

[20] Mintzberg et al (1976:255) could show the differences in the development phase between the search for ready-made solutions and the design or modification of custom-made ones, which they claim is exactly the distinction between convergent and divergent thinking.

(Hofstede 1980; Misumi 1984; Takahashi/Takayangi 1985). Hence, structuring of activities through standardization, specialization, and formalization (Uncertainty Avoidance), group practices versus individual initiative (Individualism), collaboration between managers on different ranks (Power Distance), and the type of information processing (Organizational Learning) may result in differences in and between the strategic planning phases.

2.33 Summary and Conclusion

This chapter dealt with the notions of strategy, planning, strategic decisions, and strategic decision and planning process. For each of these terms, conceptualizations were critically reviewed, both from their origin and with regard to their applicability to comparative research. Strategy was defined as 'pattern in the stream of actions and decisions.' Planning was defined as 'frame of action and decision making.' Strategic decisions were defined as important, complex, novel, open-ended, messy, and ill-structured issues. Normative and empirical views with regard to decision and planning steps let to the conclusion that they are highly interrelated flows. Throughout the discussion, comparisons of the conceptualizations with cultural dimensions were undertaken.

After basic concepts of strategic planning were defined in this chapter, the next chapter will use this terminology to distinguish between different approaches to strategic planning. Whereas here the emphasis was on normative, rational-analytical views about planning and decision making, alternative views will be integrated in the next chapter on approaches to planning systems.

3 STRATEGIC PLANNING SYSTEMS

This chapter introduces a culture-based conceptual framework for classifying and analyzing strategic planning approaches. The aim is to show how this theoretical framework can help to predict the likely impact of contextual factors on planning approaches.

3.1 Categorizing Planning Systems

To clarify contextual influences on planning frameworks, several authors proposed conceptualizations of planning approaches as shown in the following. While these approaches to categorize strategic planning systems may be quite useful for delineating several contextual influences on strategic planning frameworks, they do not tie cultural dimensions to underlying assumptions and outcome differences of the planning approaches.

Based on the cultural aspects of a process-oriented model of managerial functions as depicted below, these planning conceptualizations were summarized and categorized into <u>five underlying planning approaches</u>: action-vision, avoidance-emergent, incremental-adaptive, political-power, and action-vision-approaches to planning.

Concept	**Explanation**
Individualism (Quasi-Resolution Conflict)	Individual subunits that create consistency through "local rationality vs. uniform of of systems
Uncertainty Avoidance	Solve pressing problems and anticipate short-term reactions of other parts of the environment to reduce uncertainty rather than develop long-term strategy.
Power Distance (Problemistic Search)	Satisficing to find solutions to problems as perceived in the usual power structure and environment
Organizational Learning	Adaptive change as the result of experience

Table 3.1 The Cyert/March (1963) Process-Oriented Model of Managerial Functions.

<u>Cyert/March</u> (1963:113-123) proposed four components of a process-oriented model of managerial functions as shown below. <u>Hofstede</u> (1980), based on the works by Cyert/March (1963), Mulder (1971), and the Aston group (e.g. Pugh/Hickson 1976), developed similar dimensions to describe differences between organizations in an international context. Organizational learning was emphasized by <u>Sullivan/Nonaka</u> (1986, 1988) for comparative research in strategy. <u>Dutton et al</u> (1983:85,318) similarly suggest heterarchy, the involvement of individuals at multiple levels), and masculinity-

Author	**Rational/ Analytical**	**Avoidance/ Emergent**	**Incremental/ Adaptive**	**Political/ Power**	**Action/ Vision**
Ackoff (1981)	Research Approach/ Problem Solving	-	Clinical Approach/ Problem Resolving	-	Design Approach/ Problem Dissolving
Allison (1971)	Rational Classical Model	-	Org. Process Model	Political Process Bureaucratic Politics Model	-
Boulding (1956), Pondy & Mitroff (1981)	Machine	Cultural	Biological	-	-
Bourgeois & Brodwin (1984); Scholz (1987)	Commander Model	Cultural Model	Collaborative Model	Crescive Model	Change Model
Butler et al. (1979)	Rational	Non-decision	Incremental	Garbage Can	-
Camillus (1982)	Synoptic Formalism	-	Logical Incrementalism	-	-
Chaffee (1985)	Linear	Interpre-tive		Adaptive	--
Gluck et al (1982)	Strategic Planning	-	-	Strategic Thinking	Opportu-nistic Dec.mkg.
Lyles & Thomas (1986)	Rational	Avoidance	Adaptive	Political	Decisive
March (1981)	Rational Change	Rule	Learning	Conflict Contagion	Regenera-tion

Table 3.2 <u>Categorization Derivations</u>
Existing classifications of planning approaches were reclassified into five approaches, following four underlying cultural dimensions (UA, PD, IDV, OL).

Author	Rational/ Analytical	Avoidance/ Emergent	Incremental/ Adaptive	Political/ Power	Action/
Mintzberg (1973b	Planning	-	Adaptive	-	Entrepre- neurial
Mintzberg (1981)	Formalized Procedure & Articulated Result	Pro- gramming	Integrated Decision Making	-	Future Thinking
Mintzberg (1985)	Deliberate; Planned	Emergent; Imposed; Cultural	Process	Consensus, Umbrella Unconnected	Entrepre- neurial
Nutt (1984a,b)	Historical	Search	Nova	Off the Shelf	Appraisal
Quinn (1978)	Formal Systems Approach	-	Incremental	Power- Behavioral	-
Shrivastava & Grant (1985)	Systemic Bureaucracy Model	-	Adaptive Planning Model	Political Expediency Model	Managerl. Autocracy Model
Steinbruner (1974)	-	Cybernetic Model	-	-	Cognitive Model
Steiner, Miner, Gray (1982)	Formal structured Approach	-	Incrementing and Adaptive	-	Intuitive- Anticipatory Entrepreneurial- Opportunistic
Taylor (1987)	Central Control System	-	-	Political Planning	Futures Research
Thompson (1967)	Computational	Compromise	-	Judgmental	Inspirational

Table 3.2 <u>Categorization Derivations</u> cont'd
Existing classifications of planning approaches were reclassified into five approaches, following four underlying cultural dimensions (UA, IDV, PD, OL).

femininity (dominant values for division of social roles). So does Zutshi (1981:93) in describing the structural characteristics of planning by authority relationships (power distance), departmentalization (individualism), and the extent of formalization (uncertainty avoidance).

If we use these dimensions as qualitative scales, the relative positions of cultures can be compared.[21] Here it is argued that five different planning approaches correspond to certain values of the four underlying cultural dimensions. For clarification, they are depicted below in a simplified way with regard to planning frameworks. It is argued that certain approaches are more prone to be applied in specific cultural settings than others. For example, rational/analytical planning systems under conditions of low uncertainty avoidance, low power distance, high individualism, and specific organizational learning, as is the case in the USA (Hofstede 1980; Sullivan/Nonaka 1986).

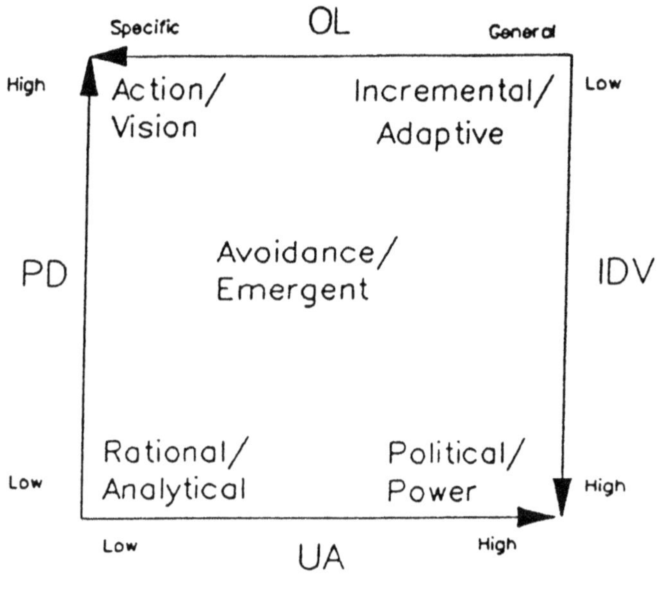

Figure 3.1 Categorization of Strategic Planning Approaches.

The individualism-collectivism (IDV) dimension refers to the participative-ness of decisions, and emphasis on tasks and

---

[21] It is not suggested, that these dimensions determine strategic planning approaches. However, it is argued, that they influence strategic decision making and planning. Following Zutshi (1981:86) in applying the systems approach, a strategic planning system (SPS) can be expressed as a function of dimensions and their interaction with the company, e.g. as SPS = f(UA, PD, IDV, OL, 0), where 0 is a residual value to represent that planning systems are open rather than closed systems. For a further discussion of systems concepts, see Ackoff (1971).

individual initiative versus emphasis on relations and on loyalty and duty to the organization (Mintzberg 1980:238). Uncertainty avoidance (UA) is the extent to which unstructured, unclear or unpredictable situations result in the adoption of institutionalized security through formalization, standardization, specialization, and ritualization (Hofstede 1983a:81). Organizational learning (OL) refers to the acquisition, sources, types, spread and use of information by organizations (Fiol/Lyles 1985; Hedberg 1981; Shrivastava/Grant 1985). Power distance (PD) refers to the degree of acceptance of inequality, centralization of authority and autocratic leadership (Hofstede 1983:81).

The advantages of this classification scheme are manyfold. First, it allows much of the empirical work on strategic management to be considered within a rigorous theoretical framework. It is useful because it deals with fundamentally different perspectives for explaining strategic planning approaches. Second, the different approaches are widely known and used. What is new is the introduction of elements that distinguish between the approaches. This framework, therefore suggests new research questions and directions as well as interesting implications for practicing managers.

Third, the proposed categorizations cover both models that emphasize strategy formulation (i.e. problem setting; e.g. Lyles/Thomas 1986), and those which focus mainly on strategy implementation (i.e. problem solving; e.g. Bourgeois/Brodwin 1984). Due to the characteristics of the planning process, decision process models (e.g. Nutt 1984) were included to reflect the decomposition of strategic decisions into their process components (Witte 1972:157). It includes categorizations both derived from business settings (e.g. Steiner et al 1982) and politics (Allison 1971).

It is intended to provide a "lens" for examining relevant issues, the relationships and relative importance of these issues, and for simplifying assumptions with this construct (Hofer et al. 1980:3). The distinction between the approaches labeled above is neither intended to be normative, nor exhaustive or clear-cut; it shows extremes.[22] This categorization is not intended to be a hierarchical model as some of the frameworks from the literature review propose (e.g. Boulding 1956). There are overlaps on some dimensions, as the review of similar categorizations in table 3.2 showed. Therefore, each of the five planning approaches is discussed seperately in the following.

---

[22] The graphical representation in Figure 3.1 serves only as a guide for the reader. It is not suggested by the author that there are strict correlations, as they could wrongfully be read into the graphical representation. Individualism and Power Distance are negatively correlated (r = 0.-67) in the way Hofstede (1983b:50) used the dimensions. Uncertainty avoidance and Power Distance are only marginally (r = +0.28) correlated (Hofstede 1980).

3.2 Rational-Analytical Models

The essential property of this approach is the view of planning as the outcome of intended, rational conscious choice (Schwenk 1988:7). Executives identify opportunities and threats, predict change, formulate strategic plans, and consequently guide implementation (Kagono et al 1985:217). The assumption is that organizations behave as rational individuals. In analogy to Foster (1986:181), the first point concerns the problem of delineating what constitutes a "rational planner." Central to the rationality concept are complete information and foresight, the absence of uncertainty, complete mobility, pure competition, and objectivity (Kantona 1969:92). This includes both substantive (content) and procedural (process) rationality (Simon 1959).

Formality is supposed to reduce uncertainty (Fischhoff/Goitein 1984:505). Some authors adhere these models to comprehensive rationality (Allison 1971:71), while others limit it to instrumental rationality (Murray 1978:10). "The process described .. assumes that strategists are analytically objective" (Andrews 1980:25), impartial, amoral (Mintzberg 1980:110) and, as a result, agree upon events and implications (Stubbard 1986a:8).

Thus, the rational-analytical models of the strategic planning process are characterized by the formalized, explicit order of ends, ways, means that are achieved in a linear, integrated, tightly coupled, purposive process with distinct static phases as shown below to maximize proactivly the future output of the whole organization following a known order of priorities (Ansoff 1969; Fredrickson 1986a:474; Hayes 1985:112; Stubbard 1986b:5). Implementation by the "doers" is no problem in an environment that is assumed to be predictable due to analytic, specific hard data the "thinkers" have, leading to quantifiable results (Bourgeois/Brodwin 1984:244). "If the analysis was right, .. the correct strategy would pop out automatically" (Gluck 1986:20). Each step is undertaken in an impersonal way, emotions are screened out of planning (Stubbard 1986b:5; Mintzberg 1980:110).

Author	**Phases, Routines, and Path Configurations**
Glueck (1976)	Appraisal (set objectives; determine threats, opportunities & comp. advantage); choice (evaluate; decide); implementation (develop structure, corp. culture and medium & short range plans); evaluation; back to appraisal. <u>The</u> textbook example. A strategy is a unified, comprehensive, and integrated plan (ends-orientation).

Table 3.3 Phases in Rational/Analytical Planning Systems

3.3 Avoidance/Emergent Strategy Models

Central to this approach is the assumption that goals can emerge from the decision-making process rather than exist as given inputs to it (Mintzberg 1980:112). Realized strategies that never were intended or formally articulated emerge implicitly through natural convergence over time (Mintzberg 1978:945; 1981:322). The organization "carries itself" through cycles of innovation, learning, passive waiting and defense (Bourgeois/Brodwin 1984:251; Nutt 1984a:438). Strategy evolves gradually over time, as a result of market feedback to managerial judgments and trial and error. The table below depicts this phase theorem.

Author	**Phases, Routines, and Path Configurations**
Cowan (1986)	Gestation (latency, scanning); categorization (arousal, discrepancy, perceived urgency, clarification, accumulation of discrepancies, discrepancy classification); diagnosis (familiarity, priority, search, inference), activity. This model makes a distinction between opportunity, crisis and problem decisions (Mintzberg et al 1976:251), and emphasizes attention, readiness to respond, attempts to understand, and attachment of labels.

Table 3.4: Phases in Avoidance/Emergent Planning Systems

Accepting uncertainty helps to make tentativeness legitimate. Vagueness can be intentional in itself, for example to reserve the decision on what course of action to pursue, without the need for immediate clarification (Pascal/Athos 1981:140). Emergent actions are pragmatic, less guided by sophisticated planning procedures (Kagono et al 1985:2216). Management needs to be open, flexible and responsive, close to the market (Mintzberg/Waters 1985:271). Beliefs of management and workers are the key to setting the long-term direction.

Strategy is developed by the masses, not by the few. Managing the corporate culture is seen to be possible and gives the necessary orienting metaphors and frames of reference (Bourgeois/Brodwin 1984:250). Thus, strategy is an organization-wide activity, not just top-managements' concern (Chaffee 1985:93). This requires motivation and assumes informed and intelligent people that can make and inplement consistent, satisficing decisions at all levels within an open system of organization and environment (Bourgeois/Brodwin 1984:252).

Size, homogeneity and inbreeding can hamper flexibility and creativity, and lead to the maintenance of the status quo through the avoidance of problems or the ignorance of uncertainty (Lyles/Thomas 1986:10; Stubbard 1986a:13). To overcome such "calm placidity" of a non-decision-making organization (Butler et al. 1979:6) in organizations in the Western hemisphere, decision aids, e.g. the concepts of devil's advocate (Schwenk/Cosier 1980), dialectical inquiry, strategic assumption analysis, (Mason/Mitroff 1981) or risk analysis (Hertz/Thomas 1983:28) were proposed to detect strategic problems over time (Thomas 1984: 152). Alternatively, strong corporate cultures and commitment were suggested (Deal/Kennedy 1982; Peters/Waterman 1982). Exactly to combat this avoidance, let-it-emerge-type behavior.

3.4 Adaptive/Incremental Models

Incremental decision-making contrasts with rationality assumptions (Butler et al 1979:31). Individuals and groups are subject to heuristics and biases that lead to limited mental capacities for noticing and reacting to available information (Hogarth/ Makridakis 1981; Schwenk 1984; Stubbard 1986a:10). Decision-makers are seen as limited information processors subject to representational simplifications and "bounded rationality" (March/Simon 1958; Cyert/March 1963). Thus, only small parts of the complex problems can be dealt with at one point in time (Lindblom 1968; Quinn 1978).

Changes are introduced in a stepwise fashion. As lead times for implementation are extended, frictions are reduced (Schierenbeck 1987:37). For each major class of strategic issue, a different subsystem is used to formulate strategy (Quinn 1980:18). Problems are continually redefined as the organization must change with the environment (Chaffee 1985:91). The planning process is geared at achieving an alteration of the current state, not at a specified goal (Fredrickson 1983; Johnson 1988).

Authors	**Phases, Routines, and Path Configurations**
Denning (1971)	Simultaneous environmental and corporate appraisal; generation of alternatives; evaluation with simultaneous test against environmental factors and estimation of resources; decisions. Development of alternatives and evaluation are very close intertwined in this model. It includes interrupts, delays and recycles.

Table 3.5: Phases in Incremental/Adaptive Planning Systems

Strategic adaptation is no smooth process. Discontinuous, "revolutionary" changes in strategy occur after periods of relative stability (Miller/Friesen 1983). However, due to the emphasis on mutual agreement on the definition of a problem, change must be introduced slowly and incrementally (Lyles/Thomas 1986:12). Only a restricted number of alternatives is considered (Steiner et al 1982:285). Maximizing or optimizing behavior is replaced by satisficing (March/Simon 1958; Murray 1978:14) and search for more security promising short-run feedback as the environment is less susceptible to prediction (Chaffee 1985:92).

Decision processes consist of a plurality of subdecisions without simple sequential relationships between them (Witte 1972:177; Mintzberg et al 1976:252). This means-ways-ends approach requires somewhat dispersed expertise and responsibility (Hayes 1985:118). Organizational learning is broad in nature, supported by high collectivism. Alternatives are approached incrementally through try and error. This is made possible by a low level of uncertainty avoidance.

3.5 Political/Power Models

Contrary to the rational/analytical approach, the strategic planning process mirrors individual and group interests (Pettigrew 1977). "Power relationships and organization alignments become evident in the formulation of plans; and bargaining and negotiation processes characterize many decision processes" (Fahey 1981:52). Plans are the outcome of bargaining about the allocation of resources between interdependent coalitions.[23] This is reflected in the phases of the process as depicted in the table below.

Authors	**Phases, Routines, and Path Configurations**
Paine/Naumes (1982)	Individual awareness and sense making; collective mobilization; coalitions for action; coalition management; strategy making. Coalitions pursue in incremental steps of political activity to formulate and implement strategies. Awareness, possession, control and tactical use of power function as an overlay over the "normal" planning phases. Scanning is the process of assessing what people with power think about the problem and weighing their influence potential.

Table 3.6: Phases in Political/Power Planning Systems

Managers sometimes use planning to gain control over others (Armstrong 1982:201). Politics in the organization can distort or hinder the use of analysis (Mintzberg 1980:105). Scarcity, criticality, and uncertainty of resources lead to bargaining

[23] A quite dramatic, nevertheless realistic view provides Taylor (1987:29): "Planning decisions affect people's lives. Strategic planning determines where investments are made and where businesses stop investing; where jobs are created and where employees are made redundant; ...salaries, promotion and advancement, recognition and status - these are what planning is about."

routines among those who have control over choices (Salancik/ Pfeffer 1977:13; Mintzberg et al 1976:262). The distribution, acquisition and influence of power and authority leads to social pressure and influences all steps of the planning process the flow of information and the outcome of decisions. (Allison 1971:146; Mintzberg 1976:263; Lyles/Mitroff 1980:110; Guth/MacMillan 1986:314). Organizations that favor competition assume that competing ideas produce superior decisions (Nutt 1984a:434). Managers in such organizations need to learn how to apply power in the planning process to rise in the organization. As everybody tries to act authoritatively (high individualism), there is collective behavior, but on different levels within the organization. Political behavior, often masked in rigid structuring of activities anf formalization (high uncertainty avoidance) can only emerge in decentralized organizations, where it is possible to challenge upper management (low power distance). Subjective views and qualitative information are integrated in analytical information.

3.6 Action/Vision Models

In Mintzberg's (1980) entrepreneurial mode, a powerful leader takes bold, risky decisions towards his vision of the organizations future (Mintzberg 1980:934). Strategy making is dominated by the active search for new opportunities rather than problem solving (Steiner et al 1982:285). Power is centralized to move forward towards growth in the face of uncertainty (Mintzberg 1973a:45). "Management by involvement" with emphasis on implementation to put decisions into action is driven by a vision that does not require exhaustive analysis (Bhide 1986:65; Gluck 1986:22).

Under conditions of uncertainty, nonanalytical mental operations will appear, and the cognitive inference mechanism will tend to eliminate trade-offs from the belief system" (Murray 1978:25). Detailing activities are assumed to be carried out on the job (Nutt 1984a:436). Uncertainty is reduced through the belief in the self-fulfilling prophecy: the vision. Implementation and formulation are approached parallel, because 'clear, imaginative visions depend on an involvmement with detail, on intimate knowledge of specifics (Mintzberg/Waters 1982:496).

Authors	**Phases, Routines, and Path Configurations**
Mintzberg & Waters (1982)	Uneven progress, with very long cycles of major reorientations; periods of pause, following periods of sprinting; test-the-water with controlled boldness, always sensing an environment with minor probes before plunging in. Intuition and vision based on wisdom - detailed, personalized knowledge of the market.

Table 3.7: Phases in Action/Vision Planning Systems

Thus, driven by vision (which essentially is a kind of plan) and activities of intra- and entrepreneurs, strategic issues are defined informally, and attacked through high levels of activity and of trial and error (low uncertainty avoidance). Based on the central vision (high power distance), participation is an outcome of these shared beliefs (low individualism). Implicit decision premises and experience-based, subjective information lead to personal visions (specific organizational learning).

3.7 Summary and Conclusion

In this chapter, a model to categorize strategic planning approaches based on four cultural dimensions, namely uncertainty avoidance, power distance, organizational learning, and individualism was introduced. These dimensions were applied to distinguish between planning conceptualizations. Five major planning approaches were identified: rational/analytical, avoidance/emergent, adaptive/incremental, political/power, and action/vision-approaches.[24] Several conclusions were drawn from this framework.

First, specific approaches should be used in specific cultural environments. Both the planning system can generate corporate objectives, and, in turn, corporate objectives can generate the appropriate planning system (Schwenk 1988:46). However, as was shown above, both components are influenced by culture.

Second, we need to be careful in the evaluation of the strengths and weaknesses of each of these approaches to planning. In each of the approaches, theories of effectiveness are imbedded (Quinn/McGrath 1985:328). For example, whereas the rational/analytical approach tries to reach some specific goals, the adaptive/incremental model may have been set up (consciously or not) to adapt continuously to the changing environment. Therefore, the measure of effectiveness has to be contingent on the planning approach. And, planning systems themselves need to be adaptive.

Third, one of the things that were made clear in the delineation and comparison of the planning approaches was that we need to pay attention to the heuristics that take place during the strategic planning process: "In the case of uncertainty, the definition of rationality becomes problematic" (March/Simon 1958:138). Managers don't always act as 'economic man' (rational/analytical); strategies can emerge from unconnected actions and decisions (avoidance/emergent); issues are broken down into small, incremental parts, and approached in incremental steps (adaptive/incremental); power and politics are an important part of management, and hence, planning (political/power); intuitive visions take on their own life (action/vision).

---

[24] The author agrees with Amey (1986:130) who states that "By modeling the planning process of such systems we abstract from reality, and such abstraction is seen to be necessary in order to gain greater insights into the nature of the reality."

4 HEURISTICS IN STRATEGIC PLANNING PROCESSES

In the last chapter, approaches to strategic planning were reviewed. Four cultural dimensions (uncertainty avoidance, power distance, organizational learning, and individualism) were found to be useful parameters to distinguish different approaches to planning. One of the conclusions from that chapter was that we need to pay attention to the heuristics that take place during the strategic planning process. Mangers don't always act as 'economic man;' strategies can emerge from unconnected actions and decisions; issues are broken down into small, incremental parts, and approached in incremental steps; power and politics play an important role in planning; intuitive visions take on their own live. Therefore, this chapter will take a closer look at the heuristics and biases that "happen" during the strategic planning process.

4.1 The Nature of Heuristics in Strategic Decisions

Weick (1979b:64), contending that the "human actor does not react to an environment, he enacts it," and Herbert Simon's notions of "satisficing" and "bounded rationality" (Simon 1976; March 1978) were of big impact on writers in strategic management (Hogarth/Makridakis 1981; Steiner et al 1982, Barnes 1984; Schwenk 1984, 1985b, 1988), and general management (e.g. Mintzberg 1975; Isenberg 1984), especially on empirical research (Mintzberg et al 1976; Lyles/Mitroff 1980; Kotter 1982; Duhaime/Grant 1984). However, normative writers still depart from this notion, e.g. in making the concept of "impartiality" central to strategic management (Andrews 1980:15). Moreover, with a few notable exceptions, (Barnes 1984; Bazerman 1986; Schwenk 1984, 1985b, 1988) empirical research did not take into account the impact of heuristics on process dimensions of strategic decisions. Thus, in explaining strategic decisions, behavioral, emotional, perceptual and rational impacts on the decision process must be taken into consideration (Bazerman 1986:11; Duhaime/Schwenk 1985:187; Moag 1973:91).

"Heuristics" are simplification processes (Schwenk 1984:112), rules of thumb (Meffert 1979:487), or general inferential rules (Barnes 1984:129) decision makers use to simplify the decision situations (Simon 1957; Tversky/Kahneman 1974:1124). An excellent overview of cognitive simplification processes is provided in Kahneman et al. (1982) or Bazerman (1986). In the following, both cognitive biases that derive from judgmental heuristics and motivational effects (Tversky/Kahneman 1974:1130), and biases resulting from social interaction (Aronson 1984) will be summarized under the term "heuristics."

4.2 The Relativity of Rationality and Heuristics

As national culture is represented in the managers' frames of reference and decision making (Elbing 1978; Lammers/Hickson 1979b:403; Redding 1980:129; Shrivastava/Mitroff 1983:165,) it should be represented in the heuristics during planning, too.

Among the empirical studies on planning pitvalls reviewed below,[25] Orpen (1984) found differences in perceived benefits of planning. Steiner/Schollhammer (1975) found variations on the most important planning pitfalls across six countries.

Study	Description of Study	Questions & Content
Ringbakk (1969)	350 companies in U.S. and Europe; 65 interviews, remainder questionnaires	Reasons why formal planning systems may not function properly
Steiner/ Schollhammer (1975)	460 Multinationals headquartered in the USA, Canada, Australia, Japan, Italy, and U.K.	Pitfalls encountered in long-range planning
Naylor/ Schauland (1976)	346 corporations in the U.S., Canada, and Europe; questionnaires.	Shortcomings of corporate simulative planning models
Orpen (1984)	64 indian and 72 U.S. questionnaire responses of companies with at least 1.000 employees	Perceived problems in long-range planning efforts
Sethi (1987)	US and other multinational companies; questionnaire and interviews	Sources of conflict during the planning process
Moormann (19881,b)	46 questionnaires from Austrian, German, and Swiss banks	Reasons for not including branch managers in planning

Table 4.1 Planning Heuristics reported in Multi-Country Studies

Hofstede (1980:155) therefore argues that

> [w]hat is non-logical to a larger public may seem logical or rational to the actor. What is rational for people sharing the same culture may be non-rational to people not sharing that culture.

---

[25] In a review of 22 empirical studies of planning pitfalls and problems with planning processes, thirteen most frequent issues were identified. These are uncertainty and data, organization, upper management, participation, climate, personnel, goals, time, flexibility, overconfidence, control, approach, and power & politics. These pitfalls relate to the cultural dimensions applied here. For details, see Haiss (1989:71-81).

Bazerman (1986:87) similarly argues that '[m]any of the cognitive assumptions that we make about how to solve the problems arise from the culture and environment that surround us." Kumon (1984:8) considers the impact of cognitive aspects of culture on managerial practice, while observing that

> the nature of Japanese reasoning is "analytical" whereas that of Westerners can be characterized as "comprehensive." Thus the cognitive process of Japanese, in most cases, goes from the whole to its parts. For them to understand something is to divide it into parts ..[T]he cognitive process of Westerners tends to proceed from individual elements to a larger whole ... [W]hen individual objects which were first taken separately are put together forming one whole, Westerners say they comprehend it. Comprehension is just the opposite of division.

However, we need to be careful in evaluating findings about differences in cognitive modeling behavior between cultures in order not to misinterpret the meaning of other cultures' decision making and planning behavior (Adler et al 1986:26). Therefore, the argument here is twofold.

- At first, it is suggested that <u>some heuristics are more prone to happen in specific cultural settings</u>, for example groupthink in highly individualistic environments.

- Second, <u>what behavior is regarded as logical-rational or as non-rational heuristics is subject to cultural influences</u>, for example with regard to fatalism (domination or submission).

4.3 Conceptualization

In the preceding chapter on planning systems, it was argued that four cultural dimensions (uncertainty avoidance, power distance, organizational learning, individualism/collectivism)[26] can be used to conceptualize different planning approches. Combining this with the arguments presented above, it should be useful to link heuristics that influence decision processes with cultural

---

[26] <u>Individualism</u> as a measure of the forces towards integration and of the amount of freedom and support of a subsystem (Hofstede 1983a:79) refers to participation and the value of inidvdual initiatives. <u>Uncertainty avoidance</u> as the extent to which unclear, unstructured, or unpredictable situations lead to risk avoidance and acts of insittutionalized security (Hofstede 1983a:81) is reflected in the formalization, standardization, and specialization of tasks. <u>Organizational learning</u>, which is the experience resulting in adaptive change (Cyert/March 1963:123f) refers to used information sources and respective wazs of information processing. <u>Power Distance</u> is the degree to which people accept a hierarchical order or strive for equality (Hofstede 1984b:83).

dimensions (Hofstede 1980, 1984a). Here it is proposed that different values of these four cultural dimensions correlate to specific planning heuristics.

Dimension	Heuristic	Influence
Organizational Learning	Availability, Representativeness, Adjustment and Anchoring, Hindsight Bias, Illusory Correlations	necessary prerequisite for emergent strategies; may lead to adaptive rationality or learned helplessness.
Collectivism/ Individualism	Escalating Commitment Towards the Organization, Groupthink, Parochialism, Face Saving	Enactment, detachment activity trap, game rationality, egocentrism.
Power Distance	Escalating Commitment Towards Actions, Paternalism, Power Alliences, Obedience	entrapment, power struggles, defensive reasoning, selective rationality.
Uncertainty Avoidance	Illusion of Control, Reasoning by Analogy, Wishful thinking Certainty effect, Dogmatism, Fatalism, Ritualization	overconfidence, resistance to change, quantification, quick-fix- solutions, repressed uncertainty

Table 4.2: Heuristics and Cultural Dimensions

4.4 Organizational Learning

Organizational learning is a process of changing organizational behavior. It includes both the establishment of action-outcome relationships (Duncan/Weiss 1979), and Argyris's (1977) "double loop learning," the process of determining what questions to ask and what is the range of useful answers (Michael 1973). Organizational learning was portrayed in terms of adaption (Cyert/March 1963), creation of "theories-in-use" (Argyris/Schön 1978), and institutionalized information processing patterns (Hedberg 1981; Mitroff/Emshoff 1979).

However, there are systemic barriers to learning (Shrivastava/ Grant 1985:98). Organizational learning implies fits and starts through experimentation and trial and error (Fischhoff/Goitein 1984:506; Lenz/Lyles 1985:64; Uyterhoeven 1972:82). It also implies "learning from the accidents of past experience, and pragmatic inventions of necessity" (Cohen et al 1972:1). This experimentation needs some leeway and causes vulnerability. There is a specific mix of problems that have access to the organization, as well as a mix of solutions looking for problems

(Cohen et al 1972:16). Organizational learning is subject to selective attention, established search sets, and subjective familiarity and saliency of issues that are rooted in the availability and transformation of past experience through anchoring and adjustment (Isenberg 1984:86; Shrivastava 1983:9; Slovic et al 1977:5; Tversky/Kahneman 1974:1127f). This can result in illusory correlations about representativeness in case of positive outcomes, or in social deadlocks (Barnes 1984:131; Brunsson 1982:41; Chapman/Chapman 1969) and learned helplessness, the "perception of independence between actions and outcomes" (Langer 1975:323), in case of negative outcomes. Both are forms of adaptive rationality which can infer perceptions about the inevitability of events (Fischhoff 1975:288; Barnes 1984:130; March 1978:592)).

To the extent that strategic decisions draw upon the acquired knowledge base, they are influenced by learning processes (Shrivastava/Grant 1985:98). If there is no leeway for organizational learning, strategic patterns that often evolve from discrete steps cannot emerge. Strategic learning is a necessary requirement for emergent strategies (Mintzberg/Waters 1985:271).

4.5 Individualism

Individualism/collectivism is a measure of the integration of a society or societal subsystem seen in the relation between an individual and his or her in-groups (Hofstede 1984b:390). This dimension brings the group-related biases (political, bargaining, and power-heuristics) in the decision process that were discussed above in connection with the individual and his orientation. Planning behavior in organizations with high attachment of the managers to the organization may seem irrational and incomprehensible to those who assume self-interest to be the ultimate motivation (Hofstede 1984a:86).

In highly ambiguous situations, decision makers tend to align themselves to judgments of other people (Murray 1978:27). Where there is a strong perceived need for group solidarity, collective patterns of shared rationalizations occur (Janis 1973:16; Gibson et al 1985:278). In that case, commitment to an organization (Porter et al 1974) is directly transferred to commitment to a course of action (Salanzik 1977). Thus, escalating commitment (Staw/Fox 1977) on the side of the individual can be transferred into "social corroboration" (Murray 1978:27), also termed "groupthink" (Janis 1973). Groupthink seems to occur more frequently in highly individualistic environments, with homogeneous ingroups. Whereas the heterogeneity of ingroups in collectivist environments (as is the case in Japan) allows for extensive, "real" discussion.

The fear of being blamed for negative outcomes (e.g. sunk costs) increases the probability of such failures (Whetten 1980:580; Leatherwood/Conlon 1986), reduces innovativeness, (Chakravarthy/Lorange 1984:45), and leads to face-saving compromises (Brockner et al 1981:68; Earl 1984:50) through defensive attribution of responsibility (Fischhoff 1975:289) and defensive reasoning (Argyris 1985). In cultures low on individualism, people are very face-conscious (Hofstede 1984a:89). Whereas in highly individualistic contexts, communication and blame are open and direct, maintaining harmony in order to protect face is important in low individualism organizations (Hofstede 1984a:89). Thus, under high individualism, there is selected rationality (March 1978:593) under which the sponsor instead the alternative itself gets evaluated in a dogmatic shortcut (Daft/Steers 1986:40; Mintzberg 1973:89).

Such "self-other" judgments can lead to the selective use of data to create a particular focus in support of parochial self-interest through game rationality (Baumol 1959; Bradley/Korn 1984:206; Dutton et al 1983:311; Guth/MacMillan 1986; Kotter/Schlesinger 1979:107; Porac et al 1985:5; March 1978:592; Salter/Weinhold 1982:68; Sapp/Smith 1984:199). However, ego-centrism cannot occur in cultures high in collectivism, because there the individual does not even have an ego. High collectivism, expressed in shared selective attention to (and use of) information, then, will lead to "enactment" (Weick 1977). Heuristics are likely to occur when there is a great deal of consensus among the decision-makers (Schwenk 1984:124). This relativates recent calls (Ouchi 1981; Deal/Kennedy 1982) for increased commitment within organizations (Stubbard 1986b:19). If however the adhesive forces are low, "detachment" can occur (Murray 1978:11).

4.6 Power Distance

Power distance describes the degree of inequality. In organizations, it is expressed in the degree of centralization of authority and the degree of autocratic leadership (Hofstede 1983a:81). Mintzberg et al (1976) suggested that the examination of the relationship between decision making processes and organizational structures is the key to studying ill-structured problems. Segmentation of the decision structures in hierarchical, unsegmented and specialized issue access can result in decreased latency at higher levels of activity for a longer time period, depending on the type of task (Tversky/Kahneman 1974:1129; Cohen et al 1972:5,19). Thus, the opportunity cost of attending to an issue is influenced by the power distance involved (March 1978:592). If there is a clear-cut hierarchy with individual responsibilities, it is likely that commitment to a course of action escalates, due to the reduction of cognitive dissonance (Conlon/Leatherwood 1986:6; Festinger 1957; Staw/Fox 1977:431). While in the case of individualism/collectivism, commitment to an organization escalated through visible public commitment of the individual, in the case of power distance it is the perception about "equal" hierarchical levels that leads to entrapment towards an action (Staw 1981; Brockner et al 1981; Conlon/Leatherwood 1986:9).

High power distance can lead to what was termed 'obedience' in western cultures with a slightly negative connotation (Hofstede 1984a:90). It is the expression of the acceptance of formal dependence through paternalism. Large power distance by itself need not necessarily lead to more power abuse than low power distance. "A paternalistic superior who respects the norms of his or her society for the behavior of a good father or mother does not abuse power; a consultative superior who manipulates consultation rituals does" (Hofstede 1984a:90).

4.7 Uncertainty Avoidance

Decision making involves several sources of uncertainty: unknown problem structures, unknown preferences about consequences, and unknown cause-effect relationships (Thompson 1967; Mason/Mitroff 1981). This relates to equivocality, the environmental conditions (e.g. volatility and diversity) under which the decision making takes place, as well as it relates to probabalistic conditions of the results itself (Leblebici/Salancik 1981:580; Weick 1979). Uncertainty avoidance/tolerance for ambiguity, or reduction of equivocality as it was termed by Daft/Weick (1984:291), then is the extent to which members of the organization feel uncomfortable in situations they perceive as unstructured, unclear or unpredictable, and the extent to which they try to avoid risk by adopting strict codes of behavior and by creating institutionalized security (Hofstede 1983a:81).

Consequences that are obtained with certainty are valued higher than uncertain outcomes (Slovic et al 1977:10). This is influenced by personal risk-taking propensities which lead to a trade-off between the amount of evidence searched for, and speed of decision (March/Simon 1958). Similar conclusions for the time horizon of planning systems were drawn by Das (1987). Strategic decision-making typically involves the employment of analogies from prior experience, e.g the personal background (Mintzberg 1973b:38; Mintzberg et al 1976:247; McNamee 1985:3) to current problems, even if the problem structures do not fit (Schwenk 1985a:76). Reasoning by analogy helps to reduce the uncertainty perceived in the environment (Schwenk 1984:117; Steinbruner 1974).

When environmental uncertainty cannot be reduced by organizational action, decision makers may repress this uncertainty by altering their perceptions so that issues seem less inconsistent (Michael 1973; Isenberg 1984:87). Their thinking becomes "wishful" as the changed preferences for outcomes of events affect the evaluation of the issues involved (Hedberg/Jönsson 1977:98; Murray 1978:26; Fischhoff/Goitein 1984:506). Overconfidence in their own judgment (Slovic et al 1977:5; Fischhoff/Goitein 1984:506; Barnes 1984:133) may be bolstered by a reliance on experts or quantification (Paul et al 1978:125; Whetten 1980:578; Lenz/Lyles 1985:66, 1986:57). Both support the illusion of control, the belief that success is due to one's own efforts, while failures happen due to environmental impact (Langer 1975; Larwood/Whittaker 1977). "Planning activities are often undertaken to give strategic decision-makers the illusion of mastering and controlling their environment" (Gardner/Thomas 1985:34).

The contrary is fatalism, the belief that one is under outside control, not under one owns command, which of course is not conducive to planning (Schneider 1987:7). On the other hand, overestimations of the impact of personal skills on outcomes of events and the overestimations of the skills itself result in the events and the overestimations of the skills itself result in the assumption that additional effort can solve issues (Langer 1975:311; Schwenk 1985a:78). Planning or forecasting, i.e. tools to reduce uncertainty, can create such illusion of control over ambiguous future events (Barnes 1948:133). Pragmatism, opportunism and ritualization can help in such situations (Hofstede 1984a:93). Similarly, tendencies toward rigidity and dogmatism relate towards intolerance of ambiguity (Hofstede 1980:155).

4.8 Summary

In this section, a link between heuristics and national culture was established. The argument was twofold. At first, it was suggested that some heuristics are more prone to happen in specific cultural settings. Second, it was argued that perceptions about what behavior is logical-rational or heuristical are subject to cultural influences. A model that clarifies the interaction of the cultural dimensions uncertainty avoidance, organizational learning, individualism and power distance was proposed. Heuristics were discussed within each of these dimensions. It was found that these four dimensions are good discriminators for planning heuristics. The conclusion was drawn that we need to pay attention to national culture in order not to misinterpret findings about planning behavior.

5 CONTEXTUAL FACTORS OF PLANNING

As was clarified in the introductory chapter, the main theme here is the interdependence of societal culture and planning systems (Scott 1983:156).[27] However, culture is just one contextual factor in which every company is embedded. Both companies and their managers interact with environmental stimuli and strive to mold them and benefit from them (Parsons 1961). Strategic planning is usually based on information about, and the interaction and experience with aspects of the environment (Lenz/Engledow 1986:33). We therefore need to identify the relevant external environment, in order to compare managerial practices in different surroundings (Farmer/Richman 1964:58).

In the following, environmental constructs are reviewed. Specific attention is paid to the task environment or industry in which firms compete. Different typologies of industries are discussed. The concept of industry influences is investigated both from a theoretical view and from empirical research. As the current study was undertaken with banks, previous multi-country research on strategic planning in banks is reviewed. Economic, technological, and legal influences on planning practices are briefly discussed.

5.1 Environmental Constructs

Based on the concepts of open systems (e.g. Von Bertalanffy 1950), systems theory (Katz/Kahn 1966) and contingency theory (e.g. Lawrence/Lorsch 1967), Negandhi (1983:21) has contributed a useful interpretation of the environment by distinguishing between three layers: the organization environment, the task environment, and the societal environment.[28] His integrating model is shown in figure 5.1.

The organization environmental layer marks the boundaries of a specific company, i.e. its size, technology, corporate culture, human and capital resources. The task environment is "the total setting within which the organization is competing and transacting" (Miller 1984:75), i.e. the market setting with customers, suppliers, competitors, regulatory agencies, and other stakeholders and client groups supplying resources, information and know-how (Astley/Fombrun 1983:579; Howe 1986:33; Scott 1983:158). The societal environment includes the economic, cultural, social, technical, legal, and political surrounding of the firm (Negandhi 1983b).

---

[27] The emphasis here is on interdependent and interact. Managers are not seen as passive agents (England/Negandhi 1979:2). "The manager and the organization do influence the environment, and in a proactive manner" (Miller 1984:73).

[28] For a review of the development of environmental concepts, see for example Scott (1981, 1983), Negandhi (1975a,b) or in a different vain Lenz/Engledow (1986).

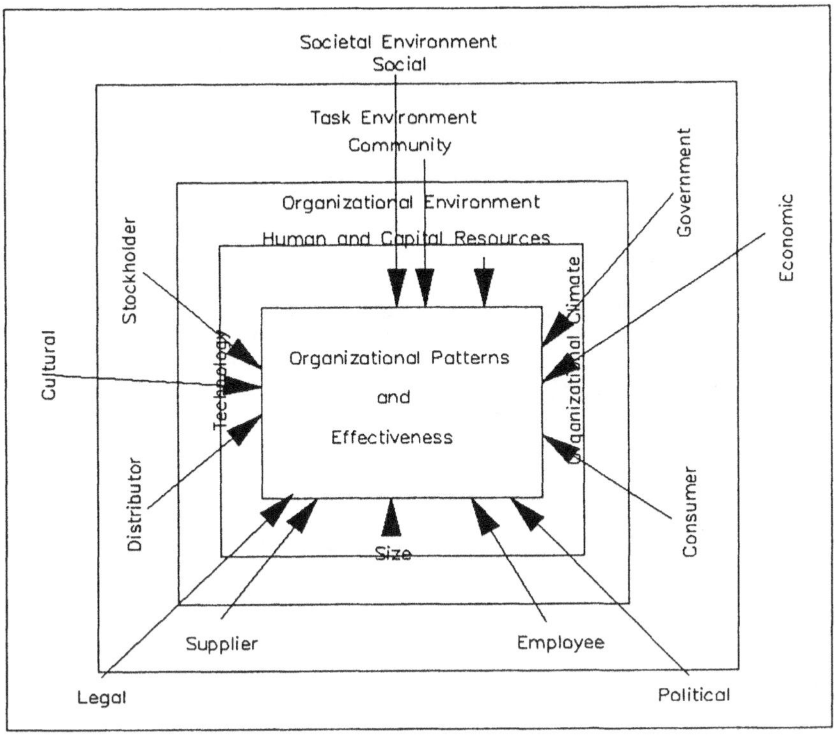

Figure 5.1 Environmental Layers

Source: Negandhi, Anant (1983b:21): Cross-Cultural Management Research: Trends and future Direction. In: Journal of International Business Studies, Fall 1983, pp. 17-28.

The discussion in previous chapters on planning processes, systems and heuristics dealt with the organization environmental layer. The task environment will be discussed in the following in terms of the concept of the industry system (Hirsch 1972:642) as a sector of organizations which perform similar functions and provide similar services and products (DiMaggio/Powell 1983).

5.2 Industry Influences

While reviewing empirical studies about the relationship of strategic planning to performance, Pearce et al (1987:671) and Rhyne (1986:427) emphasize the need to control for industry effects. Kudla (1981:5) similarly states that "[i]t is important that industry effects be controlled so that the effects of planning on risk can be measured." The basic argument is that it is necessary to portray the role the selected industry's task environment, i.e. its industry or product/market sector (Fombrun/ Astley 1983:129), plays for corporate planning. The first issue, then, becomes the selection of the relevant <u>criteria</u> upon which <u>to characterize the task environment</u> of the firm.

Different sets of dimensions are offered. The attention to a collection of organizations providing similar services is represented in the organizational population model (Aldrich, 1979; Hannan/Freeman 1977), in the industrial organization paradigm (Porter 1980, 1985), in research on strategic groups (Hunt 1972), and in research on shared industry concepts (Spender 1980). These concepts are briefly reviewed in the following.

5.21 Industry Paradigms

In the industrial organization paradigm, the environment is referred to with respect to the industry, or market, in which a firm competes (Lenz 1981:132). Industry generally is defined "as the group of firms producing products that are close substitutes for each other" (Porter 1980:5). The essence of the paradigm is, that a firm's performance depends on the characteristics of the industry environment in which it competes, i.e. entry/exit barriers to new entrants or substitute products (e.g. product differentiation, access to distribution channels etc), the bargaining power of buyers and suppliers (e.g. their rates of concentration and integration), and the rivalry among existing firms (industry life cycle, number and size of competitors etc.; Porter 1980).

The main argument is that "there are some fundamental structural parameters of an industry dictated by the basic product characteristics and technology, but that within those parameters industry evolution can take many paths (Porter 1981:616). The industrial organization-paradigm offers a conceptualization of the environment useful for determining the content of an appropriate strategy.

Somewhat similar, but on a different level, Spender (1980) argues that it is not the product/market scope that defines an industry, but rather the shared experience of the managers interacting in that particular environment. The argument is that the industry supplies a set of possible strategic frameworks which serve as building blocks for "industry wisdom" through which managers filter their perceptions of environmental events (Huff 1982:125; Goodman/Newell 1989). As this refers to the heuristics already discussed in the last chapter, this argument will be used later on with regard to the industry culture of the banking industry.

In research on populations of organizations providing similar services, primary attention is given to the change in number and characteristics of the members of these populations in response to changes in resources (Dess/Beard 1984). This approach is somewhat covered in the industrial-organization paradigm.

While the latter three paradigms emphasized differences between industries, research on strategic groups has pinpointed differences within industries. A strategic group is a cluster of companies within an industry, whose members follow similar though not identical strategies according to their strategic posture (Gardner/Thomas 1985:26; Huff 1982:126). Variations in intraindustry profitability and growth were found to be related to strategic group membership (Dess/Davis 1984). For the U.S. financial services industry, Fombrun/Zajac (1987:45) identified three strategic groups: commercial banks and financial service firms; thrift institutions; and niche players with specialized product lines. The discriminators that proved significant in their study were posture vis-à-vis the environment (technology, political, competitive), size, the pursuit of interorganizational linkages, and institutional function (Fombrun/Zajac (1987:44).

For an extension of the current research, splitting the responding financial institutions in strategic groups might lead to interesting conclusions. Such groups could for example be built with regard to the markets served, i.e. wholesale vs. retail banks; or, with regard to their legal statute, i.e. savings & loan associations vs. cooperative institutions vs. commercial banks. However, as will be shown later on, these distinctions can hardly be operationalized in an international context (Revell 1985:3).

5.22 The Industry-Planning Link: Empirical Findings

The industry approach refers to the relative performance of industries and determinants of institutional effectiveness (Hirsch 1975:328; Scholz 1987:16) and as industries as important factors in organizational adaptation (Hrbeniak/Snow 1980:750). Rhyne (1977:121) argues that the level of economic activity within industries influences different industries to a varying extent, which, in turn, affects planning practices (Rhyne 1986:427). It is further argued in the literature that in different industries, certain decision areas and functions may be considered more serious for success than in others (Child/Francis 1977:121). As Davidson (1982:316) put it,

> [d]ifferent businesses exhibit different planning needs, in terms of the focus, frequency, formality, time frame and format of the planning function. Differences in business success factors and needs frequently frustrate attempts to initiate uniform planning procedures for diverse firms. Every business has different planning needs, just as every business has different organizational needs. The unique nature and needs of each business unit should be addressed in designing and executing the planning process.

Empirical findings about this claim, however, are mixed. In <u>earlier studies</u>, Golling (1977:22) and Töpfer (1976:7) indicate that German firms within different industries place various emphasis on strategic planning. Similar results are reported by Litschert/Nicholson (1971, 1974) and Rue (1973) for U.S. companies. In the following, several studies that were undertaken in the <u>last decade</u> are reviewed.

Gouy (1978:47) reports differences in the formality of planning process across heavy and light industries in Europe. Sais/ Montebello (1980:340) attribute the lag of European companies in the introduction of strategic planning partly to differences in industry structure.

Study	Description of Study	Conclusions
Gouy (1978)	Interviews with 55 top managers in 47 companies in France, the U.K. and Germany	Differences in the formality of the planning process across industries
Kudla (1978)	Questionnaire survey of 272 U.S. companies in 15 industries	Minor differences across industrial/ consumer sectors in content of plans & frequency of review
Al-Bazzaz/ Grinyer (1980)	48 interviews with planners in large U.K. companies in 19 industries	Different value of contributions & degree of problems between planning in manufacturing and service companies
Koehler/ Uebele (1986)	334 questionnaires from large German manufacturing companies	Different intensity in use of planning techniques across sectors
Poensgen/ Hort (1986)	88 interviews with chief executives, in four German industries	Different average size accounts for different planning
Chinta/ Jenster/ King (1987)	1.184 questionnaires from members of the North American Society for Corporate Planning from seven industries	Planning tasks vary by their content across four industries
Ramanujam/ Camillus/ Venkatraman (1987)	207 questionnaires from Fortune 500, Fortune 500 Service, and Inc. 500 companies in five industries in the U.S.A.	Higher emphasis on strategic planning in service sector than in manufacturing sector
Seeger/ Shuman/ Teebagy (1987)	242 questionnaires from Inc. 500 companies with 1978 sales between $m .1 and 25 in the U.S. (New England & California)	Wholesalers and service firms differ in factors factors of planning that load on formulation and implementation
Fredrickson/ Iaquinto (1988)	Questionnaire survey with 65 U.S. firms in two industries; one stable, one unstable	Comprehensiveness of strategic decisions varied significantly across environments

Table 5.1: Studies on Industry Influences on Planning

Berthel/Moews (1970:69), however, explain differences in planning practices across their industries with different average firm sizes for the industries in their sample.

Minor differences across industries in the types of quantified objectives, environmental factors, plans, and financial statements contained in the plan, and in the frequency of review of long-range planning are reported by Kudla (1978:49). The significance of these differences remains to be tested yet. The first four content-related factors slightly vary between consumer and industrial goods-sectors, as does the frequency of reviews.

Al-Bazzaz/Grinyer (1980:38) and Ramanujam et al (1984:30; 1987:625) indicated differences in planning systems between manufacturing and service companies. Al-Bazzaz/Grinyer (1980:38) report that corporate planners take a more creative and influential role within service companies; however, they experience greater difficulties. In comparing their findings with other studies, they refer to societal culture to explain difficulties with planning. Both Al-Bazzaz/Grinyer (1980) and Ramanujam et al (1984, 1987) state that planning was later introduced in the services industries, which in turn may explain the differences. Service industries in their samples were dominated by banks.

Differences in the intensity of the application of planning techniques (e.g. decision tree analysis, linear programming etc.) between the consumer goods sector and the industrial goods sector are reported by Köhler/Übele (1986:149). They attribute these findings to differences in customers, customer predictability, and to the different spread of marketing practices across these two industrial sectors (Köhler/Übele 1986:150). However, they did not make any indication with regard to the planning process.

Pönsgen/Hort (1986:274) investigated differences between the planning processes in four industries. Their planning index showed significant differences between the textile industry and the other industries. Differences between other industries were not significant. These differences, however, disappear, when they control for the time horizon of middle- and long-range plans, size, detaildness of planning, and formalization. They attribute the differences found in the first place to differences in the average firm size between the four industries.

Profiles of planning tasks most positively and most negatively associated with specific industries were developed by Chinta et al (1987:544). The emphasis put on a task was measured by the time spent for accomplishing that task as reported in the questionnaires. Banks, for example, emphasize designing and administering the planning system, implementation and scanning, while in durables, most time is spent on strategic business unit planning and acquisition analysis in their findings. Again, these differences could be attributed to a later introduction of planning by banks.

Seeger et al (1987) set out to study cultural differences in the planning approaches between Inc. 500 firms located in the states of New England and California. The average firm in the sample had

1982 sales of $m 8.8 with 115 employees. Service firms differed from others in one third of the behavioral items. One fourth of the items discriminated manufacturers and retailers from the rest. Two dimensions, labeled 'formulation' and 'implementation' appeared in factor analysis which significantly differed between industry types. Both dimensions include both strategy content and planning process items. They finally conclude that wholesalers and service firms are different in their planning behavior. However, they attribute this result to differences in societal culture between New England and California.

While using data from two earlier studies, Fredrickson/Iaquinto (1988) attempted to determine whether firms in stable environments make and integrate strategic decisions using significantly different processes compared to firms in unstable environments. They report significant interindustry differences in the comprehensiveness of strategic decision processes used to make the same decision (Fredrickson/Iaquinto 1988:11). It needs however yet to be proven, if the same conclusion holds true with matched pairs of companies in other industries.

Evaluating these studies is no easy task. One has to acknowledge that only a few of the studies reviewed here were conducted to investigate industry effects on the planning process. A drawback that results from this notion is that the number of companies per industry in some of the studies is not enough to reach significant conclusions. However, there seems to be evidence enough to argue that industries differ somewhat in their planning approaches. What could be shown is that minor differenes exist between the content of plans across industries. Some planning process differences could be shown at least between service sector companies (i.e. banks) and manufacturing companies. This could be the reflecttion of an evolutionary aspect (Ansoff 1984:14; Canon 1968:525; Downs 1967; Quinn/Cameron 1983; Wells 1972), with planning introduced in the manufactorung sector and later on transferred to the service sector.

However, there are several mediating factors for industry influences: company size, experience with planning, average company size in the industry, and the current industry life-cycle position (i.e. stability of the environment). And, we need to apply some caution in interpreting the research findings reported above. They only refer to formal planning. Moreover, they do not indicate the application of alternative, functionally equivalent tools and means. Industry is just one of the influencing factors. Still, it is important in empirical research to control for these possible industry effects.

5.3 Economic Influences

The economic environment of a company is both a source of opportunities as well as of serious threats and therefore pertains to strategic planning (Steiner/Miner 1982:47). Inflation, GNP trend lines, consumer expenditure, savings patterns and the like have to be considered (Kotler 1984:96; Sapp/Smith 1984:48). Economic instability is one of the many factors that influence the perceived environmental uncertainty. Therefore, economic factors can be important determinants of managerial practices.

Unemployment, inflation and social unrest can affect managers risk propensity (Cyert/March 1963). Negandhi (1987:229) conducted a comparative study with fifty-six U.S. subsidiaries and fifty-five comparable local firms in six developing countries. He concludes that the existence of a sellers market (i.e. the lack of competition), the availability of raw materials, and high inflation adversely affected the firms ability to plan for a longer time horizon. Negandhi (1983a:21) regards the impact of the seller's market on managerial decision-making higher than other factors, as it makes planning less necessary for firms to achieve high profitability. However, the factors he mentions vary among different countries (Negandhi 1975a:75).

Orpen (1984:22) conducted another comparative study on planning practices with 64 indian managers and 72 American managers. He concluded that Indian managers had experienced greater difficulties with planning due to the volatility of the economic and political environment, and the lack of experienced managers. The latter point, the lack of qualified management personnel as a handicap to the formulation and implementation of strategy, is advocated by Lasserre (1983:41), Godse (1986) and Mrema (1987). Hofstede (1984a:94) argues that less economically developed countries tend to be fatalistic, which is not conducive to planning. However, he states that he still sees cultural differences in planning practices in the more economically developed countries (Hofstede 1984a:94).

And, firms adjust to these volatile economical conditions with their planning practices (Shipper/White 1983:106). Banks reacted with the creation of contingency plans and economic audits, when the cost of funds soared above yields on long-term, fixed rate assets in the early eighties (Pohlman 1982:142). Horovitz (1980:151) reports that British companies reacted with more frequent revisions of projections to higher levels of inflation.

5.4 Technical Influences

Technology can be regarded as the defining characteristic of organizations in applying techniques to accomplish something (Perrow 1967:194). Several authors (e.g. Woodward 1962; Perrow 1970) focused on the influence of technology on management processes. The creation and distribution of goods and services depends upon an organization's knowledge-technique base. Hence, rapid technological progress can be another reason for perceived environmental uncertainty.

Miles et al (1978) and Birnbaum/Wong (1985:2268) stress the importance of technology for strategy and structure. Scholz (1984:96) argues that technological dynamics reduce the horizon for planning. Rockart/Morton (1984:139) suggest that technology drives strategy and managerial processes. Litschert (1968) relates the degree of formal planning to company size and technological variables. He argues that larger firms in more technologically dynamic environments exhibit higher degrees of formal planning. Grinyer et al (1986) found that, among other contextual variables, the vulnerability of the core technology was related to planning system characteristics, such as the use of more specialist planners. Technological change has resulted in increased planning efforts by banks (Bienkowski 1985; Malmstrom 1986; Raphael 1986). However, the type of technology a firm applies is determined by the market environment (Kagono 1985:29). And, it was argued that attitudes towards the use of technology are culture bound (Hofstede 1980:154).

5.5 Legal/Political Influences

In many countries, the government takes a strong role in business decision making. Ramamurti (1986:62) distinguishes between four types of government-dependence: ownership, regulation, market (purchasing power), and financial (resource-based). For firms operating in such environments, the strategic decision process is often slowed down by bureaucracy. The government is added to the process as a strategist (Higgins 1984:209; Lassere 1983:40). In regulated environments, entry and exit barriers are weakened, and the focus of planning shifts from customers and competitors to the regulatory body itself (Mahon/Murray 1981:255).

Regulatory agencies acting as buffers encourage companies to detailed, programmed planning (Mahon/Murray 1981:256). Ramamurti (1986:62) argues that government-dependency limits the relevance of planning models, due to fragmented strategic decision making authority, heightened goal ambiguity, politization of strategic decision making, short-term orientation and internal bureaucratization. Kallmann/Shapiro (1978) suggest that formal planning may be less important in regulated industries, because strategic alternatives are more limited. From a study with 56 US subsidiaries and 55 local firms in less developed countries, Negandhi (1987:229; 1983a:19) concludes that governmental control of prices and political instability affect a firms' ability to plan negatively.

Governments both can support and restrict business (Steiner/Miner 1982:46). An often quoted example of support is the interplay in strategic planning between the MITI, other government leaders, and Japanese industry (Allen 1981:86). This networking with regulators and competitors is typical for the Japanese culture (Kagono et al 1985:77).

European governments used planning as method to interfere with the operations of the private sector (Sais/Montebello 1980:339). Such behavior may be culture bound (Hofstede 1980). As Weber (1946) put it:

> The idea that the bureau activities of the state are intrinsically different in character from the management of private economic offices is a continental European notion and by way of contrast, is totally foreign to the American way.

For political acceptability, societal responsibility is necessary in addition to economic performance in Western European democracies (Higgins 1980:230). This fact leads to a different view with regard to governmental interventions. Banks are often considered to have to pursue societal goals as well as profitability goals (Lusser 1987; Suechting 1987). As banks are currently going through major deregulation and reregulation (Fombrun/Astley 1983:138; Bröker 1986), they had to adjust their structures and planning processes - a typical adaptation of firms that move in or out of regulated environments (Mahon/Murray 1981:258).

5.6 Size

While differences in the average firm size in given industries may influence planning through the specific industry structure as an <u>external contingency</u> (Berthel/Moews 1970:69), company size itself may influence planning as <u>internal contingency</u>, as the following review shows.

Study	Description of Study	Conclusions
Klein (1977, 1979, 1980, 1981)	77 questionnaires from banks in the 7th (Chicago) Federal Reserve Bank District.	No relation between extent of planning and size, growth & profit trend found.
Wood/LaForge (1980)	17 interviews and 92 questionnaire responses from US-banks.	Large banks introduced planning earlier than small.
Giroux (1980)	259 questionnaires from U.S. banks	The use of forecasting techniques correlates positively with size.
Giroux (1981) (data from 1970)	234 questionnaires from mostly medium & large U.S. banks	Reemphasizes later published findings.
Gup/Whitehead (1983)	Questionnaires from 335 and 114 S&L's (USA)	Size is of critical importance.
Robinson/Pearse (1983)	50 questionnaires from small commercial banks in South Carolina, USA	Mixed influences of size and degree of formality.
Rule/Sedgwick (1986) (A. Anderson)	1.080 questionnaire responses from bankers in 17 European countries	Size is of major impact to planning systems.

Table 5.2: Studies on Size Influences on Planning

Klein (1977) investigated the planning practices of commercial banks in the U.S. 7th Federal Reserve Bank district which participated in the Functional Cost Analysis Program. In the analysis of 77 questionnaires, he linked the extent of long-range planning with bank size, with growth trends, and with profit trends. Banks were classified according to their total deposits. He defined long-range planning as "all planning activities that exceed a time horizon of one year" (Klein 1977:5). Bank size was not found to be a determining factor of the extent of long range planning efforts undertaken by banks (Klein 1977:179). However, the extent of planning was positively correlated with market share. And, in small banks the extent of long range planning efforts undertaken was found to affect growth trends positively. The study did not include very large banks, as these do not participate in the Functional Cost Analysis Program.

Wood/LaForge (1980) surveyed U.S. banks with regard to formal planning and financial performance. They conclude that large banks did introduce profit planning earlier than smaller ones.

Giroux (1981) set out to investigate what forecasting techniques were used in 1970 in the U.S. banking industry. The sample was stratified by deposit size. 204 of the responses were from medium and large banks (Giroux 1981:101). Large and medium-sized banks differ in their information sources and in the application of forecasting techniques. Giroux (1980) could increase his sample to 259 banks by adding responses from very large banks. Again, the use of quantitative vs. judgmental forecasts correlated positively with size, measured in deposits (Giroux 1980:53). He later again increased the sample to 711 banks (Giroux 1984:136). Large banks were found to have specialized planning departments, whereas in medium sized banks planning was found to be the responsibility of top-level line managers. Among the very large banks, effectiveness ratings were directly related to the age of the planning system. They seem to have moved up the learning curve.

Friedman et al (1983) conducted a Delphi survey. Size is of major impact to the planning system. Larger banks are more committed to using planning to run the business. These larger banks use planning specialists, link senior managements compensations to strategic plan fulfillment, and update their plans more regularly than smaller banks.

While analyzing data from banks and savings & loan associations in the U.S.A., Gup/Whitehead (1983) found that formal planning activities were directly related to the asset size of the institutions surveyed. Size was found to be of critical importance to the level at which corporate objectives were established. In very large institutions, corporate objectives were set by the CEO; in medium sized institutions, they were set up by their directors. Presidents of small institutions have greater planning responsibilities than their counterparts in larger banks. Large institutions consider management's commitment to planning most important, while smaller institutions are more concerned with productivity.

Robinson/Pearce (1983) received 50 questionnaires from small federal- and state chartered commercial banks in South Carolina, U.S.A. Most of the banks had deposits between $m 10 and $m 25. Contrary to the Wood/LaForge (1979) findings, the performance of small banks engaged in formal planning was not significantly better than non-formal small bank planners. Within their sample of small banks, the percentage of formal planners did not vary by relative size of the bank. In another sample in the U.S. savings & loan industry by Javidan (1984), size was of no significant impact on the extent (i.e. formality) of planning.

From the empirical studies reviewed above, two conclusions are drawn. First, size and recommendable formality of strategic planning seems to be somewhat linked. Up from a certain size which still needs to be investigated, some formalization of planning seems to make sense, because the bank's organizations otherwise simply gets out of control. Second, among other factors, size does influence planning. We therefore must try to compare companies of equivalent size in order to arrive at meaningful conclusions in comparative research.[29]

5.7 Bank Planning

In the sections above, the influences of economic, technical, and legal/political contingencies as well as company size on strategic planning were briefly reviewed. For comparative research, the conclusion was drawn that it is necessary to take these contingencies into account, at best by holding them constant. In order to investigate their influence on strategic bank planning, these contingencies are discussed with regard to the outcome to bank planning in the following. Thereby, empirical studies on planning practices in the banking industry are reviewed.

5.71 Banking Service Characteristics and Planning

Services are different from products. This leads to critical success factors and factor combinations strategic planning has to deal with, which are different from other industries (Carman/ Langeard 1980:7; Weigele 1983:95). "Services are defined and measured by the adequacy of a total service package consisting of tangible and intangible features" (Chase/Erikson 1988:194).

Thus, services can be explained using their extensional and intensional characteristics. Intensional characteristics of services are, that there must be reasons that cause the needs, wants and demands, that the activities or omissions performed must bear the required utilities, that they have to be available (in time and space), transferrable (receivable and sendable), and relative scarce (Scheuch/Hasenauer 1981:273). Extensional characteristics of services are their intangibility, the fact that they are the

---

[29] A third conclusion could also be drawn. Namely, that size labels are difficult to handle and very dangerous to use. For problems and opportunities with regard to measuring bank size, see Haiss (1989b).

output of a combination of factors of production (i.e. produced goods), the fact that they are a necessary condition for derived goods (i.e. original goods), and that they are real goods that get evaluated in terms of nominal goods (Scheuch 1982:75). Services, of course, can also include tangible goods. However, it is not a service if there is no intangible process which adds value to the goods (Chase/Erikson 1988:192).

"Two characteristics of services - intangibility of the offering and simultaneity of production and consumption - have important implications for strategic planning" (Carman/Langeard 1980:7). For example, it was argued that competitive strategies based on 'pull' versus 'push' marketing or brand identification for service firms have to be replaced by strategies based on franchising and image (Albrecht/Zemke 1985; Pearce/Herron 1987).

These service characteristics require the existence of a direct organization-client-relationship, and high customer involvement in the production process (Scheuch 1982:75). Market segmentation is often forced on banks by the intimacy of production, leading to short channels and standardization (Carman/Langeard 1980:8). Due to the customer involvement in the production of the service, the server as well as the facility's location and design are integral parts of the product design (Chase/Erikson 1988:195). The impli- cations of this service issues are twofold. The capacity and capability to render the service (i.e. the necessary factors of production) must exist prior to the transaction (Kotler 1980:624). And, service firms have to put a high premium on overall visi- bility, quality control, and accountability for every detail of the operation (Carman/Langeard 1980:8).

As services cannot be stored, production and consumption are interrelated and performed somewhat simultaneously (Scheuch/ Hasenauer 1981:274; Wright/Pauli 1988:25). Thus, providers of service must manipulate their productive resources, not inventories, to cope with the uncertainty of customer demands. A financial institution' most versatile resources are therefore high-quality people and readily adaptable equipment (Bhide 1986:60). Pricing, is somewhat different, too. Normally, certain quantities of products are offered, and demand regulates the market prices. For some financial goods sectors, the producers tell their prices, with the sales' quantities being defined by the customer's reactions to these given prices (Jacob 1986:25).

Many of these financial products and services are basically undifferentiated (Reidenbach 1986:19). And, financial markets bear the unique ability to generate close substitutes for existing products at low cost, as most bank products are readily and cheaply imitated (Harper 1986:37). Innovations, therefore, are often gradual improvements of existing chains of products rather than revolutionary initiatives that shake up the financial world (Bhide 1986:60; Tilston et al 1985:10). Peripheral services are normally added to core services (Carman/Langeard 1980:9). These overlaps on both customer segments and product groups cause severe problems in the establishment of free-standing strategic business units (Sapp/Smith 1984).

It is therefore argued in the literature, that several of the methodologies of strategic planning, for example the product-lifecycle concept, and market share, do not necessarily lend themselves to banking (Carman/Langeard 1980:7; Metzger/Rau 1982:58). Others, e.g. the customer-lifecycle are of special importance (Regli 1983). For evaluation, empirical studies that investigated banking industry influences on planning practices are evalutated below.

Study	**Description of Study**	**Conclusions**
Mans (1973)	154 German companies including 13 banks & insurance companies.	Banks lag behind other industries and are not satisfied with their planning efforts.
Kirsch et al (1975)	154 responses from German companies, including 10 banks and insurance companies.	Banks lag behind other industries withg regard to their planning systems.
Kono (1976) Kono (1984)	Questionnaires and interviews with US, British and Japanese companies	Most finance and insurance companies included had a long-range plan.
Kudla (1978)	323 questionnaires from 15 industries; 20 responses from finance & Services (U.S.A.).	Differences to other industries in terms of content & content ofof long-range planning.
Al-Bazzaz/ Grinyer (1980)	48 interviews with U.K. companies in 19 industries	Banks have more difficulties with planning than other industries.
Bologna (1980)	Group sessions with 308 farm and farm bank managers in the U.S.A.	Did not control for industry effects.
Ramanujam/ Camillus/ Venkatraman (1984, 1987)	207 questionnaires from Fortune 500, Fortune 500 Service, and Inc. 500 companies in five U.S. industries	Banks introduced later than other companies and are more concerned with regulatory issues.
Chinta/ Jenster/ King (1987)	1.184 questionnaires from seven industries (U.S.A.)	Banks spend most time on design, administration, implementation and scanning during planning.

Table 5.3: Studies on Banking Industry Influences

One of the first studies in this field was conducted by Mans (1973). Seven out of nine German companies which had indicated that they have no formal planning process were banks (Mans 1973:44). Banks lagg behind other industries in the application of computer models for planning, and were in general not satisfied with their planning systems (Mans 1973:51). Similar results are reported by Kirsch et al (1975). However, the small number of banks in these studies does not allow for generalizations. The same applies to Al-Bazzaz/Grinyer (1980) and Kono (1976:71). All four finance companies in Kono's (1976) sample had a formal long-range plan. In a replicate study (Kono 1984:75), he could identify 29 Japanese banks with planning systems.

Kudla (1978) reports differences across industries in terms of content of plans and planning processes. Banks are less concerned with market share, include technological and regulatory developments and competitive factors in their environmental forecasts, heavily use income statements and show no common frequency of review of long-range plans. Ramanujam et al (1984, 1987) report that many banks introduced planning later than other companies and that they emphasized regulatory issues. Chinta et al (1987) again show that banks are relative newcomers to planning. Banks in their sample spend most time of their planning efforts on designing and administering the planning system, implementation, and scanning, and the least on strategic business unit planning, acquisitions, and planning review.

The findings reported here have to be accepted with caution. Taken separately, all the earlier studies under review do not allow for meaningful conclusions due to the small sample size. However, interpreting their findings comparatively and together with the later studies, they indicate that banks on average did indeed introduce planning later than companies in other industries. There seems to exist an industry lag in the introduction of planning with regard to banks (Giroux/Rose 1984; Metzger/Rau 1982:62; Prasad 1984; Ramanujam et al 1984; Rau 1988:62; Rule/Sedgwick 1986:46; Sapp 1980:34).[30] Banks seem to have problems with strategic business-unit planning. They are more concerned with regulatory issues compared to other industries.

5.72 Regulatory and Economic Influences on Bank Planning

To understand how bank planning works, we must also understand what sort of economic role a bank plays. The place to begin is therefore the products banks offer.

---

[30] This industry lag can be attributed to the fact that bank planning was in the past largely functional, that the regulatory environment was very stable and led to protected markets with high entry barriers, that bank's top management tended to focus on short-range operational issues, and that banks were not marketing-driven (Channon 1986:6; Fredrick 1983:42; Holmberg/ Baker 1984:219; Lindsay/Rue 1980).

The core business of the banking industry is to render services on money and money substitutes. Money is a exceptionally homogeneous product (Higgs 1988:2), with banks performing closely intertwined activities as both client and supplier in the same market (Rudolph 1987:113). The very core product (money) and therefore its traders (banks) are of high stake and interest for both the respective national and supranational governments and the public at large where the bank does business (Weigele 1983:78). As Arndt (1988:74) put it:

> It is a highly competitive, though oligopolistic-competitive, industry. But banks are powerful and are therefore often able to invoke the help of government to protect their interests. Governments, moreover, have their own motives for intervention. Private market power is therefore a much less important influence on the pattern of trade in financial services than government intervention.

Restrictions on price competition, on product range competition, and on geographic competition lead to a sectoral structure of the financial services industry within most countries, reflecting the institutional coverage of products (Mitchell 1986; Bröker 1986). Financial markets, therefore, are (or at least were in the past) no free, but regulated markets with more or less secure entry and exit barriers that are now nearly world-wide subject to some deregulation (Bröker 1986:72; Zehetner 1988:201). And, financial services sectors and institutions are highly interdependent through vertical and horizontal integration, which is quite common for the service sector (Chase/Erikson 1988:192; Süchting 1987:204).

Banks, then, have to consider both financial goals and corporate social responsibilities (Steiner/Miner 1982:57). These somewhat vested interests between regulators and banks and among banks, however, influence the industries' and single banks' value chains (Porter 1985:58):

> Industry structure both shapes the value chain of a firm and is a reflection of the collective value chains of competitors. Structure determines the bargaining relationships with buyers and suppliers that is reflected in both the configuration of a firm's value chain and how margins are divided with buyers, suppliers, and coalition partners.

This difference in the system of productive factors in comparison to other industries clearly should be reflected in bank planning (Rudolph 1987:113; Weigele 1983:95). Claims are, for example, that banks are limited in their autonomy and degrees of freedom to change and adaptation due to capital adequacy requirements, which in turn may influence the planning horizon (Jacob 1986:30;

Zapotocky/Malzer 1984:308).[31] Therefore, respective empirical studies are evaluated below.

Study	Description of Study	Conclusions
Giroux (1981)	234 questionnaires from U.S. banks.	Forecasting methods independent of legal charter.
Kudla (1982)	105 questionnaires from large U.S. banks.	High importance of legal issues.
Gup/Whitehead (1983)	Questionnaire responses from 335 banks and 114 S&L's in the U.S.A.	Legal charter is of influence to planning.
Godse (1986)	Introduction of planning in 2 nationalized Indian banks.	Public-sector banks are not policy-makers but policy-takers.
Dalby (1986)	Interviews with 9 major U.S. and 15 major European banks	Stresses importance of regulatory issues in bank planning.
Ramanujam/ Camillus/ Venkatraman (1984, 1987)	207 questionnaires from Fortune 500, Fortune 500 Service, and Inc. 500 companies in five U.S. industries.	Banks are more concerned with regulatory issues.

Table 5.4.: Studies of Regulatory Influences on Planning

No influence of different legal regulations on the forecasting and planning methods were found by Giroux (1981:135). While analyzing data from U.S. banks and U.S. savings & loan associations, Gup/Whitehead (1983) found that banks put more emphasis on planning than S&L's, regardless of asset size. Ramanujam et al (1984, 1987) report that many banks in their sample were less concerned with competitive issues and put more emphasis on

---

[31] It is not the author's intention to deny the existence of regulatory influences in other industries. Telecommunications, food, textile and a variety of other industries are subject to regulation. The current climate of deregulation on a national basis and reregulation on a supra-national basis in the financial services industry (Brökner 1986; Zehetner 1988), however, provides a pervasive argument for the regulatory influence discussed here. For a general discussion of regulations and protectionism see, for example Lenway (1985); for a discussion of reasons for the existence of regulation in the financial services industry, see for example Harper (1986).

regulatory changes. Dalby (1986) found that for European banks, government policy was of great limiting influence in strategic planning with regard to the strategic options available. In a survey conducted by Kudla (1982), regulatory issues were ranked second only to economic issues in importance of consideration, with competitive and technological developments following in the ranks.

Study	Description of Study	Conclusions
Wood/LaForge (1980, 1981)	17 interviews and 92 questionnaires from U.S. banks	High importance of economic forecasting.
Giroux (1981)	234 questionnaires from U.S. banks	Econometric modeling high in use.
Kudla (1982)	105 questionnaires from large U.S. banks	Emphasis on contingency planning and environmental scanning.
Fidler (1989) (KPMG Int'l)	50 banking institutions	Increased importance of bank's ecoonomic role in planning.

Table 5.5.: Studies of Economic Influences on Planning

Wood/LaForge (1981) report that economic forecasting, financial planning, portfolio and branch location were the major tasks included. Giroux (1981) reports that econometric models and forecasting were widely used by U.S. banks in the 1970ies. Kudla (1982) found that economic factors are given most consideration in forecasting among U.S. banks. In Javidan's study on the top 200 U.S. Savings & Loan Associations, no difference between groups of extensive (i.e. formal) and limited (i.e. informal) planners were found with regard to perceived uncertainty resulting from deregulation and economic volatility. However, their responses to these perceived uncertainties were different. Moormann (1988) reports that accounting data is more frequently used than market-data in bank planning. KPMG, in a survey covering 50 large banks, stresses the finding that banks have to pay more attention the their economic and ethical role during planning (Fidler 1989:29).

In the review above, it clearly appears that senior management still is very much involved in the day-to-day operations (Beck 1987; Davis 1985; Weigele 1983). Figure-driven, short-term information, for example interest-rates or exchange-rate changes, are of prime importance for short-term profits (Rau 1987:68). Together with the characteristics of the core product (money), both the ease of imitation and the high entry/exit barriers are more conducive to planning for "business as usual" than to marketing-driven, planned bold moves and changes (Rudolph 1987:

113). The methodological orientation of the credit function was one of control, based on rules, regulations and traditions, with emphasis on security, close to accounting (Twomey et al 1988:62). Experience and success in a banks' credit department is typically one of the prerequisites for the recruitment to senior management (Davis 1985; Higgs 1988). No wonder, then, that "[i]n the traditional financial institutions the planning function lies within the jurisdiction of the accounting/reporting controllership domain" (Schmid/Eber-Schmid 1982:14), or that it is performed in a similar way.

From Davis (1985), however, it is also clear that many banks managed to change their corporate culture in order to become more externally, marketing and planning oriented, with emphasis on strategic thinking. Although many banks use a formal long-range planning process, the real important, strategic decisions seem to be based on some type of strategic issue management and contingency planning, not the outcome of a rigid, annually revised palnning process with a fixed time frame.[32] Projections of pro-forma financial statemeents (balance sheet and income statement) are widely used and are still the venture point for bank planning within a frame of regulatory, economic, and other competitive issues.

5.8 Planning Contingencies Revisited

Throughout this chapter, the importance of the interaction of contextual factors with planning systems, processes and heuristics were stressed. Environmental constructs were reviewed. The environment was depicted by three layers: the societal environment, the task environment, and the organization environment.

Industry paradigms were discussed and possible industry influences on planning in general were investigated against empirical findings. Similarly, economic, technical, legal and political influences (external contingencies) as well as company size (internal contingency) were discussed with regard to their possible interaction with planning. By reviewing corresponding empirical studies on bank planning, the impact of these issues on planning was evaluated within the banking industry.

The conclusion was drawn that it is necessary to control for these factors in empirical research on strategic planning practices. It will be argued in the following chapter, however, that national culture can be of equal importance in influencing planning.

---

[32] Besides small subsamples or possibly missleading size labels, one other factor has to be taken into consideration while comparing the findings of the studies reviewed here. Only a few studies operationalized what "long-range planning" or "strategic planning" is, exempt from Klein (1977), who accepted any plans with a time frame above one year as strategic. Similarly, Sapp (1980) regarded plans with a scope of more than two years as strategic. Therefore, we must not mix up financial planning with strategic planning.

6 CULTURAL INFLUENCES ON PLANNING

Throughout the preceding chapters, the interaction of societal culture with the concept of strategy, planning processes, systems, heuristics, and contextual-environmental influences on planning was discussed. Although the study of values and culture is not new (see, e.g. Parsons 1951; Kluckhohn/Strodtbeck 1961), there has only recently appeared an increasing awareness that we need to look at the impact of the environmental facet "societal culture," if we want to understand how organizations conduct their strategic planning and make strategic decisions (Jaeger/Baliga 1985; Sekaran/Snodgrass 1986a, 1987).

The basic argument for the culture-planning link here is, that if there are general differences in managerial behavior attributable to culture, these should be observable in any of Fayol's (1972:3) managerial activities of planning, organizing, control, and execution (Horovitz 1980:11; Triandis 1983:156). As was shown in previous chapters, strategic planning which introduces high levels of uncertainty, complexity, and exchange of information to organizations, should specifically be suited to observe these cultural influences (Hofstede 1980:383; Snodgrass/Grant 1986; Triandis 1983:156). A systematic relationship between specific dimensions of culture and the specific managerial task of strategy development and planning has not yet been established and empirically tested. Only a few empirical studies have been completed in this emerging field (Kagono et al 1985; Negandhi 1975b; Rieger/Wong-Rieger 1984).

The purpose of this chapter is to provide information about the influence of national culture on strategic planning practices. At first, the notion of societal culture is explained. Cultural dimensions that were frequently used to describe possible cultural variations in managerial practices are reviewed. Next, conceptual models that linked planning and culture are discussed. The 'culture-planning-model' used and developed throughout the preceding chapters is summarized and explained. Finally, empirical evidence concerning cultural influences on planning processes is reviewed.

6.1 Culture as Environmental Construct

6.11 Components of Culture

The inclusion of culture requires specification of its meaning. "Culture is one of those terms that defy a single all-purpose definition, and there are almost as many meanings of culture as people using the term" (Ajiferuke/Boddewyn 1970:154). In their review of conceptualizations of culture, (Kroeber/Kluckhon (1952:43) counted more than 164 definitions. Therefore, it is indispensable to be selective in applying the proper definition for comparative management studies (Negandhi 1983b:25). Early writers in anthropology focused on primitive societies in using the expression "culture." One of the earliest definitions of culture was presented by Taylor (1871:1):

> Culture is that complete whole which includes knowledge, belief, art, morals, laws, customs, and any other capabilities or habits acquired by man as a member of society.

From their extensive literature review, Kroeber/Kluckhohn (1952:181) derived a definition which became generally accepted.

> Culture consists of patterns, explicit and implicit of and for behavior acquired and transmitted by symbols, constituting the distinctive achievement of human groups, including their embodiment in artifacts; the essential core of culture consists of traditional (i.e., historically derived and selected) ideas and especially their attached values; culture systems may, on the one hand, be considered as products of action, on the other as conditioning elements of future action.

Anthropologists and researchers in organizational behavior have both narrowed and widened the definition. Distinctions have been drawn between <u>culture as a behavioral or a meaning system</u> (Jahoda 1984:140), and between the <u>content of culture</u> (the shared understandings contained in ideologies, norms, and values) and the <u>products of culture</u>, i.e. rites, ceremonies, practices and forms of communication (Enz 1986:176; Trice/Beyer 1984:654). The latter distinction was derived from Triandis (1972), who distinguishes between "subjective" culture as a "cultural group's characteristic way of perceiving the man-made part of its environment" (Triandis 1972:4) and its expression in "objective" cultural artifacts (Triandis 1984:305).

Each of these definitions recognizes that culture is something that is shared, learned, and shapes behavior Adler (1986:8). Hofstede (1980:25) arrived at a definition that became widely accepted and used in comparative research. He treats culture as

> the collective programming of the mind which distinguishes the members of one human group from another .... the interactive aggregate of common characteristics that influence a human group's response to its environment (Hofstede 1980:25)

in its function as an "adaptive-regulatory mechanism" (Smircich 1983:342) " as a filter for perceptions of the environment which sets decision premises for members of the culture group to the strategic planning process (Snodgrass 1984:3). This is the definition applied here. It concentrates on the cultural content or the set of shared values, mental programs, or societal norms, and the symbolic representations of shared meanings. This approach is <u>useful because</u> it looks at

> the fundamental differences in the way in which groups perceive the organizational regime and organizational climate, and hold values regarding general ideological factors such as competition at the workplace, and certain job aspects such as

> earnings, security, and the like. His having mapped out these differences has helped us to delineate the differences to delineate the differences in the cultural orientations or the collective mental programming of organizational members in different countries, and segregate culture as an independent variable rather than confounding country with culture (Sekaran/Snodgrass 1986a:212).

It depicts the values which have led to patterns of institutions in a society with particular structures and ways of functioning and is therefore meaningful for managerial behavior (Hofstede 1980:26). This political-value paradigm differs from structural-functionalism by claiming the independence of values (Child 1972:19) and assuming equifinality and cultural relativity (Adler 1986:43). The functional equivalence argument claims that "..societies can achieve similar objectives through different but parallel institutions" (Pascale 1978:91) and points to the fact that similar objectives can be achieved through different ways and functions (Negandhi 1975b). Scott (1981:335) argues that **equifinality** as part of the open systems concept was often overlooked by contingency models. The cultural relativity argument claims "..that there is no a priori dominant culture which is superior in coping with reality in any situation (Hessling 1973:129). These two assumptions imply that we have to accept both culture-specific and culture-general facets of the planning process (Adler 1986a:43), as particular management functions are facilitated and others are restrained in particular cultures (Triandis 1983:156).

From the discussion above follows, that the cultural contingencies of reinforcement result in particular cognitive structures and cause maps, information processing strategies, and perceptual selectivity (Doktor 1983:607; Triandis 1984:306). This postulates that cultural dimensions influence perceptions, values, cognitions, and behavior (Adler 1986:12; Triandis 1982:88).

Orientation	**Range of Variations**			**Overlaps with**
Time	Past	Present	Future	**UA**
Activity	Being	Becoming	Doing	**UA**
Environment	Subjugation	Harmony	Mastery	**UA**
Human Relations	Individualism	Collaterality	Hierarchy	**PD IDV**

Table 6.1: Cultural Value Orientations

Source: Adapted from Kluckhohn/Strodtbeck (1961:12): Variations in Value Orientations. Greenwood Press, Westport, CT 1961.
UA = Uncertainty Avoidance; IDV = Individualism;
PD = Power Distance (Hofstede 1980)

A number of classifications have been proposed to distinguish between such sets of cultural dimensions. Among them, the Kluckhohn/Strodtbeck (1961:12) concept of value orientation has gained broad recognition and is depicted above. Glenn (1981) and Sullivan/Nonaka (1986, 1988) introduced cultural differences in information processing. For managerial functions, a model of cultural dimensions proposed by Hofstede (1980) has gained widerecognition. Hofstede (1980) empirically derived the cultural dimensions of uncertainty avoidance, power distance, individualism-collectivism and masculinity-femininity, which overlap to some extent with the Kluckhohn/Strodtbeck factors as was shown above. He analyzed some 116.000 responses to a questionnaire on work-related value differences of IBM-subsidiaries in about 50 countries. For a short summary and critical review, see Hofstede (1983b), Triandis (1982), Sekaran/Snodgrass (1986a) and Westwood/Everett (1987). As its basic tenets were already presented and discussed throughout the preceding chapters, the emphasis here is on presenting alternative views of cultural influences.

6.12 Values, Cognition and Behavior

Triandis (1982, 1983, 1984) argues that we need to look at both values, cognition, behavior and inherent perceptual information processing strategies to delineate cultural influences on management. Some of the dimensions of variation with regard to planning are briefly reviewed below.

Time is regarded as important in some cultures, and less important in others. In some societies, spontaneous actions and sure, short-term benefits are preferred, whereas in others planned activities and uncertain large, future benefits are favoured (Sekaran/Snodgrass 1987:42; Triandis 1984:319). Time horizons are clearly of importance to strategic planning (Gaelweilwer 1980: 166). Temporal orientations influence the planning horizon (Bhagat 1977:39; Das 1987:203). Triandis (1983:156) argues that planning is likely to be facilitated by an orientation towards the future and inhibited by an orientation towards the past or the present. This cultural value is related to the uncertainty avoidance dimension referred to below (Hofstede 1980).

Activity is valued in Western cultures, while being (having deep experience) and being-in-becoming (evolve to a broader level of understanding) are valued in others (Triandis 1984:320). The be-ers are more passive, the do-ers more active (Adler et al 1986). This pertains to uncertainty avoidance (Hofstede 1980:171).

In some societies, people share the beliefs that they have a dominant role over the environment, that the world is under their internal control and can or should be mastered (Adler et al 1986). In other societies it is important to live in harmony with the environment. In a third group of societies, the perception is that it is better to passively accept subjugation to nature and not to interfere with the dominant external environment (Triandis 1984:319). Different from this man/nature concept (Kluckhohn/Strodtbeck 1961), but comparable is the idea of human mutability. In some societies, people are viewed as changeable, while in others they are viewed as unchangeable. Drawing on fatalism, Hofstede (1980, 1984a) implicitly includes these concepts in his uncertainty avoidance dimension.

Personal relationships among people can be ego-centered with emphasis on individual goals and well-being, depending on the self-concept and the degree of identification and strength of affiliation with different groups. Certain people are always defined as trustworthy, worthy of cooperation. Groups of such people were termed 'ingroups,' whereas the outsiders are termed 'outgroups' (Triandis 1984:310; 1983:144). The definition of ingroups and outgroups varies from culture to culture by size, ease of change, and entry/exit barriers. In ingroup oriented societies, people do not have an individual ego, but define themselves as members of clans or organizations. Relations in such ingroups can be either collateral (peer-oriented) or lineal, with attention paid to opinions held by superordinates in the hierarchy (Triandis 1984:322). Although there is no full overlap, the cognitive structures (self-concepts) are captured by Hofstede's (1980) individualism-collectivism dimension; the perceptual differences in the ingroup-outgroup-definition can be included in Hofstede's (1980) power distance dimension. The behavioral side of these notions is captured by superordination-suboridination, which clearly corresponds to the value dimension power distance (Triandis 1984:323).

Glenn (1981) drew attention to cultural influences in the utilization and evaluation of information. Sullivan/Nonaka (1986) theorize on how managers in different societies either increase uncertainty or decrease uncertainty through the process of creating information. In some cultures, people relate the information to limited, narrow frameworks, starting the information search with only facts and empirical observation to extract generalizations. Only the most relevant aspects of stimuli are included. This inductive, particularizing (i.e. searching for the specific) and probabalistic information processing strategy was termed 'pragmatic' and 'abstractive' (Triandis 1982:89; 1983:149; 1984:313). Sullivan/Nonaka (1986: 130) use these patterns implicitly to delineate information-gathering and processing differences between Japanese and American managers. Their 'variety reduction' dimension (named after Weick 1969) is proposed to be represented in the following way:

> State policy focusing only on relevant issues and sources of information. Identify specific employees who will identify problems and opportunities. Seek only high-quality information from the environment. State a desire for the firm to attain a realistic level - a goal (Sullivan/Nonaka 1986:130).

In other cultures, people start with a broad framework, such as an ideology, and place every fact into that grid. In such cultures, people associate many related concepts to the extracted stimulus to increase their understanding. Information search is broad and diffuse, as everything is related to everything else. This pattern is deductive, generalizing and tends to be absolutistic. Such cultures were termed 'ideological' and 'associative' (Triandis 1982:89; 1983:149; 1984:313). Similarly, the Sullivan/Nonaka (1986) 'variety amplification-dimension' refers to associative, diffuse, and ideological information processing:

> Announce information gathering policy that all phenomena are relevant. Require all employers to be identifiers of corporate problems and opportunities. Seek a large quantity of information from the environment. State the desire for the firm to attain an ideal - a dream. (Sullivan/Nonaka 1986:130).

These patterns are related to Hofstede's (1980) uncertainty avoidance dimension. However, as the latter deals with values, and the discussion here showed that the emphasis is on cognition and information processing behavior, it will be treated separately.

6.13 The Interaction with Corporate Culture

Similar to societal culture, corporate culture typically is defined as a complex set of values, beliefs, assumptions, and symbols that define the way in which a firm conducts its business (Smircich 1983). Common meanings attributed to the concept center around observed behavioral regularities, espoused norms and dominant values, the philosophy that guides organization's policies, rules of the game for getting along, and the feeling or climate (Schein 1985:6).

Corporate culture has two basic components: the networks of meanings and substance, and its forms and practices (Trice/Beyer 1984:654). Schein (1985:6) argues, that corporate culture

> should be reserved for the deeper level of basic assumptions and beliefs that are shared by members of an organization, that operate unconsciously, and that define in a basic "taken-for-granted" fashion an organizations's view of itself and its environment. These assumptions and beliefs are learned responses to a group's problems of survival in its external environment and its problems of internal integration. (Emphasis original)

Several terms are used to describe these patterns of experience, e.g. cognitive maps, cause maps, theories in action, ruling myths, (Axelrod 1976; Weick 1977; Argyris/Schön 1980).

Greipel (1988:7) argues that corporate culture influences strategy. King/Cleland (1978:273) assert that the corporate culture within which planning is embedded is of higher impact to the success of planning than the specifics of the planning techniques that are used. Bigler (1986:10) claims that the corporate culture has to accomodate the value chain imperatives. Strategic planning provides a milieu in which assumptions often need to be explicated. Shrivastava (1985:105) therefore argues, that rationality in strategic planning is mediated or substituted by corporate culture and its artifacts. "By influencing strategic decision processes, organizational cultures also indirectly influence the content of strategy" (Shrivastava 1985:106). His argument is that heuristics are the outcome of corporate myths, metaphors, rituals, and value systems as depicted in figure 3.1. Similarly, Deal/Kennedy (1982:31) assert that corporate culture influences what kind of information and what matters are to be attended to.

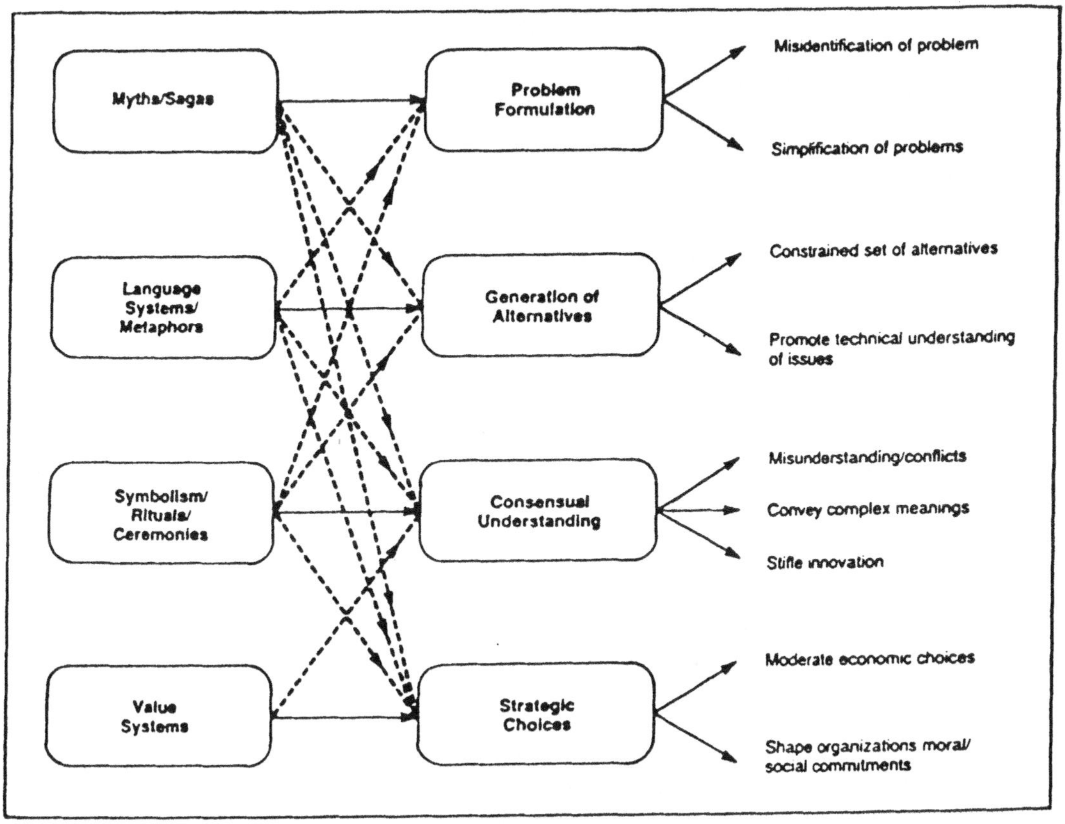

Figure 6.1 Influence of Corporate Culture on Planning Heuristics

Source: Shrivastava, Paul (1985:106): Integrating Strategy Formulation with Organizational Culture. In: Journal of Business Strategy, 5, 3, Winter 1985, pp. 103-111.

Corporate culture in that sense influences strategic planning through schemas, i.e.templates imposed to give form and meaning to the environment, shared believes, ideologies and value systems relative to tasks (Jackson/Dutton 1986:2; Hogarth/Makridakis 1981:117). Similar objects and issues are clustered together to categories during the planning process (Jackson/Dutton 1986:5). Corporate culture can affect perceptions about the environment, issue identification, activities and persons involved, and outcome evaluations throughout the planning process (Hogarth/Makridakis 1981:117; Mintzberg/Waters 1985:262). However, as was pointed out by Davidson (1982:325), the planning climate can be quite different from the corporate culture within an organization.

While these findings are quite useful, it is argued here that we need to be careful with regard to the level of observation. Corporate culture deals with values and mental programs on the company or micro-level. Societal culture deals with values and mental programs on the macro-level of national societies. Both can be explained as "the collective programming of the mind which distinguishes the members of one human group from another" (Hofstede 1980:25). Again, we need to pay attention to the level of analysis. As depicted below, companies produce their own corporate culture within the environment of the surrounding national culture (Deal/Kennedy 1982).

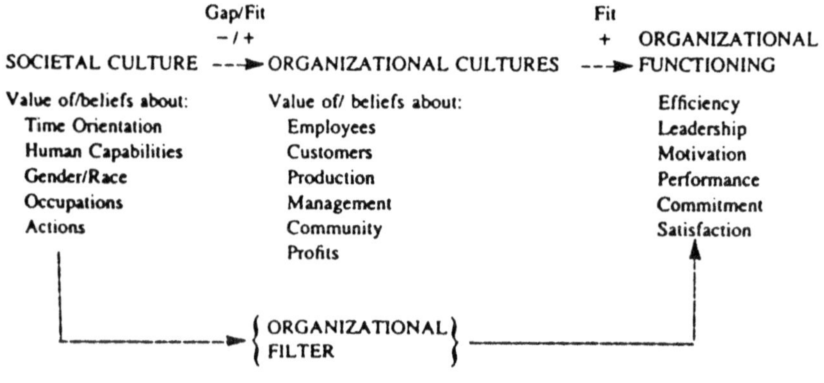

Figure 6.2: The Influence of Societal Culture on Corporate Culture.

Adapted from: Enz, Cathy (1983:181): New Directions For Cross-Cultural Studies: Linking Organizational and Societal Cultures. In: Advances in International Comparative Management, vol. 2, JAI Press, New York 1983, pp. 173-189.

Moreover, new entrants into a company are usually socialized on the macro-level (society) before the micro-level (company) socialization (Deal/Martin 1982). This is not to say that there are no sub-groups or companies with corporate cultures that are different from their surrounding national cultures (Enz 1986). Or, that there are no countercultures within corporate cultures (Martin/ Siehl 1983). Societal cultures vary in the extent to which their set of beliefs and values are dominant (Enz 1986:173). The degree of homogeneity of societal cultures (Enz 1986) and the strength of corporate cultures (Schein 1985; Peters/Waterman 1982) clearly are mediating variables. The argument here is that "societal norms have led to the development and pattern maintenance of institutions in society with a particular structure and way of functioning" (Hofstede 1980:26). Therefore, at first we need to look at the impact of national culture on planning systems

(Hofstede 1980; King/Cleland 1978: 278). Then, we can evaluate the influence of corporate cultures.

6.2 Linking Culture and Planning

While the last sections defined culture and provided a review of cultural dimensions that are relevant to planning, this section reviews conceptual models that were found in the literature. A new, comprehensive 'Culture-Planning-Model' is suggested.

6.21 Existing Conceptual Models

Several theoretical models that link cultural facets to planning and strategy making could be identified. The work by Faucheux (1977), Hofstede (1980, 1984b), Horovitz (1980), King/Cleland (1978), Orbach (1984), Redding (1980), Redding/Martyn-Jones (1979), Schneider (1989), Sekaran/Snodgrass (1986ab, 1987), Snodgrass (1984), Snodgrass/Grant (1986), and Sullivan/Nonaka (1986) is reviewed below.

Faucheux (1977) and Orbach (1984) present historical views about the <u>structural development</u> of companies in the Latin and Anglo-Saxon culture (Faucheux 1977) and the Japanese versus American culture (Orbach 1984). The argument presented there is that differences in the structural development led to different planning approaches. For both authors, the planning process clearly follows the structure, which can be explained from historical and cultural development.[33] Orbach (1984) relates the U.S. short-time orientation to the importance of short-term profit oriented stockholders, whereas in his view Japanese companies do not suffer from that constraint. One proposition that could be derived from the work of Faucheux (1977) and Orbach (1984) is that large power distance inhibits strategic thinking and supports political thinking (Hofstede 1980:384). However, no further hypotheses or propositions are developed.

King/Cleland (1978:273) draw the conclusion, that

> the success of long-range planning in an organization is less sensitive to the specifics of the

---

[33] Faucheux (1977:131) argues that the development of companies in the Latin culture was based on metaphors from institutions like the catholic Church and always followed centralized, top down policy making and control; on the contrary, companies in the Anglo-Saxon culture followed a more operational approach, based on the existence of consensus and decentralized responsibility. Similarly, Orbach (1984) refers to the Japanese history to depict the long-term perspective and close collaboration of Japanese enterprises and government to develop opportunities, following some type of nearly religious mission. U.S. companies in his view are subject to the short-run, quick-fix solution of problems due to the historical development.

> planning techniques that are used than it is tho the overall culture within which the planning process is accomplished.

They define culture as "the integrated system of acquired behavioral patterns" (King/Cleland 1978:174) and argue that societal culture influences corporate culture, which in turn determines "what the organization is able to effectively accomplish as well as how it will accomplish things" (King/Cleland 1978:275). Cultural traits they refer to are the (Japanese) emphasis on defining the issue vs. the (American) emphasis on solving predefined problems, ego involvement, and the Kluckhohn/Strodtbeck (1961) past/present/future-orientation. Similar to Ouchi/Jaeger's (1978) "Theory Z" they argue that there is an American corporate culture which is different from a Japanese corporate culture. The link between societal and corporate culture, however, is not clear.[34] No further links or operationalizations between specific aspects of societal culture and planning frameworks are offered. Nevertheless it has to be acknowledged that King/Cleland (1978) were among the first writers in strategy that introduced the culture-strategy link.

A similar, but more elaborate model was introduced by Rieger/Wong-Rieger (1984, 1986). They linked the influence of societal culture, industry culture (termed "norm"), and corporate culture (identity) to organizational structure, process, and strategy. In their view (Rieger/Wong-Rieger 1986)

> A fundamental proposition underlying the cultural domain is that organizations do not have random characteristics, but coalesce into configurations defined by certain key attributes.

Redding/Martyn-Johns (1979) developed a model of cultural influences on managerial practices, based on cognition processes. They took Fayol's (1949) functions of management and speculated about how several mental constructs (causality, probability, time, self, and morality) interfere with them, bound by societal culture. In their understanding, planning is influenced by causality, probability, and time (Redding 1980:143).[35] Cultural differences in the causality construct are the outcome of means-ends relationships and the extent of abstract thinking.

> The process of planning rests on thinking in abstracts. .. it also contains an implied linear logic to link them together .. The use of abstract

---

[34] Societal culture is a macro-level construct, while corporate culture is a micro-level construct. For a further discussion of the relation between societal and corporate culture, see section 6.13 on 'Interaction with Corporate Culture.'

[35] In the Redding/Martyn-Johns (1979) paper, no reference is made about the interference of cultural causality and planning. This is added in the Redding (1980) paper.

> categories and linear logic, while natural to the Western mind is not apparently the normal mental approach of the Chinese. Their vision is more of large numbers of interconnected specifics .. does not include formalized planning (Redding 1980:143).

Their probability-construct refers to the Western notion of predictions based on facts, whereas in fatalistic views the future cannot be calculated. The type of planning, then, depends on the view of probability (Redding/Martyn-Johns 1979:108).

In a similar way, Sullivan/Nonaka (1986:145) tie their concept of variety amplification vs. variety reduction to the process of strategy formulation. They argue that U.S. managers use either of the two concepts, but not both. Japanese managers, however, they argue, use both, depending on their hierarchical level.

	Causality	Probability	Time	Self	Morality
Planning	Not formally developed	More use of hunch and intuitive; fatalistic view	Low priority to deadlines; Non-linearity		
Organizing	Abstract entities not seperated out		Co-ordination loose	Personalistic networks	
Leading				High subjectivity. Obligation nets. Paternalism.	Sensitivity to face. Pragmatism in business ethics.
Control	'Control cycle' not perceived		Problems of urgency and common perception of co-ordinating deadlines.	Objective performance measures not used.	Use of shame mechanism.

Figure 6.3: Redding/Martyn-Johns Model of Cognition as an Aspect of Culture. Potential problem areas in applying Western management principles to Asian cultures.

Adapted from: Redding, G. / Martyn-Johns, T.A. (1979:118): Paradigm Differences and Their Relation to Management, with Reference to South-East Asia. In: England, G.W. / Negandhi, A. / Wilpert, B. (1979, eds.): Organizational Functioning in a Cross-Cultural Perspective. Comparative Administration Research Institute, Kent, OH 1979, pp. 103-125.

Time is the next culture-bound construct Redding/Martyn-Johns (1979) and Redding (1980) discuss with regard to planning. Their argument is that the view of time (linear or cyclical) and the sense of urgency finds its manifestations in the planning system. They argue that the linear view of time is represented in Western planning systems through programming (determining a sequence of activities over time) and scheduling (placing the activities into defined time periods), while "detailed organizing into the future is not highly developed in Chinese business" (Redding 1980:144). Redding/Martyn-Jones propose the following hypothesis for the influence of culture on planning:

> In oriental cultures, the fatalistic view of probabilities will result in a lower sensitivity in the calculation of future events. Processes of extrapolation will be carried out witch less conviction if they are carried out .. planning as such may not take place in any identifiable way and companies will be run more on an ad hoc basis. Oriental companies will use either less formal planning systems and/or planning systems with fewer variables than equivalent Western companies.

The Redding/Martyn-Johns (1979) model is implicitly based on the Kluckhohn/Strodtbeck (1961) value orientations towards time (past/present/future), man/nature (mastery/harmony/subjugation) and Glenns (1981) information processing strategies (ideologism-ideology/pragmatism-facts). It presents a reasonable framework for investigating the culture-planning influence with regard to some factors and develops testable hypotheses. The Redding/Martyn-Johns (1979) cognitive process model treats information as an input and behavior as an output. Cognition, however, is not the only important factor in decision making. Therefore, the model only includes some of the dimensions relevant for this link. And, it remains in the Western-Asian culture dichotonomy.

Horovitz (1980) conducted a comparative study of control and planning practices in German, British and French companies. Horovitz (1980:35) treated managerial control and planning practices as the dependent variable and related them to three independent variables: country (culture, manager's education), industry-sector (task environment), and management system. One of his hypotheses was that control and planning

> are affected by 'cultural traits' such as employees' attitudes towards authority and discipline, towards bureaucracy and centralism and towards initiative and autonomy (Horovitz 1980:35).

Horovitz (1980:39), like Faucheux (1977) above, uses the Haire et al (1966) classification of Latin-European, Anglo-Saxon and Nordic-European country clusters.[36] However, he does not explicitly deal with the underlying cultural values that lead to these attitudes. His model is more targeted towards control than towards planning.

---

[36] The Haire et al (1966) study is based on Maslow's (1943) hierarchy of human needs, which Hofstede (1980:31) defies because Maslow's (1943) hierarchy of needs itself is culture-bound.

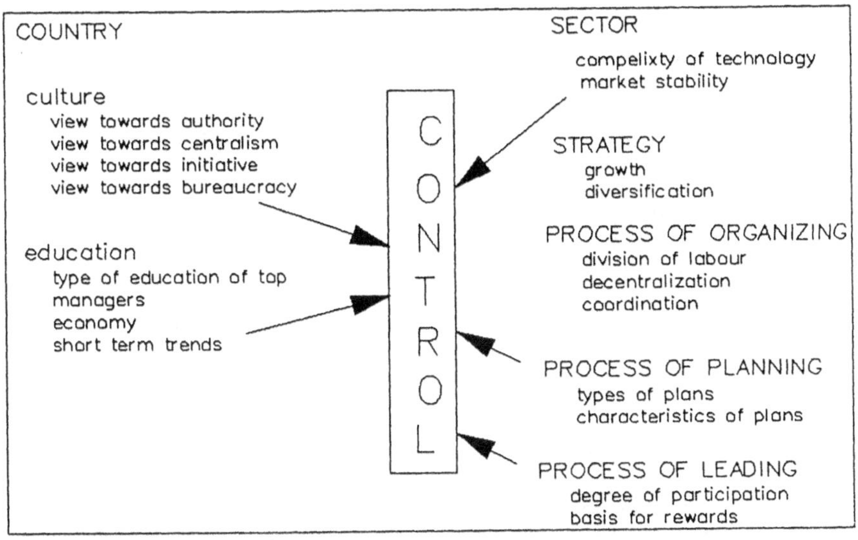

Figure 6.4: The Horovitz Control Model

Source: Horovitz, Jacques (1980:35): Top Management Control in Europe. St. Martin's Press, New York, 1980.

Hofstede (1980:383), in his landmark study, which was referred to earlier, claims that planning processes reflect the power distance and uncertainty avoidance dimensions of the dominant national culture. He argues that we have to be careful in transferring planning practices from the U.S. to other countries, because American planning systems might not fit into other environments. He claims that the criteria used to evaluate the effectiveness of planning are subject to cultural influences just as the planning practices themselves (Hofstede 1980:383). The following propositions are suggested:

> A stronger Uncertainty Avoidance norm supports a need for more detail in planning and more short-term feedback .. [and] makes it less likely that strategic planning activities are practiced .. [and] supports a tendency to leave planning to specialists. A larger Power Distance supports 'political' rather than 'strategic' thinking (Faucheux 1977) .. [and] supports personal planning and control rather than impersonal systems. This often means no formal planning at all when power distances are large.

In a related article, Hofstede (1984b:94) implicitly refers to the Kluckhohn/Strodtbeck (1961) nature/man-value of mastery, harmony or subjugation to the environment, nature, or the gods. He argues that planning in less developed countries is less developed or not practiced at all due to a fatalistic, subjugative view of the world. Contrary to the propositions in his 1980 book and based on the empirical findings of Horovitz (1980), Hofstede (1984b:94) postulates that

> [i]n the more Uncertainty Avoiding cultures, short- and medium-term scheduling and planning get more top

> management attention than in less Uncertainty Avoiding cultures. On the other hand .. the idea of strategic planning - rethinking the fundamental goals and activities of an organization - is more popular in less Uncertainty avoiding cultures like Great Britain than in than in more Uncertainty avoiding cultures like France (Horovitz 1980) because strategic planning presupposes a tolerance for great ambiguity and for taking distance from the certainties of the past. (Emphasis original)

These differences in the propositions clearly show the necessity of more empirical research in this field. Although Hofstede's (1980) dimensions are quite useful and found wide appreciation, they were criticized by Triandis (1982:88) because they mainly rely on values and only randomly include perceptions, cognitions, and behavior. Still, one has to recognize the importance of this study, since it offers an empirically derived framework. Hofstede's (1980) dimensions are applied in the Culture-Planning Model, but in a broader frame of reference than originally conceptualized by the author. As mentioned earlier, the Hofstede (1980) dimensions are linked to the Kluckhohn/Strodtbeck (1961) value paradigm and Glenn's (1981) information processing paradigm, in order to reduce the shortcomings discussed above.

In her dissertation, Coral Snodgrass (1984) explored the influence of culture on the strategic planning and control process. Her research model establishes the potential influences of culture on the management control system used in the implementation phase of the strategic planning and control process. Japanese and US manufacturing companies were shown to vary in their mode of control along an "explicit control" (laws and rules) - "implicit control" (myths and values) continuum. Snodgrass et al (1986) added a German sample to the original research. This approach is based on Child's (1981) notion of "preferred modes of action."[37] The basic argument here is that cultural influences are visible in the type and extent of control during strategy implementation, termed "mode of control" (Snodgrass/Grant 1986:207). The definition of culture was based on cognition as "a filter for perceptions of the environment which sets decision premises for members of the culture group" (Snodgrass 1984). The twelve hypotheses she tested in a sample of about 1.000 questionnaires from both workers and managers in Japan and the U.S.A. are based on the Kluckhohn/Strodtbeck (1961) value paradigm. To quote one of the four that were supported,

---

[37] Child (1981) argues that culture dictates both the preferred modes of actions (process) and the organizational structure that is consistent with these preferred modes. Both serve as a means to achieve the individual's and organizations' aims. The interesting idea here is that, as structure follows process, culture at first influences process and then, although parallel, structure. This contrasts with the view of Faucheux (1977) and Orbach (1984) discussed earlier.

> Japanese managers experience less explicit control in their firms' monitoring system than do U.S. managers.

Although this work has a huge database, it does not directly relate to strategic planning. It extensively investigates control systems on the level of workers, and is only concerned with the implementation phase. However, the application of Child's (1981) preferred modes deserves some attention. In a later research, Sekaran/Snodgrass (1986b, 1987) investigated the cultural variations in the modes of exchange with the environment (market mechanism, bureaucratic mechanism, and clan control) developed by Ouchi (1980). For planning, they used the Kluckhohn/Strodtbeck (1961) 'nature of human activity' (being/being-in-becoming/ becoming) value dimension, which they operationalized as "spontaneous vs. planned action" (Sekaran /Snodgrass 1987:42). As was shown in the discussion above, this is certainly one of the factors that should be investigated. However, a more holistic framework would be more appropriate.

Schneider (1987, 1989) developed a very comprehensive and useful conceptual model of the interaction of societal culture with strategy formulation. Strategy formulation is defined as "the alignment of the organization with its environment" (Schneider 1987:3). Her basic argument is that societal culture influences both "the nature of the relationship of an organization with its environment as well as the nature of the relationships among people within an organization" (Schneider 1987:2). These two dimensions were operationalized in the following way (Schneider 1989:152):

> Relationship with environment (external adaptation): uncertainty and ambiguity, control over the environment (domination/submission), proactivity vs. reactivity (doing vs. being, fatalism), nature of truth and reality, time orientation, and change.
>
> Relationships among people (internal integration): hierarchyl (power and statues), individual vs. group orientation; social vs. task orientation.

She then employs the information processing theory and the decision phase theorem to depict the impact of culture on specific steps of strategy formulation (scanning, selection, interpretation, validation), as shown in table 6.2 below. For most of the factors that influence the nature of the organization with the environment, and the nature of the relationship among people, value dimensions from Kluckhohn/ Strodtbeck (1961) were used.

Schneider (1989:155) then continues to delineate two different models of strategy formulation. These two models of strategy formulation seem to be similar to the distinction between rational/analytical and avoidance/emergent strategy approaches referred to in the chapter on planning systems. She proposes her "model one" for companies in cultures high in uncertainty avoidance, power distance, and individualism; "model two" is proposed for companies in environments low in uncertainty avoidance, power distance, and individualism, using Hofstede's (1980) dimensions.

Strategy Formulation	National Culture
1. Environmental scanning	
- active vs passive	relationship with environment
- broad vs. focussed	(control, activity and uncertainty)
- systematic vs nonsystematic	
2. Selection	
- type of information sought:	nature of truth and reality
quantitative vs qualitative	(fact vs principles)
	uncertainty avoidance
- sources of information:	task vs social
personal vs impersonal	power and status
subjective vs objective	individual or group
3. Interpretation	
- analytic vs intuitive	'truth and reality'
	uncertainty avoidance
4. Validation	
- personal edict	hierarchy
- bureaucratic	uncertainty avoidance
- historical precedent	time orientation
- political coalition	individual vs group
- consensus	task vs social orientated
5. Establishing priorities	
- importance	task vs social
- urgency	time orientation
- certainty	uncertainty avoidance

Table 6.2 Interaction of Culture with Phases of Strategy Formulation

Source: Schneider, Susan (1989:155): Strategy Formulation: The Impact of National Culture. In: Organization Studies, vol. 10, # 2, pp. 149-168.

The framework proposed by Schneider (1987, 1989) is among the most comprehensive models reviewed. It includes both information processing and values. Suggestions are made as to which type of strategy formulation process might be suitable in a particular environment. It resembles the Adler (1986a) cultural variations in the (normative) steps of decision making and planning, which were reviewed in the chapter on decision making processes, depicted in Table 2.1. Therefore, it shares the same critique with regard to the application of the phase theorem of decision making. Yet, its focus is somewhat different from what is pursued in this research. While here the emphasis is on strategic planning frameworks (process, systems, heuristics) with the culture-free notion of parallel <u>or</u> sequential strategy formulation and implementation process, while the Schneider (1989) model pertains to strategy formulation only, assuming a sequential procedure. While this is a very comprehensive and useful conceptualization, it is still culture-bound.

CULTURE		
Environment	controlling	adapting
- uncertainty	reduction	tolerance
- control	high	low
- activity	proactive	reactive
Relationships		
- hierarchy	high emphasis	low
- peer	individual	group
- task vs social	task-oriented	social-oriented
STRATEGY FORMULATION	**CONTROLLING**	**ADAPTING**
Scanning	search: active, focussed, systematic	monitor: reactive, broad, non-systematic
Selection		
Type of Information	quantitative	qualitative
Sources	objective, impersonal	subjective, personal
Interpretation	analytic	intuitive
Validation	personal edict bureaucratic rules	consensus political historical precedents
Priorities	urgency certain task concerns	less urgency less certainty social concerns
Overall	top down elite dominated 'strategic planning' intended	bottom up consensus based 'evolutionary' adjusting. emergent

Table 6.3: The Two Schneider Models of Strategy Formulation
Source: Schneider, Susan (1989:161): Strategy Formulation: The Impact of National Culture. In: Organization Studies, vol. 10, # 2, pp. 149-168.

Similar to Schneider (1989), the influence of cultural and strategic learning is emphasized by Greipel (1988). Strategy, for him, is something evolving, gradually shared and learned, influenced by and interacting with cultural learning. However, his level of observation permanently amplifies from the micro-level (corporate culture) to the macro-level (societal culture). While arguing about corporate culture, he actually uses concepts from societal culture. Greipel (1989:6) emphasizes that

> to live in a culture means to learn culturally, because <u>cultural learning</u> determines that fundamental (socialization-) process through which each single employee acquires and internalizes <u>his companie's</u> corporate culture. A companie's thoughts and acts are thereby always also reflections of specific cultural learning processes. (Emphasis original; translated)

The use of the term "culture" is quite difficult to evaluate in Greipel's dissertation, because he does not touch the point that companies produce their own corporate culture within the environment of the surrounding national culture (Deal/Kennedy

1982), depending on it's relative dominance (Enz 1986:173). However, the value and importance of the Greipel (1988) model as shown below lies in establishing an interaction between cultural learning and strategic learning, which is termed organizational learning here.

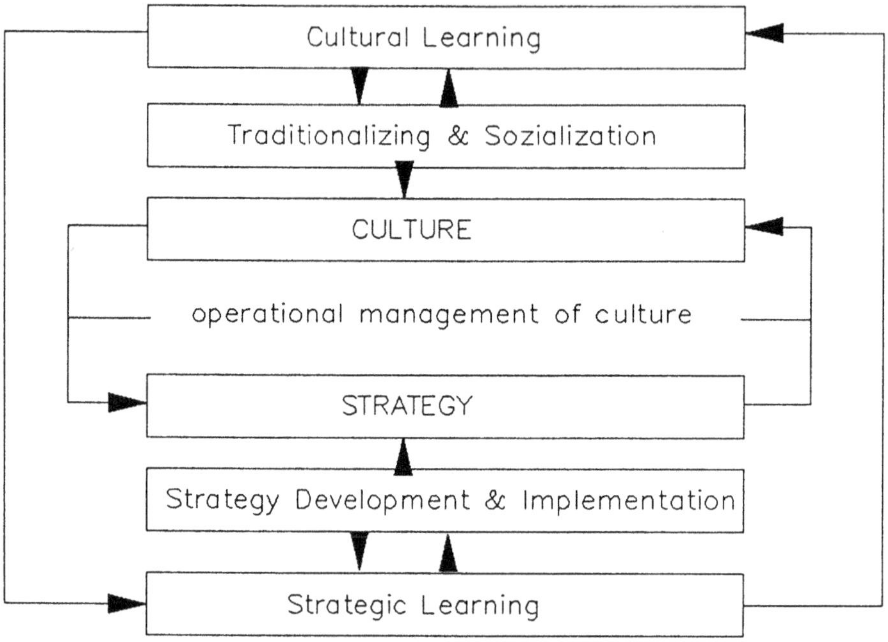

Figure 6.5: The Greipel (1988) Conceptional Synthesis of Strategy and Culture on the Learning Level

Translated from: Greipel, Peter (1988:7): Strategie und Kultur. Doctoral dissertation, University of Wuppertal/ Switzerland. Verlag Paul Haupt, Bern.

6.22 Summary and Critique

Faucheux (1977) and Orbach (1984) link planning to the historical development of culturally different societies in general. Besides the proposition that large power distance inhibits strategic thinking and supports political thinking, no further theoretical development is offered. The importance of their argument lies in the historical view.

King/Cleland (1978) argue that societal culture influences corporate culture, which in turn influences the effectiveness of planning. No specific operationalizations or links between societal and corporate culture, or between specific aspects of societal culture and planning frameworks are offered. It has to be acknowledged, however, that King/Cleland (1978) were among the first writers on strategy who introduced the culture-strategy link.

The cognitive process model, as used by Redding/Martyn-Johns, (1979) uses information as an input and behavior as an output. Cognition, however, is not the only important factor in decision making. Therefore, the model only includes some of the dimensions relevant to this link. Moreover, it remains in the Western-Asian culture dichotonomy.

Hofstede's (1980) monumental work provides a comprehensive, empirically based framework for the investigation of the impact of societal culture on managerial behavior. The propositions with regard to planning, however, are partly contradictory (Hofstede 1980, 1984). Sorge (1983:627) argues that "the great amount of cultural diversity behind each of Hofstede's dimensions was becoming just too great to be taken into account convincingly." For example, the Kluckhohn/Strodtbeck value dimensions were not explicitly included. However, given the vast amount of information about cultural influences on managerial behavior provided by Hofstede in his original (1980) and later work, one cannot expect that one study can capture all possible aspects of all the managerial functions. Hofstede's (1980) empirical work is widely acknowledged, though criticized as above. It is therefore applied as a guiding framework in the proposed Culture-Planning Model.

The work by Snodgrass, Sekaran and Grant (1984, 1985, 1986) does not directly relate to strategic planning. It investigated to a large extent control systems, and restricted itself to the implementation phase. However, the application of Child's (1981) preferred modes deserves some attention. Similarly, Horvitz (1980) is mainly concerned with control aspects. He does not explicitly deal with the underlying cultural values that lead to the cultural traits he uses.

The framework proposed by Schneider (1987, 1989) includes both information processing and values. However, the model is limited to strategy formulation only, assuming a sequential procedure, while in reality strategy formulation and implementation can also parallel each other (Mintzberg 1985). While this is a very useful conceptualization, it still is culture-bound. And, it relies on the rational-analytical understanding of decision making in applying the phase theorem. Similarly, the Greipel (1988) model emphasizes organizational learning. However, it rests on the micro-level, and it only relates to the evolutionary understanding of strategy making.

Thus, the conclusion is drawn that a model is needed which is not restricted to either the control, implementation or formulation aspects of strategic planning; a model that does not rely on the phase theorem and is based on both organizational theory and findings from comparative management; one hat includes both cultural values, cognition, and information processing perceptions and behavior; that uses an empirically derived framework and integrates other theoretical concepts.

6.3 The Culture-Planning Model

Hofstedes' (1980) dimensions include much of the value orientations discussed above and refer specifically to managerial behavior. However, the dimensions here are not used as a set of limiting specific questions, but as a guiding, broad framework encompassing much of the concepts derived above. The work of Kluckhohn/Strodtbeck (1961) is integrated in the power distance (PD), uncertainty avoidance (UA), and individualism-dimensions (IDV). Organizational learning (OL) is introduced as a new independent variable, representing the information processing notions developed by Glenn (1981) and Sullivan/Nonaka (1986).

These <u>comparative-management findings</u> can be related to the four components of the <u>process-oriented model of managerial functions</u>, developed by Cyert/March (1963). Their first component is "quasi-resolution of conflict" (individual subunits that create consistency through 'local rationality' vs. uniform systems; Cyert/March 1963:117). The second component is "uncertainty avoidance," i.e. solving pressing problems and anticipating future reactions of other parts of the environment in order to reduce uncertainty rather than developing long-term strategies (Cyert/March 1963: 118). "Problemistic search," the third component, refers to "satisficing" to find solutions to problems as perceived in the usual power structure and environment (Cyert/March 1963:120).

Source & Content	**Derived Concepts**			
Organizational Behaviour Concepts:	Uncertainty Avoidance	Problemistic Search	Quasi-Resolution of Conflict	Organizational Learning
Cultural Concepts: Values, Cognitive Structures, Information Processing Behavior	Man/Nature Time Activity Uncertainty Avoidance Tight/loose	Ingroup-Outgroup Power-Distance Superordination/ Subordination	Self-Concept Group Identification Relational Orientation Individualism	Ideologism-Pragmatism; Associative-Abstract Specificy-Diffuseness
Dimension Labels	**Uncertainty Avoidance**	**Power Distance**	**Individualism -Collectivism**	**Organizational Learning**

Table 6.4: Derived Concepts

Source: Compiled by the author from: Cyert/March (1963); Glenn (1981), Hofstede (1980); Kluckhohn/Strodtbeck (1961); Triandis (1984)

Organizational learning points to adaptive change as the result of experience (Cyert/March 1963:120). Combining these diverse streams of research, the models given above and below are suggested.

Lammers/Hickson (1979:401) propose that societal culture influences the manner in which organizations are evaluated (through values, norms, and roles), designed, (through premises about what is possible and wanted), and how roles are enacted. For the framework suggested here, this was operationalized in terms of planning systems (structure, reasons), heuristics (behavioral issues), and process (characteristics, acts), as outlined previously.

Independent **Dependent** **Dependent**

CONTEXT ------> STRATEGIC PLANNING ------> OUTCOMES

Depicted by:

CULTURE ------> SYSTEMS & HEURISTICS ---> PROCESS

Explained by:

-Power Distance	Structure	Behavior	Characte-ristics
-Uncertainty Avoidance	Goals& Reasons		Acts
-Organizational Learning			
-Individualism/ Collectivism			

Dimensions **Questionnaire Indicators**

Figure 6.6: The Culture-Planning Model

In the stepwise refinement, each group of factors has to be read columnwise from top to bottom, e.g. planning-systems-structure. Existing labels for the dimension labels were taken from other authors to ease understanding, although the interpretation is much broader here as was already pointed out.

The model consists of independent, exogenous variables and dependent, endogenous variables, following the tradition of theory building often utilized (Friedrichs 1980:86; Scheuch 1982:22). Following Lazarsfeld (1967), it flows from theoretical constructs to a partition in dimensions, to the choice of indicators and their integration, and is explained in three stages.[38]

The first stage argues that the context influences strategic planning frameworks, which in turn influence the planning outcomes. The second stage takes out culture as one contextual, exogenous variable, which - among others - influences strategic planning frameworks as depicted by systems, process, and heuristics, which in turn influence the effectiveness of planning frameworks as outcome measure. The third stage is designed to capture the distinct aspects of culture, planning frameworks, and planning effectiveness.

Culture is operationalized by the dimensions of power distance, uncertainty avoidance, individualism/collectivism, and organizational learning as outlined above. Exogenous variables are treated as given in within-country comparisons. However, in the cross-cultural model depicted here, these dimensions differ from one culture to another in their interactive effect on planning frameworks (Sheth/Sethi 1981:371). Planning system refers to the time frame, structure, and reasons (goals) of planning frameworks. Planning processes are depicted in terms of characteristics and activities performed. Schemas, assumptions, and non-rational behavior form what was termed "heuristics".[39]

6.4 The Culture-Planning Dimensions

The dimensions derived above are explained in this section with regard to their interaction with planning. The model draws on concepts that were developed in the preceding chapters.[40]

Uncertainty Avoidance (UA), as introduced by Cyert/March (1963), refers to the absorption of ambiguity (March/Simon 1958) and reduction of anxiety (Schein 1985:82) through tight control, formalization and the structuring of activities, e.g. separation of strategy formulation and implementation (Hofstede 1980:384; 387). Depending on the beliefs about the relationship between man

---

[38] The model is largely conceptual. In practice, the dynamics of interaction are, of course, much more complex. Such a conceptual model, however, provides a good overview of major interactions and allows for the detection of patterns (Miles/ Huberman 1984:34; Mintzberg 1979a:584).

[39] This concept is used to avoid value judgments with regard to the rationality of planning frameworks. Due to the wide differences in values among cultures, the question of rationality is less meaningful in a cross-cultural context. (Sheth/Sethi 1981:371). For further details, see the chapters on planning systems and on heuristics.

[40] Therefore, it was decided to include in a holistic frame what had so far been developed in various chapters. The overlaps in content resulting from that aim are thought to aid in the derivation of underlying concepts.

and nature (mastery, harmony or subjugation), managers try to control the future or to let it happen (Hofstede 1983:81; Strodtbeck/Kluckhohn 1961).

Low	**Uncertainty Avoidance (UA) High**
loosely-coupled strategic issue management	tight, formalized long-range planning system
planning process based on on informal rules	planning process based on printed planning manual
longer time horizon	shorter time horizon
long-term feedback & goals, e.g. market share	short-term feedback & goals, e.g. profit; time is important
line managers plan	planning staff plans
future orientation	past/present orientation
simple, bold monitoring system	detailed, comprehensive monitoring system
planning to benefit from opportunities	planning to master the environment
control the environment	defend against the environment
willingness to accept risk	concern for security & stability
deviant ideas are welcome	deviant ideas are dangerous
practice counts	principles count
variability	standardization, specialization
less structuring of activities	more structuring of activities
less ritualistic behavior	more ritualistic, formalized behavior
strategic planning actively practiced	strategic planning as unwelcome duty

Table 6.5: Uncertainty Avoidance and Planning

High UA refers to a high concern about stability, security, and activity aiming at having everything under control, whereas low UA refers to a positive view towards innovation and risk taking, and allows for events to evolve loosely-coupled through trial and error. In high UA environments, time is an important, scarce resource. The emphasis is on short-term benefits and the climate is not favorable to planning (Triandis 1984:319). Precision as well as formal and informal principles count more under strong UA, leading to more formalization, standardization and ritualization (Jackofsky et al 1988:40). Under high UA, planning will be more concerned with details and short-term feedback and carried out by specialists (Hofstede 1980:384). The structuring of planning activities is performed either through explicit formalization, standardization, and specialization or on the basis of implicit rules and rituals (Hofstede 1980:187). The appropriateness of broad planning guidelines versus rigidly specified procedures is equally widely discussed in the strategy literature (e.g. Kühn 1985).

Power Distance (PD) refers to concentration of authority and task specialization (Hofstede 1980:384). It is the degree to which people accept a hierarchical order in terms of superordination and subordination or strive for equality (Hofstede 1984a:83; Triandis 1984:323). Participative or consultative decision making and two-way communication are preferred in organizations in a low-PD environment. Status differences and the absolute power of the superior are reflected in centralization in high-PD contexts (Hofstede 1984a:88).

Low	**Power Distance (PD)** **High**
decentralization	centralization
flat organizations	tall organizations
strategic thinking	political thinking
two-way communication	one-way communication
bottom-up planning	top-down planning
control system based on trust	planning used for control
planning is just a managerial function	planning is a prestigious position
planning as practice	planning as training
use of consultants (expert power)	use of in-house experts (referent power)

Table 6.6: Power Distance and Planning

For planning, these contrary positions are reflected in political vs. strategic thinking, in the value of more or less centralization, and in taller or flatter planning hierarchies (Hofstede 1980:135;384). In this context, bottom up, bottom-down or a combination of the two extremes are widely discussed planning process elements (e.g. Steiner et al 1982).

Individualism versus collectivism (IDV) is a measure of the integration of a society or societal subsystem seen in the relation between an individual and his or her in-groups. It relates to people's self-concept, their orientation and commitment towards the 'I' or the 'we' in organizations (Hofstede 1984a :390). Under the notion of individualism, employees are 'factors of production,' which are only involved in a calculative and not in a moral way. Openness and directness are the way problems get solved (Hofstede 1984a:87). In individualistic contexts, people put emphasis on self-interest, individual initiative, self-actualization, and the task to be performed. In collectivist organizations, belongingness, loyalty and relationships in the company as an in-group are the things that count in business. Trust and faith as means of maintenance of the proper forms and harmony are preferred to openness and directness of task completion (Hofstede 1984a:88).

For planning processes, this dimension refers to the participativeness of decision making (Hofstede 1980:226), the value of individual initiatives (Hofstede 1980:229), emphasis on orderliness or variety (Hofstede 1980:230), and security versus autonomy (Hofstede 1980:235), reflected in the strategy literature, for example in Hax (1984) or Lorange (1986).

Low — **Individualism (IDV)**	**High**
participative decision making	authoritative decision making
emphasis on loyalty & duty	emphasis on individual initiative
emphasis on relations	emphasis on tasks
planning for the well-being of the companies' members and stakeholders	planning for financial strength of the company

Table 6.7: Individualism and Planning

Organizational Learning (OL) refers to how organizations create, acquire, communicate, share and interpret information and knowledge (Fiol/Lyles 1985; Hedberg 1981; Sullivan/Nonaka 1986:129). OL processes form the organizational knowledge base about cause-effect relationships, key assumptions and guides to interpretation of information (Shrivastava 1983:9; Shrivastava/ Grant 1985:109). For example, it refers to how organizations adapt to environmental changes, what sources of information are used, and how information is collected and used. Furthermore, it asks whether the information is linked to limited, narrow frameworks, starting the information search with only facts and empirical observation to extract generalizations, while only the most relevant aspects of stimuli are included (inductive, pragmatic, abstract, particularizing). Or, whether information search is guided by a broad framework, associative thinking, with reliance on qualitative, personal intuition and experience (Hofstede

1980:187; Rhyne 1987; Triandis 1982:89). Whether it is deductive learning from theory (e.g. strategy formulation) or inductive learning from doing (e.g. implementation; Mintzberg et al 1976:255), if there is active search or passive monitoring (Burgelman 1988; Ginter/White 1982; Horvath/McMillan 1979; Schneider 1987:10; Shrivastava/Grant 1985), if the emphasis is on issue diagnoses or issue solution (Drucker 1971; King/Cleland 1978:275), and if issues are categorized as threats or opportunities (Mintzberg et al 1976:251;253; Sullivan/Nonaka 1986).

Broad Organizational	**Learning (OL)** Specific
qualitative, associated, diffuse information used	quantitative, abstract specific information used
variety amplification	variety reduction
experience, personal and subjective sources	empirical, objective information sources
emphasis on defining issues	emphasis on solving the issue
broad conceptual framework (universalism, ideologism, deductive thinking)	specific conceptual framework (particularism, pragmatism, inductive thinking)
all phenomena are relevant	focus only on relevant issues
implicit decision premises (myths, values)	explicit decision premises (laws, regulations)
face-to-face communication	impersonal communication
intuitive interpretation of information	analytical interpretation of information

Table 6.8: Organizational Learning and Planning.

6.5 Empirical Evidence

In the sections above, culture was defined and a link between planning system characteristics and culture was established. The literature was reviewed for conceptual models and a more comprehensive Culture-Planning Model was proposed. In this section, comparative studies about planning practices are reviewed.

6.51 Case Studies

Several authors offer qualitative insight into possible cultural influences on planning practices. Most of these articles center around Japanese management practices.

Orihata (1985:17) on the basis of his consulting experience argues that mission statements are very broad in Japan; they avoid giving specific direction, which allows for free discussion within the respective company. Similarly, Ohmae (1982:225) claims that Japanese companies conduct business in a less planned, less rigid, but more vision-driven way than Western organizations. In his view, this is due to the fact that

> the Japanese concept of a corporation, based on .. commune or village concept, is fundamentally different from the Western model, which sees the stockholders as the owners of the corporation and the work force as employed labor (Ohmae 1982:218).

Leontiades (1986:149) reports that Japanese companies have no elaborate planning processes or large planning staffs and that planning is conducted much more informally than in U.S. corporations. Misumi (1984:537) finds that routine matters of strategic importance are handled by line managers in Japan, whereas strategic decisions are made by top managers solely. Similarly, Tsurumi (1976) finds that Japanese middle management is substantively involved in making strategic decisions, whereas the presidents' task is more to cope with crisis situations. The same issue is treated by Yang (1982). He claims that we must

> distinguish long-range planning from long-term vision setting. Japanese top executives are really facilitators rather than planners. The CEO first announces a long-term vision that members of his organization are to follow (Yang 1984:182).

Yamaguchi (1988:36) sees lifetime employment as a basis for a broad diffusion of information along non-specific carrier paths as conducive to this type of planning in Japan. Most of the arguments presented so far are supported by Pascale/Athos (1981) and Chinn et al (1986). Chinn et al (1986) argue that the Japanese view corporations as a social entity, not as a financial entity, which shapes the process that Japanese corporations follow to reach strategic decisions.

> In Japan strategic issues are usually not singled out as such for special treatment but are handled within the context of the overall participative decision-making process. Planners are involved in this process, but they are regular managers assigned to planning departments .. planning is closely linked to implementation. (Chinn et al 1986:7.17).

Lassere (1983:41) argues that strategic planning methods do not fit with the prevalent managerial culture in South-East Asia. Instead, companies in this region pursue incremental adjustment (learning by doing, deployment of resources, information directly linked to action; Lassere 1983:38). Vernon (1977) argues that in comparison with American and Japanese companies, German companies approach strategic decisions "as if they were the sum of a series of technical questions" (Vernon 1977:31). Durstberger (1985, 1987) concludes that US banks plan in a more centralized fashion than their European competitors. Similar anecdotal evidence about planning in international banks can be found in Davis (1985).

Most of these observation-based comments on differences in planning practices across countries rest in the Japanese-American dichotonomy. Hardly any of them offers a theoretical basis for the reported observations, e.g, specific differences in values or cognition. However, this cannot be the aim of such qualitative studies. Their merit lies in the rich description that may help in interpreting the large-scale studies reviewed next. Although the findings are to some extent contradictory, they seem to confirm the culture-boundness of rational-analytical vs. incremental strategic processes proposed in the chapter on planning systems.

6.52 Large-Scale Studies

Numerous single-country studies were conducted to investigate planning practices, for example Hayashi (1978) in Japan, Montebello/Buignes (1982) in France, Wright (1982) in New Zealand, Scholz (1984) in Germany, and Csath (1989) in Hungary. Others were reviewed in previous chapters or can be found in Shrader et al (1984); for a historical review, see Hofer (1976).

From a comparison of contemporary comparative planning studies, three patterns emerge. One group of multi-country studies did not pay attention to different origins of responses, for example Rhenman (US-Sweden; 1973), Naylor/Schauland (US-Canada-Europe; 1976), and Boulton et al (US-Canada; 1982b).

A second group of studies, notably the landmark work of Negandhi and associates (e.g. Negandhi/Welge 1984), were conducted either with multinationals or with subsidiaries of multinational companies, comparing planning practices transferred from developed countries with planning practices in less-developed countries. They will be reviewed first, because their focus is somewhat different.

A third group of comparative studies was conducted in countries with similar levels of economic, market, and regulatory environment and will be reviewed next. Most of them were explicitly comparative (e.g. Kono 1984), while others only controlled for country influences (e.g. Rule/Sedgwick 1986).

6.521 Planning at Multinational Companies and in Countries on Different Levels of Development

A number of authors conducted studies about differences in managerial functions between multinationals' subsidiaries and the respective host country companies. Most of this admirable work was performed by Negandhi and associates. Negandhi (1973) conducted a study on management practices of 29 US and Japanese subsidiaries and local firms in Taiwan. He found that US subsidiaries had long-range plans (time horizons 5-10 years), while Japanese subsidiaries and local firms had only short to medium range (1-2 years) plans (Negandhi 1973:125). In U.S. subsidiaries, policy-

Study	Description of Study	Conclusion
Negandhi (1973)	27 American, Japanese & local companies in Taiwan	US subsidiaries' plans had a longer time frame and were much higher in formalization.
Negandhi (1975a)	650 interviews with mangers in 15 US parent companies, 56 US subsidiaries 7 countries (Far East, Latin America) and 55 local firms.	Country differences in extent of planning, participation & information sharing due to market, legal, and economic differences.
Sim (1977)	American, British and Japanese subsidiaries in Malaysia	More participation & information sharing in US subsidiaries than in others.
Gouy (1978)	Interviewed 13 West German, 16 British, and 18 French top managers in in 55 companies in 11 industries	Planning varies among countries, but stronger among size, industry, and ownership.
Hulbert/ Brandt (1980)	US, Japanese, and European Subsidiaries in Brazile	Japanese subsidiaries used the annual operating plan less as a starting point for long-range planning.
Bazzaz/ Grinyer (1981)	48 interviews with planners in companies in 19 industries with parent companies in the UK, US, and EEC.	Companies owned by US or Swiss parents tended to have significantly more written plans than the UK-owned.
Negandhi/ Balige (1981) and Negandhi/ Welge (1984)	158 subsidiaries and 39 headquarters of US, UK, German, Japanese and Swedish multinational companies	American multinational companies and their subsidiaries differ in their planning practices from the other companies.
Christodolou (1984) and Christodolou (1986)	Interviews & questionnaires with a sample of 63 large manufacturing companies in Australia, out of which 31 were foreign subsidiaries; UK (12), US (12), other (11)	Mixed findings; in original work no differences are reported; in the later paper, home office culture is found to influence the planning process.

Table 6.9: Comparative Planning Studies at Multinationals & Subsidiaries

Study	Description of Study	Conclusion
Orpen (1984)	64 Indian and 72 U.S. questionnaire responses from companies with at least 1.000 employees	Differences in perceived benefits, time horizon, frequency of updating due to economic, market, and value influences.

Table 6.9: Comparative Planning Studies at Multinationals & Subsidiaries Cont'd.

making was formally stated and used as guidelines and control measures, while this was not the case for the other samples.

Negandhi (1975a) later on conducted a monumental study with 650 interviews in more than 110 companies in seven countries with similar results. While two-thirds of the US subsidiaries undertook formalized, detailed, and systematic long range planning, and had their managers participate and share information, only one third of the local companies did so (Negandhi 1975a:66). Latin American local companies engaged less often than Far Eastern companies in comprehensive long-range planning. Negandhi (1975a:70) vehemently refutes to relate these findings to culture. He concludes that the existence of a seller's market, governmental control of prices, availability of raw materials, inflation, and political instability adversely affect the firm's ability to plan for a long duration and therefore explain the differences in planning emphasis and characteristics (Negandhi 1975a:81; 1987:229).
A similar, though smaller study was undertaken by Sim (1977), who found that American subsidiaries in Malaysia had their managers participate and share information to a larger extent in long-range planning than British and Japanese subsidiaries.

Goy (1978) conducted 55 interviews with managers in 47 European companies. British firms emphasized the role of the marketing department for strategic decisions, the finance department was most important in France, and a pretty even spread was found in Germany. Strategic decisions in French companies are more decentralized and bottom-up driven. From factor analysis Goy (1978:45) concludes that the differences (e.g. in formalization) are more attributable to size, industry, and ownership (e.g multinationals, subsidiaries, nationalized) than to nation.

Hulbert/Brandt (1980) conducted a study on planning of US, Japanese and European multinational subsidiaries in Brazile. While most companies used the short-term plan for rolling forward the long-range plan, the Japanese subsidiaries did so to a lesser extent. For the annual plan, over 90% of the American and Japanese firms followed a highly formalized process (type of information to collect, sequencing of activities, and timing), while this was only the case for 73% of the European subsidiaries.

While the Bazzaz/Grinyer (1981) study was undertaken solely in the UK, it included subsidiaries from both US, British, and other

European mother companies. While technology and industry were of impact, companies with American or Swiss parents tended to have significantly more written plans than those with British owners.

Negandhi/Baliga (1981) and Negandhi/Welge (1984) together with Swedish associates undertook yet another large-scale study in 16 countries with 158 subsidiaries and 39 headquarters of American, British, German, Japanese, and Swedish multinational corporations. Swedish and Japanese subsidiaries had much less influence on strategic decisions (appointment of CEO, expansion, new products) than US or German subsidiaries, with the Swedish somewhere in the middle. American multinational companies used their planning process to a much greater extent as integrating and controlling device. American subsidiaries engaged to a greater extent in long-range planning with higher levels of formalization and detaildness than subsidiaries with mother companies in other countries in the sample.

Orpen (1984) conducted a comparison of the extent to which comparable firms in a developed country (U.S.A.) and a less-developed country (India) employ long-range planning. Other than many of the other studies reviewed above, he starts with a hypothesis: Indian firms make less use of long-range planning than do their US counterparts. US managers perceived greater benefits from planning. Other differences emerged in the frequency of updating, time horizon, time spent on planning and issues included. While US planners were more concerned with financial data, Indian planners were more attentive to socio-economic factors (e.g. government actions and raw material procurement).

While Orpen (1984:22) regards the differences as "due to the different nature of the values and customs that characterize the two societies," it is suggested that the arguments Negandhi (1975a:76) found in comparing planning practices of multinational's subsidiaries (from developed countries) and local companies (in less developed countries), for example governmental control of prices, availability of raw materials, inflation, political instability, and the like, are of more value here.

Christodolou (1984) used interviews and questionnaires in a sample of 63 large Australian manufacturing companies, out of which 31 were foreign subsidiaries. In his doctoral dissertation (1984:5), he only reports minor differences between Australian and subsidiary-companies with respect to the development of corporate strategy, corporate goals and other planning process aspects. However, in a paper presented in 1986, he argued that he found differences between US and UK subsidiaries with respect to home office planning information requirements and the extent of home office influence on the long term direction of the subsidiary. He concluded that these differences are a genuine reflection of cultural differences between US and UK multinational companies. In a later companion paper with the same data base (Capon et al 1987:54), differences in the planning approaches between home country (Australian) companies and foreign subsidiaries are attributed to influences from regulators (entry/exit barriers for foreign subsidiaries), ownership (different home office expectations), and market restrictions.

6.522 Comparative Planning Studies in Developed Countries

While the section above dealt with comparative planning studies among multinationals, subsidiary-local company comparisons, and companies in countries of different economic development, the studies below deal with independent companies' planning practices in developed countries.

Steiner/Schoellhammer (1975) conducted a study on planning pitfalls in six countries, extending from a US-database. They found variations in most important pitfalls and in degrees of formality and documentation between countries. US companies were found to be the most formal, Japanese the least formal planners.

Nicholson/Litschert (1973) interviewed with six American and four American banks "as part of a larger study which looks at some of the cross-cultural differences in planning" (Nicholson/Litschert 1973), which, to the best knowledge of the author, unfortunately was never published. In their small sample, they show that planning was introduced later at British than at American banks. They attribute the broader coverage of planning activities by American banks to differences in the regulatory environment.

Kono (1976) conducted a study with 26 US and 74 Japanese companies, out of which 23 US and 57 Japanese companies conducted long-range planning. The US companies used the planning process for integration and control purposes. Planning was found to be decentralized (bottom-up), with longer time horizons, updates about every year, and close follow-ups, and with one strategic plan plus project plans. In Japanese companies, the planning process is an interactive, centralized process (more top-down) with two different time horizons planned for parallel. The strategic plan is more qualitative, the mid-range plan is more quantitative. The implementation is often ensured through project plans, to a lesser extent through follow-ups. Some of the findings not covered in this review are quite contradictory. Kono (1976:64) argues that the differences stem from the more stable US business environment, the more decentralized and diversified structure of US companies, and the higher orientation towards the individual in the US. His sample is no true Japanese-US comparison, because the US data solely relies on responses from Southern California (Kono 1984:76).

Horovitz (1980) conducted 175 interviews in three European countries, while controlling for industry. While the work by Negandhi (e.g. 1975) drew on various interviewers, Horovitz was accompanied by a translator in Germany. His findings fit into the Hofstede (1980:188) framework. Both in British and German companies the planning process is bottom-up; in British companies, however, more people participate, the planning cycle and the planning horizon are longer, and both operational and strategic issues are treated simultaneously. Corporate plans are prepared before short-term budgets. German companies were found to use a shorter time horizon, they were more strongly oriented towards operational details and figures than towards strategic thinking. Corporate plans are often prepared simultaneously with the budget or even afterwards, a procedure that Horovitz (1980:71) attributes

Study	Description of Study	Conclusion
Nicholson/ Litschert (1973)	Interviews with 6 major U.S. and 4 major U.K. banks	Less planning activities of British banks due to to different regulatory environment.
Steiner (1972) and Steiner/ Schoell-hammer (1975)	Questionnaire survey 460 responses: Japan (118), Canada (42), UK (32), Italy (31), Australia (22); US (215)	Degree of formality and documentation and types of pitfalls among planning systems varies by country.
Kono (1976)	Questionnaires from 23 US and 57 Japanese companies with long-range planning; 33 interviews with US companies	In the US, planning is decentralized, often updated, and used for control; in Japan, it is more centralized, with emphasis on implementation.
Horovitz (1980)	175 interviews in West German (61), French (49) and British (66) companies in three industries	German and French companies focus more on detail and short-term feedback; British engage more in strategic activities.
Christodolou (1984, 1988)& Capon et al (1984, 1987)	Questionnaires and interviews with 63 large Australian and 113 US Fortune 500 manufacturing companies	Planning in Australia is more participative due to differences in size and level of market competition.
Rieger/ Wong-Rieger (1984, 1986)	Observation & interviews with 2 European and three Asian Airlines top management and employees	Societal culture influenced the content of strategy more than industry culture.
Kono (1984)	Data from Kono (1976) and additional 437 questionnairs from two mailings (1979, 1982) from Japan and 122 from the UK (1981)	Minor variations in planning systems by style, centralization & emphasis due to market, company, economic & legal differences. Weak methodology.
Snodgrass (1984) Snodgrass/ Grant (1986)	Semistructured interviews with 25 managers and 25 workers in 11 Japanese and 11 US large manufacturing & construction firms	The design of strategic control systems is subject to cultural influences.

Table 6.10: Comparative Planning Studies in Developed Countries

Study	Description of Study	Conclusion
Snodgrass et al (1986)	Added a German sample to the above study	Same results as Snodgrass (1984)
Sekaran/ Snodgrass (1986b, 1987)	28 Singaporean and 128 Malaysian junior & senior university students	Differences in time and action orientation are not statistically significant.
Rule/Sedgwick (1986) (A. Anderson)	1.080 questionnaire responses from bankers in 17 European countries	Minor differences in emphasis on strategic planning by country.
Suzuki (1986)	225 Japanese and 193 US questionnaire responses from engineering and non-engineering CEO's	US planning is more formalized top-down, while Japanese companies use less quantification & plan bottom up due to culture.
Kagono et al (1985)	227 questionnaire responses from US-Fortune 1.000 companies and 291 from comparable Japanese companies plus extensive interviews and case studies	Japanese strategy evolves as a result of incremental adjustments; US firms analytically develop strategies through formal planning and implementation. The study downplays culture
Dalby (1986)	Interviews with nine major U.S. and 15 major European banks	Found more similarities than differences; considerable market and government influence.
Hegarty/ Hoffman (1987)	Questionnaire responses from 407 top managers from 109 European manufacturing companies in 10 countries	There is more impact of expert power in the US, more legitimate, expert power in European firms in strategic decisions.
Seeger et al (1986, 1987)	242 questionnaires from Inc. 500-companies with 1978 sales between $m .1 and 25 in the US States of California and New England	Culture accounts for differences in formality; other differences were due to industry and market type.
Sullivan/ Nonaka (1986)	76 questionnaire responses from 75 large US companies; 75 responses from 40 Japanese firms in eight industries;	US companies follow a strategy-making process that is either rational-analytical or messy; In Japanese both occur simultaneously.

Table 6.10: Comparative Planning Studies in Developed Countries

Study	Description of Study	Conclusion
Moormann (1988a,b)	46 questionnaires from Austrian (6), Germany (29) and Swiss (11) banks	Differences attributed to legal, market and size influences; sub-samples too small for meaningful conclusions.

Table 6.10: Comparative Planning Studies in Developed Countries Cont'd

to the fact that in Germany the controller is responsible for both long-range planning and budgeting. Less than half of the French companies in the sample engaged in long-range planning. The time horizon is as short as for German companies, even fewer people participate; no planning manual exists. Control as a consequence of planning was high in Germany, but low in the UK and France (Horovitz 1980:103). Half of the French companies prepare the corporate plan after the budget. The use, content, horizon, subjects, process, and organization of planning was found to differ substantially across the three countries (Horovitz 1980:78). He argues that these differences are attributable partly to technology, industry, and culture. Higher technology leads to more sophisticated planning in the UK and Germany, but not so in France (Horvitz 1980:172). Industry sector influences are larger on the operational than on the strategic management level (Horvitz 1980:177). Using the same data base, Horovitz/Thietart (1982:70) include the degree of diversification as a contingency variable.

In his doctoral dissertation, Christodolou (1984) included a comparison of planning practices between Australian and American manufacturing companies. In that sample, nearly 80% of Australian companies either prepared the corporate plan first and then the budget, or developed both simultaneously, while only half of the American companies did so (Christodolou 1984:383). Lower level managers in Australian companies are more likely to have access to their corporate plans (Christodolou 1984:393); the planning process is more participative than in the US, the CEO is more involved. The US companies were about 8 times larger than their Australian counterparts. 35 of the Australian companies were subsidiaries. He attributes the differences in planning practices to the more dominant position of the Australian companies in less competitive, more protected markets in comparison to the American companies, which are more diversified and introduced planning earlier (Christodolou 1984:360). He thereby supports Negandhi's (1975) argument. Capon/Christodolou et al (1984, 1987) and Christodolou (1988) repeatedly report the same findings. They argue that apart from these market and size effects on planning, no major difference in planning approaches could be expected because the US and Australia cluster in the same groups for three of Hofstede's (1980) dimensions (Capon et al 1984:42).

Rieger/Wong-Rieger (1984, 1986) conducted five case studies in the airline industry. They set out to research the relative influence of societal, industrial and corporate culture on both strategy formulation (process) and strategic actions (content). They find that the content of competitive strategies is more influenced by societal culture than by industry norms. The three Asian airlines were found to be more autocratic, while the two European counterparts were found to be more bureaucratic. However, the two European airlines (Alia, Lufthansa) are quite larger compared to the three Asian airlines (SIA, Thai Int'l, Garuda). I attribute the findings to the size differences.

Snodgrass (1984) in her dissertation and in companion papers (Snodgrass/Grant 1986; Snodgrass et al 1986) investigated the influences of societal culture on strategic planning and control systems, based on Ouchi's (1981) Theory Z. Originally, managers and workers at large Japanese and American manufacturing companies were surveyed with interviews and questionnaires. Later on (Snodgrass et al 1986), a German sample was added. However, the emphasis is on aspects of control only, and findings are mixed. While the US companies measured high on explicit control in the interviews, Japanese companies measured high on both explicit control (in the questionnaires) and implicit control (in the interviews; Snodgrass/Grant 1984:222). They attribute their findings to structural and cultural differences. Their notion of explicit/implicit information and control patterns can be referred to the organizational learning dimension as introduced above. As they controlled for size and industry effects, their findings are important with regard to control practices.

Sekaran/Snodgrass (1986b, 1987) analyzed questionnaire responses from Singaporean and Malaysian university students to organizational scenarios. They used the Kluckhohn/Strodtbeck (1961) value dimensions to investigate to what extent Ouchi's (1980) market mechanisms, bureaucratic mechanisms, and clan control are used as mechanisms for interfacing with the external environment in strategy implementation. Of interest here are the findings with regard to focus of time (past, present, future) and nature of human activity (spontaneous vs. planned action), as operationalized by Sekaran/Snodgrass (1986b:42). The spontaneous vs. planned action-item shows no significant difference; the "focus of time"-differences are neglegible. While their framework helps in understanding what kind of cultural factors influence control mechanisms, it suffers from several shortcomings. At first, it used students only; the samples varied in size; the link to strategy implementation is not clear. And, Ouchi's (1980) framework deals merely with corporate culture.

Kono (1984) reports findings based on a mix of surveys. He again used the US data from 1976, made two mailings (1979, 1982) in Japan, and compared this data to mailings to the UK from 1981. He finds a great number of similarities and several differences. Integration through planning is more important in the UK sample than in the Japanese. While the Japanese plan more issue-oriented, the British tend to integrate strategic projects into long-range plans. The UK companies that did plan in 1981 had longer time horizons than their Japanese counterparts. Kono (1984:61) attributes this to the fact that the Japanese business environment is more volatile than the environment in the UK in 1981 (which was in a state of crisis at that time). The frequency of review is higher in the UK, while in Japan the plan is more seen as a goal. Planning is more centralized in Japan, with plans often prepared not by line, but by a specific staff department. However, only a minority of the Japanese companies show the two-plan-system Kono (1976) found. While in Japan management committees play an important role for review and final decision, this is not the case in the UK sample. He reasons - quite overlapping with Negandhi (1975) - that the minor differences are due to different levels of diversification (variety of product/market scope in the average company), regulation (functions of the board of directors), organizational structure, dependence on the import of raw materials, and competitiveness. The one interesting piece of analysis he presents is the distinction of analytical versus intuitive styles of strategic decision making (Kono 1984:68). Contrary to him, the author interprets the findings as follows. The Japanese plan more what he labels "intuitively" (what was termed "broad organizational learning" in this study), while the UK-based companies plan more analytically (what was termed "specific organizational learning" here). Kono (1984) tries do depict similarities and differences of planning systems, but he is normatively oriented and does not pay attention to the culture-boundness of the theories he uses, for example motivation theory (Kono 1984:70). He compares data from 1975 (USA) with data from 1982 (Japan) and then only provides absolute figures to numerous items; the items themselves vary across samples (Kono 1984:61). Anecdotal data from single companies is added. The operationalizations are unclear. For example, what is the difference between strategic issues (more Japanese) and strategic projects (more UK)? Just like most of the studies reviewed above, it lacks the theoretical foundation.

Suzuki (1986) investigated the relative influence of nationality versus functional education and experience on the strategic planning process.[41] He classified engineering managers as those who had an educational background in engineering or long-term assignments in engineering or manufacturing (i.e. not sales or service). From a sample of 225 Japanese and 193 US managers with either of the two functional orientations, a 2 x 2 matched-pair sample was established (e.g. US engineers vs. Japanese engineers). The strategic planning process was depicted by the contents of strategic planning, primary recipients of plans, planning time horizons, participation and planning stages, degree of formality in implementation, and the existence of a reward/ penalty system for success/failure of strategy implementation. Nationality, not the differing functional orientation, was found to be the major variable to explain the difference in planning processes among companies. Functional orientation only accounted for differences in strategy content. Type of market (related/ unrelated) was of some influence. US planning was more top-down, higher in formalization, directly tied to compensation, overall more "tight"

---

[41] The business success of Japanese companies has been attributed to the fact that many Japanese managers have an engineering background or experience, while many US managers - on average - have a different functional orientation (Suzuki 1986:70).

in Suzuki's (1986:81 terminology. Japanese planning was more bottom-up (more for business unit than for corporate strategy) and less quantified. Among many of the other studies reviewed here, this paper clearly stands out. Propositions were the venture point, dimensions were operationalized, the samples were large enough, and the analysis is comprehensive. However, no explanation is given for what makes up nationality or culture, while both expressions were used. Industry or size effects were not investigated or reported.

Kagono and associates (1985) present a comprehensive, contingency-theory based, empirical study of strategic management in the U.S. and Japan. Archetypal modes of structural adaptation tend to be more organic for Japanese firms and more mechanistic for U.S. firms, resulting from different competitive environments. The U.S. business environment with intensive rivalry, discontinuous jumps in technology, and high mobility of labor and capital, is different from the Japanese competitive environment with less rivalry, more continuous change in demand for products, and lower mobility of labor and capital.

U.S. strategy adapts to discontinuous change through analytical, formal planning and implementation processes, with strong direction from the top management. Japanese strategy evolves as a result of incremental adjustments to continuous changes in the environment, with the locus of origin closer to the plant level, and it is more production oriented. U.S. companies are oriented towards a wider scope of activities, within a shorter time frame (Kagono et al 1985:30).

> [S]trategies are better formulated and stated more clearly in U.S. companies than in the Japanese companies ... Japanese firms' mode of strategy formulation differs from the U.S. mode in that the latter emphasize the judgment of experienced executives in formulating strategies and the former seek more diverse and redundant information. This difference suggests that the strategy formulation process in Japanese firms involves interaction of various people rather than being based solely upon executive's judgment and, therefore, contains more slack and redundancy (Kagono et al 1985:33).

This quote asserts the importance and relevance of the information processing dimension which was labeled "organizational learning" above in explaining differences. Attributes Kagono et al (1985:49) use to describe differences in strategic processes resemble the Hofstede (1980) dimensions of "power distance," "uncertainty avoidance", and "individualism" in the broad interpretation applied here, which confirms the culture-planning model presented above.

Kagono et al (1985) find that many U.S. and Japanese firms share similar characteristics. Within-country variations are observed along the two dimensions of "product vs. production" and "bureaucratic vs. group." Product-market diversity, degree of discontinuity in the environment, factor mobility, size, technology, and culture affect the mode of adaptation to environmental demands. They assert

> that the characteristics of firms in each country are derived .... by a common adaptation mode consistent with and largely a result of the country's cultural and institutional setting (Kagono et al 1985:47).

This remarkable piece of research is theory based and empirical in nature with well-matched samples. It downplays, however, the cultural perspective. Although inter-country differences in strategic management are only partly attributable to economic, market, legal and size differences, they do not investigate possible underlying cultural differences.

Hegarty/Hoffman (1987), using the work of Miles/Snow (1978) as a basis, investigated the influence of different power bases and the content of strategic decisions (product/market, technological, administrative) on the process of strategic decisions. US companies placed a greater value on expert power, whereas European companies emphasized legitimate (position) power, which reflects the stronger European traditions of social stratification. This finding relates to Hofstede's (1980:121) power distance.

Seeger et al (1986, 1987) set out to investigate differences in planning behavior between North-Eastern and Sout-Western states of the U.S.A. - New England and California. Based on the work of Garreau (1981) on intra-country cultural differences in the U.S.A., they investigated the planning practices of 71 Inc. 500 companies.[42] Their discriminant analysis shows industry influences (service firms plan differently from wholesale companies) and cultural influences. Contradictory to their expectations, New Englanders were found to be less formal in their planning, while Californians tended towards more formality. This piece of research is unique in two ways. Relatively small, entrepreneurial companies were investigated, and therefore the factor size plays a main role. And, differences within one country with a heterogeneous culture were investigated. However, the shown cultural influences are not really convincing.

Sullivan/Nonaka (1986) investigated differences in the information processing behavior during strategic decision processes between Japanese and U.S. companies. They started with hypotheses. Size, industry, and market were controlled for, the samples are large enough, chi-square and stepwise discriminant analysis were the analytical tools applied. Therefore, in terms of methodology, it is an outstanding paper among the many studies reviewed here. Differences in information handling between American managers in focus (opportunities vs. problems), in type of guidelines (specific vs. general), in amount of learning through trial and error, and in degree of reliance on past experience (conservative vs. creative) emerged. Japanese managers more strongly preferred the creation to the reduction of uncertainty (what they termed

---

[42] Inc. Magazine annually ranks and rates the fastest growing privately-held firms in the U.S.

"variety amplification," following Weick 1969) in their information-processing behavior. Whereas American managers were found to follow a strategy-making processes that was either rational-analytical or messy (incremental), in Japan both types of strategy formation processes occured simultaneously. While Japanese senior strategy managers fostered the variety-amplification (messy, incremental) process, Japanese junior managers engaged in variety reduction. The differences were attributed to culture and organizational structure. This research confirms the importance of the information processing dimension outlined above, which was labelled "organizational learning" here.

Moormann (1988a,b) investigated the planning practices of Austrian (6), German (29) and Swiss (11) banks. Planning was started earlier in Germany and Austria than in Switzerland. German bank planning is more qualitative in nature. Swiss and Austrian bank planning is more formalized. Legal, market and size influences are mentioned, but not as explanatory variables for the planning process differences. Due to the small number of responses in the Austrian and Swiss subsamples, no reliable conclusions are justified.

6.523 Summary of Comparative Planning Studies

In order to account for economic, legal/political, technology, and market influences on planning practices reviewed in the last chapter, it was found appropriate to distinguish between three groups of studies. The case studies reviewed seem to confirm the culture-boundness of rational-analytical vs. incremental-adaptive strategic processes proposed in the chapter on plannins systems.

The second group consists of studies that compared planning practices among multinational companies, or that compared subsidiaries of multinational companies with local practices of mostly less-developed countries. These studies are difficult to assess, because both the cultural and the economic, market, and regulatory environments that led to the development of the respective planning practices differ considerably between developed and less developed countries. Doz (1980:37) argues that the role top management plays varies in multinationals. And, multinationals from some countries are open for host country managers and therefore have an international management team (Negandhi 1987). Others, for example Phillips, are kept in the hands of the home countries' managers only (Doz 1980:39). This is not to say that the 'open' multinationals may not reinforce a strong corporate culture that is rooted in the home countries societal culture (for example Proctor & Gamble). However, comparisons of this kind are difficult. Even Hofstede's (1980) landmark study was criticized because its sample relies on one multinational corporation only (Westwood/Evered 1987:197). Also, following Horovitz (1980) and Hofstede (1984a:94), the countries' level of development should be kept stable.

In some of these studies, differences between planning systems (structure, reasons), processes (characteristics, acts) and heuristics emerged. Negandhi (1975b:70) vehemently refutes to relate these findings to culture. He concludes that the existence of a seller's market, governmental control of prices, availability of raw materials, inflation, and political instability adversely affect the firm's ability to plan for a long duration and therefore explain the differences in planning emphasis and characteristics (Negandhi 1975b:81; 1987: 229).

Still Christodolou (1984:245) was able to show differences in the content of strategy between comparable home country (Australian) companies and foreign (US, UK) subsidiaries. Foreign subsidiaries often face other entry/exit barriers, act somewhat subject to home office expectations, and are restricted in competing against brother subsidiaries in third markets (Capon et al 1987:54).

Therefore, following the recommendations by Horovitz (1980), Hofstede (1984b:94), Capon et al (1987:54) and Doz (1980:37), it was found that true comparisons should be made only between independent companies, holding industry and the other factors of the societal environment constant as much as possible.

The third group was formed by studies that held constant the level of development of the respective countries in consideration. However, several of the studies reviewed suffer from methodological drawbacks. Often, comparisons are made without underlying theoretical foundation or hypotheses. The lack of a priori theory, which has guided the selection of input variables in many of the studies has condemned the output of many pieces of research to triviality. In some of the studies, data treatment or sample populations are inappropriate. There is a temptation to report differences where there are much more similarities. Often these differences are at random, but still reported as important. Within the samples, several studies did not control for market, industry, economic, legal and political influences. Some of the studies start out by investigating factors influencing the planning process, but then are only concerned with control, grossly over-interpreting their otherwise valid findings. Culture is often only treated as a residual variable, or not operationalized with regard to underlying perceptions, cognitions, values, and behaviors (Triandis 1984). Most of the studies had only two or three cultures in their sample, which is not large enough to randomize variance on nonmatched cultural variables or eliminate rival hypotheses (Adler 1986:52). Most often, nation is used as a surrogate for culture. Many studies suffer from what Hofstede (1980:29) termed ecological and reverse ecological fallacy, mixing up correlations on the individual with higher levels, or wrongfully constructing higher-level indices from variables correlated at the individual level. Many of the studies are ethnocentric in nature, i.e. they attempt to replicate American management research in foreign countries (Adler 1986). The concept of functional equivalence is hardly applied (Hofstede 1980:41; Adler 1986:42). Thus, many of the studies report results on cultural influences on planning that are neither reliable nor valid, or both.

However, there are several valuable exceptions from the critique above, notably Horovitz (1980), Snodgrass (1984), Suzuki (1986), Kagono et al (1985), and Sullivan/Nonaka (1986). This is not to say that these studies are all-encompassing or perfect. No study ever will.

Summing up the findings of the studies reviewed above, planning processes may vary in their systems (structure, reasons), process (characteristics, acts) and heuristics (behavioral problems) across industry, economic, legal/political, structural, **and** cultural variables. These studies emphasize similarities and differences in planning processes that resemble the dimensions the culture-planning model introduces above. Important issues were, for example, participativeness (individualism), bottom-up vs. top-down (power distance), formalization, time and action orientation, planning horizon (uncertainty avoidance), type, source, spread, and use of information (organizational learning). While the types of cultural influences are confirmed, the direction of influences is not yet clear. For example for the U.S.A., the following patterns emerge in US-Japanese comparisons (without paying attention to the methodological issues raised):

	Kono (1984)	**Suzuki (1986)**	**Kagono (1985)**	**Case Studies**	**Multi-nat'l**
SYSTEM					
Structure	decentralized		mecha-nistic	centra-lized	
Reasons	integration & control	tied do control			guidelines & control
Time Horizon	longer		shorter	mixed	longer
PROCESS					
Flow	bottom-up	top-down	top-down		bottom-up
Formali-zation	high	high	high	high	high
Partici-pation	high				high
Infor-mation	quanti-tative	quanti-tative	wide range	specific	detailed & shared
Adaptive Orienta-tion	frequent reviews	Snodgrass: explicit			tight sequencing
HEURISTICS					
Over-emphasis	analytic informa-tion		analytic		systematic

Table 6.11: Mix of Findings for Planning in U.S. Companies

Differences can be seen in structure, time horizon, and flow, although the studies above are thought to be representative for the U.S. planning systems. While there is at least considerable overlap on the other factors, the situation is worse for other countries in the studies reviewed here, for example for Japan. This clearly shows the need for an empirical study that covers these issues. Still, so far there is no study that controlled for the other influences (for example concentrates on one industry only), had a thorough theoretical base with an appropriate number of cultures included, reasonable large sample populations, and the like. The current study tries to fill this void.

6.6 Summary and Conclusion

The purpose of this chapter was to provide information about the influence of national culture on strategic planning practices. Various definitions of culture were reviewed. It was found appropriate to use Hofstede's (1980) definition. Next, components of culture were described. Specific attention was given to the Kluckhohn/Strodtbeck (1961) value dimensions and to Glenn's (1981) information processing approach. The conclusion is drawn that these value dimensions can be integrated in Hofstedes' (1980) dimensions to form a more comprehensive model. However, it was argued that we need to pay attention to the level of analysis, in order not to mix up the macro-level (societal culture) and the micro-level (corporate culture).

The next section provided a literature review of existing conceptualizations that link societal culture and planning. The conclusion was drawn that a model is needed which is not restricted to either the control, implementation or formulation aspects of strategic planning. A model which does not rely on the phase theorem and is based on both organizational theory and findings from comparative management. A model which includes both cultural values, cognition, and information processing perceptions and behavior. A model that uses an empirically derived framework and integrates other theoretical concepts.

The Culture-Planning Model was introduced as such an approach. Its advantage is the empirical base (Hofstede 1980), the broad conceptual framework (Cyert/March 1963; Glenn (1981); Hofstede 1980; Kluckhohn/Strodtbeck 1961), and a set of cultural dimensions not restricted to values (Triandis 1982, 1984). The delineation of the model was described. Propositions for each of the four dimensions (uncertainty avoidance, power distance, organizational learning, and individualism) were developed, depicted in tables.

Next, an extensive number of both case-study and large-scale research projects that investigated the influence of culture on planning were reviewed. The qualitative studies seem to confirm the culture-boundness of rational-analytical vs. incremental strategic processes proposed in the chapter on planning systems. The studies reviewed emphasize similarities and differences in planning processes that resemble the dimensions the Culture-Planning Model introduced above and therefore guarantees a good fit of the model.

From Negandhi (1975a:70) the argument is accepted that the existence of a seller's market, governmental control of prices, availability of raw materials, inflation, and political instability adversely affect the firm's ability to plan strategically. Therefore, following the recommendations by Horovitz (1980), Hofstede (1984b:94), Capon et al (1987:54) and Doz (1980:37), it was found that true comparisons should be made only between independent companies, holding constant industry and the other factors of the societal environment outlined in the last chapter as much as possible.

While cultural influences along the dimensions proposed in the Culture-Planning model could be found in the studies reviewed here, there is no clear-cut evidence yet. Still, there is no study that controlled for the other influences (for example concentrates on one industry only), had a thorough theoretical base, with an appropriate number of cultures included, reasonable large sample populations and the like. The current study tries to fill this void.

One word of caution at the end of this chapter. It is not the authors' intent to advocate environmental determinism.[43] Such an inherent reductionism would eliminate much of the richness that characterizes the strategic management process (Bourgeouis 1984:586). Management is not perceived as passive, but as mediating, while drawing on the open systems perspective (Channon 1977:41). However, there should be some common ties between environmental dimensions and those of strategy (Miller 1987:62). What is supported here is functional equivalence in planning approaches (Adler 1986:42; Pascale 1978:91; Smircich 1983:347)

While this chapter elaborated the link between planning and culture and compiled the conceptual framework developed throughout the preceding chapters, the next chapter will explain the methodology of the empirical research undertaken.

---

[43] For recent reviews about choice vs. determinism, see, for example Bourgeouis (1984), Dunphy (1987) or Hrbeniak/Joyce (1985).

7 RESEARCH DESIGN AND METHODOLOGY

To explore the culture-specific influences and outcomes to the planning process, an introductory case study, a pilot study, interviews and a questionnaire survey were undertaken. This chapter reviews the methodology of the interview and the questionnaire survey. At first, instrument selection and overall research design are described. The development of the research tools is discussed. Sample issues and populations as well as data handling and statistical procedures are explained. Finally, specific attention is given to methodological difficulties arising from cross-cultural comparisons and variations within the world-wide banking industry.

7.1 Research Design

Methodological issues must always be answered within the context of a particular research setting (Downey/Ireland 1979:630). Field research methods were chosen as the major tool for carrying out this research. Four rationales led to the combination of different methodologies in the study of the same phenomenon, following the concept of "triangulation" (Denzin 1978; Haiss 1983:78; Hofstede 1980:18; Jick 1979:602; Smith 1975). The research design is depicted in table 6.0. below. It is essential that diverse types of data are linked in the development of models of decision processes (Schwenk 1985:501). Independent and multiple measures provide a more certain portrait of the phenomenon and allow for verifications and cross-checks, if they reach the same conclusions (Jick 1979:602; Hofstede 1980:18). The various methods give distinct sorts of information that can complement each other (Gordon 1980:12). Multiple measures may reveal variations which otherwise may have been overlooked by single methods (Jick 1979:603). Following Mintzberg (1979a:586), it was tried to find measures managers themselves use within organizations.

Participative observation through an internship with an Austrian bank and interview sessions with two American banks gave the researcher a chance to reveal patterns of responses, topics and questions the bank planners themselves brought up (Piore 1979:566). Capturing situative definitions and frames of reference of the managers themselves was regarded as being very important in order to avoid the construction of abstract categories forced on the processes observed, and to allow for the derivation of the interviewed managers' phenomenologies (McClintock et al 1979:613; Mintzberg 1979a:586).

Based on this experience, semi-structured interviews with senior managers of 14 participating banks were conducted by the researcher. During the development of the questionnaire from the interviews, the suggestions made by Sudman/ Bradburn (1982:207f) and Friedrichs (1981:238 for questionnaire construction were followed. The larger samples are intended to enhance the reliability of the findings, facilitate replication studies and assure external validity (Hofer 1976:281; McClintock et al 1979:612).

Step	Content
1 **Desk Research**	on literature from the fields of strategy and policy, decision process, comparative management, organizational behavior, culture, and banking. A preliminary list of questions was developed.
2 **Participant Observation**	with an Austrian bank in a summer internship as an external staff member in a department which was highly involved in the design a corporate planning system.
3 **Case Study** before 3: informal pretests	with a local US (IL) bank, to get insight into the US banking system; to learn which factors managers use to describe their planning process; to see the bankers' reaction to types of questions in order to develop an interview tool.
4 **Pilot Study** before 4: informal pretest	with a major bank in the Chicago area. Reasons as mentioned for the case study, to pretest an interview schedule and a preliminary version of the questionnaire.
5 **Semi-structured Interviews** before 5: informal pretests	with senior managers on different levels and of different areas at major banks in North-East and Mid-west of the U.S.A. to examine the topic in depth and to formally pretest the questionnaire.
6 **Questionnaires** before 6: informal pretests	a mail survey with a refined questionnaire was conducted in seven languages in 33 countries.

Table 7.1 Research Design Overview

In order to investigate the contextual impact on strategic planning practices (systems, heuristics, and processes), the survey questionnaire consisted of four principal parts.[44] Each section starts with an explanation of the question and the answer categories. In all but sections A (structure) and D (position and area), the items were constructed using five-point Likert scales (Friedrichs 1981:175), ranging from one (not at all important/ strongly disagree) to five (very important/strongly agree). Respondents simply had to write the appropriate number to the left of each statement.

[44] Copies of the questionnaire are available from the author upon request.

Section A examines the types of plans prepared by the respective respondent banks, and the structures involved for its preparation, review and decision. The intention was to learn about the extent to which plans are prepared, what time frames are regarded as "strategic," and who participates in the strategy development process.

Section B asks for the importance of reasons for strategic planning, characteristics of the planning process, and its activities. The intention here was to empirically test, what systems (structure, goals, reasons) banks use for their strategic planning, and what the process (characteristics, activities) looks alike in the participants' perceptions.

Section C inquires about the human behavioral problems occurring during the strategic planning process. The intention here is to define, which heuristics (schemas, assumptions, and behavior) are of negative impact to the effectiveness of the planning process.

Section D contained questions to the respondent's position and area, and how long the respondent was with the bank in how many positions.

7.2 Sample Issues

This section portrays the rationale for sampling decisions and selected target groups. Interview and questionnaire sample populations are described by continent, country, and size.

7.21 The Banking Industry

There are structural differences within the worldwide financial services industry (Revell 1985:25). Banks were operationalized as "deposit taking institutions recognized by a central bank" (Blanden/Jones 1988:144), that is "institutions which primarily take deposits from the public at large and provide finance for all purposes" (Revell 1988:3). For the U.S.A., the Standard Industrial Classification system of the United States Federal Government as set forth by the U.S. Office of Management and Budget (1987) was used.[45] Included were commercial banks, SIC numbers 602 (U.S. Office 1987:336), i.e. "commercial & stock savings banks central banks" (Wards 1983:A92). Not included were non-bank banks, building societies, finance and insurance

---

[45] Business and government organizations that produce a product or service are classified in SICs when the U.S. bureau of Census conducts its sensus to develop an industry input-output model. The classification for each company is prepared in terms of the primary (largest single) product or service. The SIC system is arranged in hierarchical levels, and each level is assigned a numerical code. The larger the number of digits, the more detailed the level of classification (U.S. Office of Management and Budget 1987).

companies which do not mainly perform the above described retail and wholesale banking businesses. For other countries, the same criteria were applied.

Where banking is the main activity of a financial services group, the main operating bank, or bank holding company was approached. Subsidiaries were only treated separately from the home-country holding company, if they are run pretty independently, as is the case for Harris Bank, Chicago (subsidiary) and Bank of Montreal (holding). Similarly, banking group members that are in different product markets, and which are run independently from the parent company were treated independently. This, for example, is the case for the Österreichische Credit Institut, Vienna, Austria (fully owned subsidiary) and its parent, the Österreichische Länderbank AG, Vienna, Austria. And, for Crédit du Nord, a subsidiary of the French Paribas group.

7.22 Interview Sample

The principal criteria for deciding about the banks in the sample were size (among the top 200 in the USA), and geographical location (US-Midwest or Northeast-Area). Thus, in 1986, semi-structured interviews were held with 28 senior managers on different levels and of different areas of 14 major banks in the Chicago area, in St. Louis and at the East Coast to examine the topic in depth and to pretest the questionnaire.

Bank[46]	Rank Within Country	Rank World-Wide	Assets US-$mil
Chase Manhattan, NY	2	33	99,133
Chemical Bank, NY	4	50	78,189
Manufacturers Hanover, NY	6	58	73,348
Bankers Trust, NY	8	76	56,521
First Chicago, IL	10	91	44,209
Bank of Boston, NE	12	109	34,117
Continental Illinois	14	112	32,391
Fed'l Reserve, Chicago[47]	-	-	27,984
CoreStates, PA	39	231	15,036
Harris Bank, IL	49	218	10,556
Northern Trust, IL	56	324	9,326
Mercantile Bancorp, MO	70	412	6,766
LaSalle Nat'l Bank, IL	184	-	1,692
Busey Bank, IL[47]	-	-	0,205

Table 7.2 Interview Sample Characteristics

46 Figures correspond to the fiscal year 1987. World rankings were taken from The Banker (1988a:113); national rankings and asset size (including contra accounts) were taken from Business Week (1988b; 1988c)

47 Not included in the surveys mentioned above.

7.23 Questionnaire Sample

To compare the distribution of big banks around the globe, the number of banks of each country that made it into the Banker's top 500 ranking in 1986, 1987, and 1988 was used to select several countries for the study (The Banker 1986a:85; 1987a:81; 1988a: 113). The cutoff-point in total assets less contra accounts for the top-500 ranking was $m 3,076 in 1986, $m 3,712 in 1987 and $m 4,954 in 1988 (ibid). The selected countries are discussed continent by continent below.

The same was applied to Latin America with regard to the top 100 Latin American banks (The Banker 1986b:89; 1987b:61; 1988c:125), with a cutoff-point of $m 214 in 1986, $m 212 in 1987 and $m 247 (ibid). From these initial lists, countries were chosen that would allow large enough sample populations, both by languages used and per country. For Latin American and European countries, however, comparably smaller banks were included in the survey in order to reflect the structural realities in the respective countries' markets for financial services, following Giroux (1981:97). This is justified with reference to the relative strength of their competitive environment, especially with regard to Latin America. These smaller banks were accepted, following the rankings in Wards (1985) and Bankers' Almanac (1985a), with a cutoff point of $m 100 in assets. Therefore, to balance the size distribution, comparatively smaller banks were included in the U.S. sample, too, following Bartlett (1986:65), with total assets (including contra accounts) of $m 1,414).

Following these criteria, a total of 996 banks was selected, out of which there were 355 European, 96 Australasian, 319 Latin American and 226 North American institutions. Addresses were retrieved from a variety of sources: Bankers' Almanac (1985b), Hambro Euromoney (1985), Polk's (1986a; 1986b), and Rand McNally (1982). Several names and addresses of planners with Latin American banks not found elsewhere were gratefully made available to the author by Prof. Louis Flores of Northern Illinois University, Dekalb, U.S.A.

	Number of Banks (3)	Quest's Mailed (4)	Quests/Bk (4/3) (5)	Banks responding (6)	Bks in% of sent (6*100)/3	Quest's received (8)	Response Rate (8*100)/4	Quests/Bk (8/6) (10)
Europe	355	1,082	3.05	130	36.6	190	17.6	1.5
AustralAsia	96	330	3.44	46	47.9	59	17.9	1.3
Latin America	319	465	1.46	65	20.4	74	15.9	1.1
North America	226	519	2.30	131	58.0	178	34.3	1.4
Sum/Mean	996	2.396	2.41	372	37.3	501	20.9	1.3

Table 7.3: Mailings and Responses per Continent
(Quest's = questionnaires; Bks = Banks; resp-ing = responding)

The mailings were made during the second half of 1986 and the first half of 1987. Wherever possible, questionnaires were sent to both the chief planning managers and senior executives on the board of managing directors. This approach purposively resulted in multiple responses for banks where the positions above could be identified and separated. This increases the representativeness of the data (Ramanujam/Venkatraman 1986:22).

Mailings were done in English, French, German, Italian, Japanese, Portuguese, and Spanish. The language that is predominant in the region where the bank is headquartered was used. In order to ensure that the questionnaires were answered in the respondents native language, French, Italian, and German versions were sent to Switzerland; English and French versions to Canada; German and Italian versions to Italy (The Southern Tyrol), the Spanish version to Puerto Rico (USA).

Therefore, a total of 2,396 questionnaires were mailed in two mailings. As it is shown above, to European banks 1,082 questionnaires were sent, 330 to Australasia, 465 to Latin America, and 519 to North America.

Out of that, a total of 515 questionnaires were received, of which 501 were usable. This corresponds to an overall response rate of 21%. Given the sensitivity of strategic planning itself, and the large number of mailings to countries where questionnaire surveys are not as much in use as in the USA (i.e. Latin America and several European countries), the rate of responses is quite good.

For all responding banks, their "assets less contra accounts"[48] as of Dec 31, 1987 (for Japanese banks of Sept. 30, 1987) were collected to allow for size comparisons. The responses cover 372 banks worldwide, with assets of $8,750 billion.[49] Of the whole 501 usable responses, 279 were from 187 banks ranking in the top 550 of the world (Banker 1988a).

Continent	# of Banks	# of Responses	Assets (US-$mil)
Europe	130	190	3.491,138
AustralAsia	46	59	3.151,615
Latin America	65	74	174,557
North America	131	178	1.932,498
Total	372	501	8.749,808

Table 7.4: Responses per Continent

[48] Contra accounts are defined as bonds, acceptances, or other securities held for customers; guarantees, letters of credit, and similar instruments (Institutional Investor 1987:143). Total assets less contra accounts are a widely used measure for banks size, e.g. applied in the Banker's annual surveys (The Banker, 1986, 1987, 1988). A variety of bank rankings in the Australian Business (Burr 1987:81), The Banker (1986a,b; 1987a,b,c; 1988a,c,d,e,f), Bankers Almanac (1988), Business Week (1988a,b,c; Bartlett 1986:66), Euromoney (1987:121; 1988:75), Fortune (Blank/Gustke 1988:D41), Institutional Investor (1987:143), Le Nouvel Economiste (1987), Die Bank (1987), as well as annual reports were consulted to collect this data.

[49] Million (billion) US-$ is abbreviated by "$m" ("$b").

These 55.7% of the responses (50.3% of the responding banks) in the top 550 cover $b 8,303 in assets. This means, that one third of the world 550 biggest banks responded to this survey.

	TOTAL Banker Top 550				TOTAL Remainder to Banker Top 550		
Continent	# of Banks	# of Responses	Assets (US-$mil)	Continent	# of Banks	# of Responses	Assets (US-$mil)
Europe	83	138	3.354,583	Europe	47	52	136,555
AustralAsia	29	44	3.131,196	AustralAsia	17	15	20,419
Latin America	7	10	131,991	Latin America	58	64	42,566
North America	68	87	1.685,923	North America	63	91	246,575
Total	187	279	8.303,693	Total	185	222	446,115
In% of All	50.3%	55.7%	94.9%	In% of All	49.7%	44.32%	5.1%

Table 7.5: Coverage of the Top 550 Banks Worldwide

Within each continent, responses from several countries were lumped together to arrive at meaningful samples. For the same reasons, Hofstede (1983:49) formed multicountry regions for which the number of available responses from the individual countries was insufficient. The regroupings here were done following economic and cultural considerations.

The 1987 inflation rate (INFL) and the gross domestic product per capita (GDP) for 1987 were used as indicators of economic similarity (Economist Intelligence Service 1988). Three of Hofstede's (1980:223;316) dimensions which influence managerial practices, namely individualism (IDV), uncertainty avoidance (UAI), and power distance (PDI), were used as indicators of cultural similarities.[50]

7.231 Responses per Continent

From 130 European banks a total of 190 questionnaires were received, corresponding to assets of $b 3.491. The average response rate was 17.6%, ranging from 9.8% (Switzerland) to 48.6% (Belgium). The exact response rate for each country can be seen in table 7.5 (Europe-All) below. 72.6% of these European responses, covering 96.6% of the European banks assets, were from banks which made the Banker's (1988a:113) top 550 listing.

Three regroupings which follow the economic and cultural criteria explained above were found to be necessary due to the number of responses in each country. French-Belgian, British-Irish, and Spanish-Portuguese country clusters were formed. As the German sample was large enough by itself, it was used treated without the Swiss answers.

---

[50] Exact figures for the original and regrouped countries' values on these variables are available upon request.

EUROPE-ALL

Country	Symbol	# of Banks	# of Responses	Assets (US-$mil)
Austria	AUT	16	31	170,840
Belgium	BEL	10	17	188,084
France	FRA	12	17	703,410
Germany	GER	30	43	914,610
U.K.	GBR	11	19	557,893
Ireland	IRE	2	2	29,763
Italy	ITA	22	27	479,825
Portugal	POR	5	6	30,010
Spain	SPA	14	19	164,147
Suisse	SWI	8	9	252,552
Sum		130	190	3.491,138

REGROUPED EUROPE

Country and Country Group	# of Banks	# of Responses	Assets (US-$mil)
AUT	16	31	170,844
FRA BEL	22	34	891,494
GER SWI	38	52	1.167,162
GBR IRE	13	21	587,656
ITA	22	27	479,825
SPA POR	19	25	194,157
Sum	130	190	3.491,138

Table 7.6: European Responses

A total of 59 responses from 46 Australasian banks, covering assets amounting to $b 3.150 were received.[51] The over-all response rate of 17.9% varies between 12.% (Japan) and 44.7% (Australia). 74,6% of the Australasian responses, including all Japanese, are from banks which made the Banker's (1988a:113) top 550 ranking in 1987.

AUSTRALASIA-ALL

Country	Symbol	# of Banks	# of Responses	Assets (US-$mil)
Australia	AUL	14	17	97,061
NewZealand	NZL	1	2	8,269
Indonesia	IND	3	3	16,380
Philipines	PHI	4	4	3,301
SouthKorea	KOR	1	1	20,500
Japan	JAP	25	32	3.006,104
Sum		46	59	3.151,615

REGROUPED AUSTRALASIA

Country and Country Group	# of Banks	# of Responses	Assets (US-$mil)
AUL NZL	15	19	105,330
JAP	23	32	3,006,104
IND PHI KOR	8	8	40,181
Too few answers to be used for analysis by countries. Used only for size and economic impact analysis.			
Sum	46	59	3.151,615

Table 7.7: Australasian Responses

Too few responses were received from Indonesia and the Philipines be included in the analysis. Responses from Australia and New Zealand were grouped together according to the above described economic and cultural criteria.

---

[51] For four Australian responses, however, it could not be identified from which banks they were. Their minimum assets were estimated with $m 250 each.

From 65 Latin American Banks, 74 responses, covering $m 172 in assets were received. This corresponds to an response rate of 15.9%, which is regarded high for Latin American countries.

Of these responses, 13.5% were from countries which made the Banker's (1988a:113) top 550 list. However, 62.2% of the responses are from banks which made the Banker's (1988c) Top 100 Latin American listing. Two country clusters which reflect the above explained economic (especially inflation and size) and cultural indicators were built. The high-inflation, big Latin American countries Argentina, Brazil, Mexico and Peru were put into cluster one. The remaining countries (Bolivia, Chile, Colombia, Costa Rica, Dominican Republic, Ecuador, El Salvador, Guatemala, Honduras, Panama, and Venezuela) form the second Latin American cluster.

LATIN AMERICA-ALL

Country	Symbol	# of Banks	# of Responses	Assets (US-$mil)
Argentina	ARG	4	4	2,420
Bolivia	BOL	1	2	631
Brazile	BRA	7	9	105,217
Chili	CHL	4	5	3,680
Colombia	COL	9	9	5,107
Costa Rica	COS	2	3	3,660
DomiRepublc	DOM	1	1	355
ElSalvador	ELS	7	8	544
Guatemala	GUA	1	1	68
Honduras	HON	5	6	775
Mexico	MEX	12	14	45,367
Panama	PAN	1	1	981
Peru	PER	5	5	1,773
Venezuela	VEN	3	3	3,663
Sum		65	74	174,557

REGROUPED LATIN AMERICA

Country and Country Group	# of Banks	# of Responses	Assets (US-$mil)
LatAm1: high inflation states			
ARG BRA MEX PER	28	32	154,777
LatAm2: middle inflation, smaller states			
BOL CHL COL COS DOM ECU ELS GUA HON PAN VEN	37	42	19,780
Sum	65	74	174,557

LatAm1: ARG (4), BRA (9), MEX (14), PER (5) = 32 answers from high inflation, middle PDI, middle IDV states.

LatAm2: 42 answers from middle inflation, high PDI, low IDV states

Table 7.8: Latin American Responses

From 131 North American banks, a total of 178 responses were received, covering $b 1,933 in assets. The overall response rate is 34.3%, with 45.1% for Canada. 48.9% of the responses are from banks which made the Banker's (1988a:113) top 550. For the USA, the ratio of responses from banks which made the Banker's (1988a:113) list to those who did not is 76 to 79, which shows a quite even distribution of responses.

Regionally, a good spread of responses from US banks was achieved. There are 46 responses from the Northeast, 26 from the Southeast, 27 from the West & Southwest, and 56 from the Midwest. This will allow for within-country-comparisons with the USA data in later research (Seeger et al 1987; White/Jensen 1987).

NORTH AMERICA-ALL					NORTH AMERICA BANKER TOP 550			NORTH AMERICA REMAINDER TO BANKER TOP 550		
Country	# of Banks	# of Responses	Assets (US-$mil)		# of Banks	# of Responses	Assets (US-$mil)	# of Banks	# of Responses	Assets (US-$mil)
Canada	16	23	332,631		7	11	316,553	9	12	16,078
US (1)	61	76	1.369,370	Top550	61	76	1.369,370	0	0	0
US (2)	54	79	230,497	Remainder	0	0	0	54	79	230,497
Sum	131	178	1.932,498		68	87	1.685,923	63	91	246,575
				% of All	51.9%	48,9%	87.2%	48.1%	51.1%	12.8%

Table 7.9: North American Responses

No regroupings were necessary in the North American sample. However, during the last years, many US banks were involved in mergers and acquisitions (Haiss 1988b). In 1987, 22 out of the 87 US banks in the Bankers' Top 500 were involved in major mergers (Banker 1988a:111). Therefore, within the U.S. sample, several mergers and acquisitions occurred between the design of the study and the data compilation (Banker 1988:111; Blanden, 1987:78; Hector 1988:89; Houldsworth et al 1987:121; Paparetto/Hamilton 1988:101,117). For these banks, the current consolidated figures were used. Responses were treated separately for each bank responding. Therefore, some merged or acquired banks (e.g. Suburban Bancorp) appear in the list of banks. For details, see the list of acquired banks in the sample below. Acquired banks were included in the sample, if the responses were made prior to the merger.

Acquirer/ Merger Partner	(Rank)	**Acquiree/ Merger Partner**	(Rank)
Chemical Bank, NY	4	Texas Commerce, TX	28
First Republic, TX	13	Interfirst, TX	19
PNC Financial, PA	15	Citizens Fidelity, KY	104
Bank of New England	17	Conifer Group, PA	150
First Union Corp, NC	19	1st Railroad & Banking, GA	114
Suntrust Banks, GA	20	Third National Corp, TN	85
Sovran Financial, VA	28	Suburban Bancorp, MD Commerce Union, TN	120 126
CoreStates, PA	39	New Jersey Nat'l Corp, NJ	175

Table 7.10: Mergers & Acquisitions in the US Sample

Source: Compiled by the author from: Banker 1988b:111; Blanden, 1987:78; Hector 1988:89; Houldsworth et al 1987:121; Paparetto/Hamilton 1988:101,117; Rankings follow The Banker (1988a:129) and Bartlett (1986:66).

7.232 Test Samples

To test the hypotheses stated in the previous chapters, two types of tests were performed, independently using two subsamples of the whole answers. Responses from U.S. and German banks that rank among the top 300 according to the Banker (1988) were used for the first test. Thereby industry, size, and level of economic development were held constant.

Country	Symbol	Banks among Top 300	Banks Responded	%	# of Responses	Assets (US-$mil)	Average Assets
Germany	GER	34	22	64.7	31	768.947	34,952
USA	USA	47	31	66.0	40	1.180,496	38,081
Total		81	53	65.4	71	1.949,443	36,782

Table 7.11: US-German Top 300 Sample

For those questionnaire items that showed significant differences in the mean responses between US and German banks, a second test was performed. According to the economic and cultural criteria described above, ten country clusters were formed to compare their respective responses. While all responses are from the same industry (banking), in this sample, size and level of economic development are not held constant. Thereby, the same questions were tested against a second subsample of responses.

10-Country Comparison

Country and Country Group	# of Banks	# of Responses	Assets (US-$mil)
AUT	16	31	170,844
FRA/BEL	22	34	891,494
GBR/IRE	13	21	587,656
ITA	22	27	479,825
SPA/POR	19	25	194,157
AUL/NZL	15	19	105,330
JAP	23	32	3.006,104
LatAm1	28	32	154,777
LatAm2	37	42	19,780
CDN	16	23	230,497
Sum	211	286	5.840,464

Table 7.12: Ten-Country Comparison

7.3 Data Handling and Analysis

Analyzing data requires three steps, i.e. data reduction, data display, and drawing and verifying conclusions (Friedrichs 1981:376; Griggs 1987:17). The interviews were analyzed following the theoretical framework of Glaser/Strauss (1967) and Miles/ Huberman (1984), which suggest two categories: a-priori (deductive) categories developed prior to data analysis, and (inductive) categories or patterns that emerge from the data itself. Piore (1979:566) proposes such inductive search to take advantage of the richness of interview data, arguing that "what interviews can reveal is not a set of specific answers to specific questions, individual bits and pieces of information. What they reveal are patterns of responses" (Piore 1979:566).

'Content analysis' as a technique for coding data making inferences from identified characteristics in a systematic and objective way was used for data analysis.[52] To ensure for reliability, codes therefore were derived from the research questions and key concepts outlined in the previous chapters, and from themes that emerged form the interviews themselves.[53]

In order to analyze the questionnaire data, a menu-driven data-entry program was written in Basic, along with a codebook. National (e.g. inflation rate) and bank-specific (e.g. assets) data was added from secondary sources as mentioned above to an aggregate file. Little recoding was necessary through the regrouping of data. The data was checked for cleaning purposes.

The development of statestical procedures applied here followed the generic format of hypothesis testing (e.g. Churchill 1987:634; Glass/ Hopkins 1984:202).

Hypotheses of no difference (H_0's) and their alternatives were formulated. For example, controlling bank size and economic environment, responses from US and German banks that ranked among the world's top 300 banks as ranked by The Banker (1988a) were compared with regard to differences between the means of their responses. Similar to this two-sample test, the nullhypotheses for k-sample tests comparing more than two countries at a time were specified.

H_{01}: $\mu_1 = \mu_2$ (No differences between the two means)
H_{02}: $\mu_1 = \mu_2 \ldots = \mu_n$ (No differences between the k means)

Test statistics must be chosen to evaluate the null hypotheses, while taking the number of samples involved, the degree of independence of individual cases, and the measurement scales into account (Churchill 1987:654).

Parametric tests (e.g. t-test, F-test) are generally based on the assumptions of independent observations from normally distributed populations with equal variances, using at least interval scales (Emory 1985). Samples of $n = 25$ or more can be relied upon to yield a very nearly normal sampling distribution of means (Glass/Hopkins 1984:184). The Central-Limit Theorem, therefore, allows the application of such parametric tests, even if the assumptions stated above are not fully met (Churchill 1987:659). As parametric tests are quite robust, mean, and variance are frequently used based on Likert scales, i.e. in situations where, under strict interpretation, only nonparametric tests are

---

[52] The definition used here is close to Holsti (1968:601). For an overview of the technique of content analysis, see Brislin (1980), Kassarjian (1977), or Rust (1983).

[53] To ensure for reliability, categories must be explicitly defined, unequivocal, mutually exclusive, and have to completely represent the research question (Friedrichs 1981:93; Selltiz et al 1976:392; Rust 1983:90).

appropriate (Emory 1985; Glass/Hopkins 19884:9).

Therefore, in accordance with comparative research conducted by Christodolou (1984), Suzuki (1986), Kagona et al (1985), two-tailed t-tests were chosen to evaluate the null hypothesis H_{01} on US vs. German responses.[54] The t-tests were cross-checked with Chi-square analyses. For the ten-country comparison, one-factor analysis of variance (ANOVA) was applied and cross-checked with non-parametric Kruskal-Wallis one-way ANOVA's, following the suggestions by Emory (1985) and Norusis (1986:B-186)[55]

7.4 Methodological Problems

Many review articles provide insight into methodological problems and weaknesses of cross-cultural research (Adler 1983; Holzmüller 1986; Nath 1968; Triandis/Berry 1980). Shrivastava (1987) evaluated the rigor and practical usefulness of research in strategic management. He used conceptual adequacy, methodological rigor, and the extent of accumulated empirical evidence as criteria for assessing the rigorousness of research (Shrivastava 1987:78). Adler (1984:45) classified methodological issues in comparative management research into the fundamental dilemmas of cultural constructs,[56] research topic, sampling, translation, measurement and instrumentation, administration, and analysis.

As the interviews were all conducted by the researcher who also developed the questionnaire, a possible research bias has to be closely watched. This may be reduced due to the extensive use of pretesting and testing throughout the research process.

For the mail survey, planning managers could be identified merely for American banks. The available address material indicated that such functions exist or are reported publicly to a much lesser degree in other countries.

---

[54] For details on t-tests, see, for example: Wakolbinger (1980:89); Glass/Hopkins 1984:217; Churchill 1987:659).

[55] One-way ANOVA's are based on calculating F-values, the relation of variability within groups to variability between groups. In ANOVA all differences for all pairs of k means are examined simultaneously to see if one or more of the means deviate significantly from one or more of the other means. For advantages of ANOVA's over multiple t-tests and other details, see for example Glass/Hopkins (1987:324), Churchill 1984:668. If the sample sizes in all groups are similar (which is the case here), the ANOVA test is not particularly sensitive to violations of equality of group variance (Norusis 1986:B-158).

[56] The term "cultural constructs" here is used as a headline for the definition problem of culture, culture-specific vs. universal, culture-boundness of the researcher, identical vs. equivalent approaches, and interaction between variables, topic and approach (Adler 1984:45).

International comparisons for the financial services industry are particularly difficult due to national restrictions on price competition, on product range competition, and on geographic competition (Haiss 1989b). This led to a sectoral structure of the financial services industry within most countries, reflecting the institutional coverage of products (Mitchell 1985). However, the conclusion is drawn that in spite of the differences discussed above, the banking industry shares reasonable enough similarities to allow for valid and reliable comparisons.

The dilemma of cultural constructs was reviewed in the chapter on cultural influences on planning. Although some of the criticism raised by Triandis (1983) or Westwood/Everett (1987) may apply here, the Hofstede (1980) dimensions still provide a rich framework and venture point for the investigation. Through the inclusion of size, economic and other factors, it was not assumed that management practices are either wholly culture-specific or wholly universal (Adler 1984:49). It was however already pointed out in the chapter on strategic planning processes, that the concept of planning itself is culture-bound; functional equivalence in the means to reach the ends applies here (Jaccard/Wan 1986; Hui/Triandis 1985).

Therefore, the study is a comparative study and is not a mere replication of a single-country study. Equivalent approaches to research were undertaken. Similarly, it was purposefully tried to keep the translations equivalent, not identical. As usual, a special problem was inherent in the translation of the questionnaires. The researcher was aware of the fact that "taking an instrument designed and tested within the cultural context of one country, using it in other countries, .. and comparing the results between countries, is, in principle, a debatable form of cross-cultural research" (Hofstede/Bond 1984:412). Scales, order of questions, and outlay were kept stable over all seven language versions. Due to monetary restrictions on the side of the researcher, no backtranslations as recommended e.g. by Hui/Triandis (1985:140) were obtainable. However, to reduce problems of equivalence (Hui/Triandis 1985:133), i.e. to ensure that the different versions carry the same meaning across target populations, the translators were instructed to transfer the content of the phrases and items, not to translate literally. Only native speakers were used as translators. All translations were done from the English version. In every case, two additional native speakers were asked to revise the translation, emphasizing again the importance of meaning and content. The questionnaires were pretested with students from the countries using the respective language.

Aggregating data with society as the unit of analysis poses a tough challenge to investigations of the strategic planning process in a cross-cultural context (Sekaran/Snodgrass 1987:40). Therefore, the sample size was kept fairly large, and a sufficient number of cultures was included. Functionally equivalent samples were used. The respondent's native language was used in each country. However, it will never be possible to eliminate discrepancies in responses, construct completely equivalent items, and the like (Ayal/Hornik 1986; Candell/Hulin

1986; Hulin 1987; Marin et al 1983). Still, the researcher cannot abstain from being of Austrian origin, and that there will always be some etic influence (Adler 1983, 1984; Hui/Triandis 1985). As Smircich (1983:355) concluded,

> Because we are of our own culture, it is difficult for us, researchers and managers alike, to both live in our cultural context and to question it. It is difficult to engage in contextual, reflexive management and research, with the requirement of examination and critique of one's own assumptions and values. It is difficult; but that is what a cultural framework for management and research urges us to do.

7.5 Summary

This chapter gave an introduction to the methodologies applied, and their development. The questionnaire instrument was explained, response populations and their characteristics were critically compared by continent, country, and bank size. Data handling and statistical procedures were discussed. Finally, methodological problems were evaluated.

8 PLANNING SYSTEMS AT WORK

8.1 Findings from the Interviews

This section describes the findings from the 28 interviews that were conducted with U.S. banks in order to develop the questionnaires. The analysis presented below follows the distinction between planning systems, processes, and heuristics and is oriented towards bank planners and senior managers that assisted in the development of the questionnaire.[57]

8.11 Planning Systems

All but one of the banks interviewed had a split between corporate and business level plans. Three of the banks were very issue oriented in their plans with the focus shifting between corporate and business levels. In several banks, only those strategic business units with changing environments were included in the annual planning cycle.

These differences in the focus of corporate plans are visible in the types of plans the banks formulate. In general, the plans' time horizons varied between three to ten years. While three banks were merely issue-oriented with flowing time frames, five banks used planning horizons of five years, the remaining six banks had strategic plans with three-year time frames. Those banks using a longer time horizon made a definite split between long-term financial plans (usually covering three years) and strategic plans (usually with a time horizon of five years and above, with objectives expressed in strategic projects), while in the other cases both were included in one type of plan.

Most banks in the sample have some combination of one-year operational budgets, two to three year financial forecasts, and (in their eyes) truly strategic plans with time horizons as described above. Alternatively, three banks used a combination of action plans, rolling issue-oriented projections and position papers that are kind of strategy statements.

While one bank started as early as 1978, one as late as 1985 with their strategic planning efforts on a broader basis, the starting year for strategic planning in its current form in general was 1981/82. For several banks (e.g. Bankers Trust, Chase; Durstberger

---

[57] As was already pointed out in the methodology chapter, the interviews served as input to the questionnaire development. They functioned as a tool to learn which patterns managers themselves use to describe their planning activities. The presentation of the analysis here is therefore intentionally very practitioner-oriented. In the dissertation itself (Haiss 1989), quotes were used to make the interviewed managers' views more tangible, and to show different viewpoints in order not to overreport the average (Griggs 1987:18; Miles/Huberman 198a:238), following the example of Davis (1985).

1987:125) a crisis situation, frequently accompanied by a change in senior management was the venture point for truly strategic planning. Most of the interviewed banks overhauled or started up their planning efforts following regulatory changes in the early eighties.

So in basically all banks interviewed, a series of evolutionary steps as outlined in the table below was taken till they arrived at the current planning systems. These steps were of course intertwined and not as clear-cut as the graphic representation suggests.

Steps	**Content**
Crisis	Legal, market, or management changes
Inventory	Strategic scan within the existing structure, led by consultant s
Realignment	Definition of markets served and change in organizational structure to profit center SBUs
MIS System	Creation of management information, client profitability, & resource allocation systems
Dissolution	Refinement of planning and resource allocation units through bundling up SBU's serving the same clients into stand-alone market clusters
V	V
Current strategic planning systems	

Table 8.1: Steps Towards the Current Planning Systems.

The banks were broken up into sectors or groups. SBU's were introduced and information systems were developed that allowed to calculate and plan by customer group and decentralize accountability. As many banks felt uneasy with stringent SBU's, they changed their organizational structure again following the information they then had about their customer and revenue structures.

All managers interviewed stressed the differences between top-down versus bottom-up and line vs. staff-driven planning. i.e. centralized vs. decentralized planning systems. In general, planning systems had moved from both extreme ends of the scale towards a very interactive type of process. Corporate, over-all strategy in the banks interviewed was more top-down, staff-driven. Business unit level strategy was more bottom-up, line driven. However, the picture is not as clear cut, as there is planning staff in the lines of many banks and important SBU issues that come out of the line analysis influence corporate strategy.

There is also wide recognition of the necessity to draw from the experience and market knowledge of the line managers to formulate long-range strategies. However, some of the banks seem to have overdone this bottom-up approach in the past and therefore revamped their planning process accordingly.

All banks have some sort of policy committee, that consists of the very senior managers of the bank and meets several times a year off-site to discuss strategic issues. Depending on the management style of the president, CEO and chairman, such a committee develops or further details the strategic direction. One bank actually brought clients into its planning process by interviewing them about their future financial services' needs, and by integrating them in competitive analysis workshops.

Staff groups are always involved in the process. One staff group typically runs the process, depending on the orientation of the planning process towards truly strategic, long-term issues or financial, mid-term issues. A corporate development group that acts like internal consultants and catalysts, introduces long-term issues through environmental scans, competitive analysis and position papers. That generates ideas and provides project managers where it is required for business studies. This group typically is involved in the review process, which serves as a tool to derive at a combined, truly strategic picture from both the line plans (which are often mostly financial in nature) and the policy committee's views in the resource allocation. Second, a controller or management science group that specializes in quantitative analysis, statistics, computer modeling, with emphasis on a shorter time frame. The latter group also is responsible for the link with operating budgets. Alternatively, this function is fulfilled by some market research people. Third, within the lines there are frequently planning representatives, that work for the preparation of the strategic plan as well as for the operating budget. If such a type of planning staff within the lines exists, it is usually responsible for the implementation within the lines. However, in banks with only small corporate planning staff, these line planners also have the functions of a corporate development group described above. Implementation usually rests within the lines. Corporate follow-up, especially of resource allocation, proved to be a problem for most of the banks interviewed.

The power base for the strategic planning efforts in nearly all cases was the direct support from the highest level of management. In two banks, the planning obviously already is part of the corporate culture and need not be enforced anymore by senior management. As there seem to be some problems with that back-up by top management, several banks developed alternative approaches. In two banks, the corporate planning group could only operate based on voluntary relationships with line managers. The planners' credibility arose from beeing experienced, well-know, former line managers. In one bank, the planning department has control over the market research budget and thereby influences what strategic issues are dealt with.

In nine of the 14 banks interviewed, the planning staff reports directly to the chief executive officer (CEO), president or chairman. In the remaining five banks, it reports to the chief financial officer (CFO). The outcome of the planning process is usually communicated down to middle management. Most frequently a management summary of the general outcome (corporate issues) is generally distributed. Alternatively, managers are given the plans of related areas (business issues).

8.12 Planning Processes

8.121 Process Characteristics

Ten of the fourteen interviewed banks had discrete annual planning cycles, with specific starting and ending points, and a flow of certain activities to be performed periodically and sequentially, step by-step. Reviews in those banks were conducted on an annual basis, sticking to a general format. The other four banks used a more continuous, issue-oriented approach without distinct phases or planning cycle. The process there was more iterative, assuring for a parallel treatment of strategic issues and financial forecasts. In those banks, reviews of the financials were conducted annually, while changes in important issues were reflected in the topics to be dealt with in the planning process.

In the banks interviewed, there was a definite organizational linkage between the strategic plans, the financial plans and the budget, while different units were responsible for these plans (Shank 1973:186) in six banks, and a split in responsibility in eight banks. Five banks had established reasonable content linkages between their plans, ensuring for the correspondence between the data presented in the budget and the strategic plan (Shank et al 1973:88), which in general posed a problem.

All banks had established time linkages in the sequencing of planning and budgeting cycles. However, three very different modes of proceeding were used. Half of the banks derive the budget from the strategic plan, although most admitted to have consistency problems. Four banks extrapolate through rolling forward from the budget to the financial and strategic plan. The remaining three banks were very issue-oriented. They merely compile the projects that are summed up to plans with different implementation stages, which can be interpreted as simultaneous or independent preparation. The surprising conclusion of half of the banks not deriving their short-range plans from their long-range ones is consistent with findings reported by Christodolou (1984:383) for the U.S. manufacturing industry.

Ten of the banks used a planning manual that outlines the planning format and content, at least at the introductory phase of planning. While all banks use standard forms for the financial projections, eleven banks provide worksheets, forms and brief explanations for the strategic part of the plan. These are sent out to line units for completion. In the remaining banks, the process is kept on a very informal level. While most banks keep the same format from year to year, three banks change it, depending on the issues to be emphasized. In general, the banks reduced the degree formalization from an initially high level in the introductory phase.

Most planning efforts were means and not ends oriented, i.e. stressed the importance of the process to keep managers open for future issues and tasks over the importance of the plan itself.

8.122 Process Activities

Five banks classified their planning systems as forecast-based, financially oriented planning, while majority of nine banks cataloged their planning efforts as externally oriented (Gluck et al 1982). Accordingly, the focus during the analysis of strengths, weaknesses, opportunities, and threats is more towards (external) opportunities and threats than towards (internal) strengths and weaknesses. Although historical data is heavily used, the process itself in general is more geared towards the future.

During the planning process, only three banks emphasized on specific details in their general information search. The remaining 13 banks looked at the larger picture in the search for consistency among long-run issues. However, for the financial plans as well as within major projects, all bank planning does eventually elaborate into detail. Over all, banks use more quantitative data than qualitative data in their strategic analysis). However, the banks in the sample are deeply split on that issue. While eight banks emphasize the use of quantitative information, six banks emphasize more qualitative over quantitative information.

To overcome this dichotonomy of planning content, the bank planners in the sample mostly provide a mixture of two activities. First, nearly all banks developed and maintain computer models as tools for strategic control. Either some type of projection model, or portfolio-and balance-sheet simulation models. Second, the planners themselves usually try to provide a "role model" for the bank with regard to how to tackle and detect issues.

Among the banks interviewed, managers stressed the aspect of providing a role model to their bank, two types were apparent. In three of the banks the planning process provided the opportunity for those involved to act as "devil's advocates" (Schwenk/Thomas 1983:245), through, for example, asking nasty questions. In seven banks, the emphasis was more to broaden the view towards the general environment. The remaining four banks put emphasis on specific issues to redirect the level of thought in that way.[58]

[58] From a conceptual point of view, such decision aids introducing heterogeneity, competition and variety to the strategic decision process are applications of what Churchman (1971) termed "Kantian" and "Hegelian" inquiry systems. Both methods of inquiry produce multiple frameworks and contrasting conceptual views of issues. For further details on related concepts, see Mitroff/Emshoff 1979: Mason/Mitroff 1981; Thomas 1984).

In half of the banks interviewed, the planning department had to do some training and coaching to pave the way for the planning process. There was a strong emphasis on development, coordination and administration of the planning process in those banks that either frequently change the process or lack a planning culture and history. Forecasts, the consolidations and reviews of line plans, the internal publication of research papers and long-term projects were most frequently mentioned. In ten banks, long-term allocation of funds was either the planning managers' direct responsibility or strongly guided by their recommendations. Although most managers stressed implementation problems, only in a few banks the planning department was actively involved in implementation.

8.13 Planning Heuristics

One group of heuristics reported has to do with the availability and representativeness of information (Tversky/Kahnemann 1974). The lack of reliable market research data often leads to a substitution by accountancy data. The amount of information to be dealt with in planning was felt to be overwhelming. And most managers were very concerned of going too much into detail and loosing the broader picture.

Drawing illusory correlations, and adjustment and anchoring to the familiar (Fischhoff/Goitein 1984), to "lending" as the core banking business resulting in a short-term time orientation, emphasis on risks, and a figure-driven style of bank management were also reported.

These issues frequently were reported to have caused some form of 'group think' (Janis 1973) and escalating commitment towards actions (Staw 1981). Power alliances and struggles between the different managerial groups involved in planning, and obedience towards conforming to the process (e.g. "complete the forms for the sake of it") were also reported.

The illusion of control, certainty effects, and ritualization (Janis 1973; Hofstede 1980:383) of planning into a bureaucratic exercise were also prevalent in the planning processes with the banks interviewed. Many managers expressed the warning not to overformalize the planning process.

8.14 Summary

The preceding sections described the findings from the interviews that were conducted with U.S. banks in order to develop the questionnaires. The distinction between planning systems, heuristics and processes and were shown to be a useful concept to describe and analyze strategic planning practices. As it was only <u>US banks</u> that were interviewed, it was <u>expected to find</u> planning frameworks that on average represent <u>low uncertainty avoidance</u>, <u>low power distance</u>, <u>high individualism</u>, and <u>specific organizational learning</u> as explained previously (Hofstede 1980;

Sullivan/Nonaka 1986; Suzuki 1986; Kagona et al 1986; Snodgrass 1984).

Although differences were stressed, the planning frameworks were split between those resembling high uncertainty avoidance (formal, highly structured activities, relatively short time horizons, staff-driven, past/present orientation etc), and those resembling low uncertainty avoidance (issue-oriented, informal, line-driven planning). Power distance, however, in general was low (decentralization, two-way communication, bottom-up planning). However, planning was also frequently used for supervisory purposes. In general, emphasis is put on tasks and individual initiative (high individualism). The use of quantitative, specific and objective information sources with a focus only on directly relevant issues was prevalent (specific organizational learning). Thus, the propositions developed in earlier chapters are not fully supported by the findings from the interviews. However, this cannot be expected with a sample of only 14 banks. Therefore, a larger database is necessary to draw meaningful conclusions.

8.2 US and German Bank Planning Practices in Comparison

This section reports the findings from questionnaire responses from US and German banks that ranked among the top 300 in the world (Banker 1988). In this sample, industry, size, and level of economic development were therefore held constant.

T-tests and Chi-square analysis were run to compare the 31 German and 40 American responses. Test statistics (means, standard deviations, t-values, degrees of freedom, significance levels, Chi-squares etc. are given in the appendix.

8.21 US vs. German Planning Systems

In the following, types of plans prepared, time frames covered, subunits involved and their respective roles, and reasons for strategic planning between US and German banks are compared.

All US and German banks in the sample prepare one-year budgets. About 85% of the banks in both samples prepare long-range plans, while German banks use slightly more medium-term plans, compared to their US counterparts.

	US-Top 300			German Top 300		
Types of Plans	Have Plan	Years		Have Plan	Years	
		μ	Mode		μ	Mode
Long-Range Plan	87.2%	4.8	5	84.2%	6.1	5
Medium Range Plan	66.7%	2.9	3	76.2%	3.3	4
Short Term Plan	100.0%	1.0	1	100.0%	1.0	1
	(n = 40)			(n = 31)		

Table 8.2 Types of Plans Prepared (US vs. German Top 300)

However, strategic plans at German banks have a significantly longer time frame of 6,2 years on average compared to the time frame of 4,8 years of US banks (α = .02). German medium-range plans have an insignificantly longer time frame. Short term plans in general cover one year.

Variables	Mean US	Mean GER	Alpha
LPYears	4,8	6,2	,02
MPYears	2,9	3,3	n.s.
SMYears	1,0	1,0	n.s.

US = responses from Top300 US banks
GER = Responses from Top300 German banks
Alpha = significance level

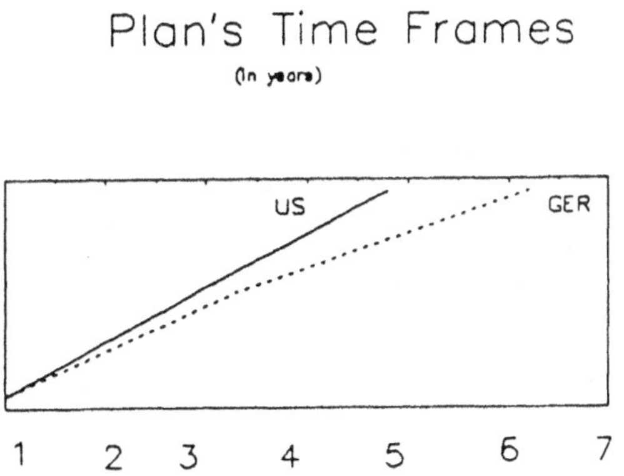

Figure 8.1 Plan's Time Frames (US vs. German Top 300)

In the next section of the questionnaire, the banks were asked to indicate <u>which organizational unit prepares, reviews and finally decides</u> the strategic plan. In US banks, the strategic plans are developed by line managers, reviewed by the planning staff and at senior executive meetings, and most frequently the final decision is made at meetings between the CEO and the department executives. In German banks, plans are prepared mainly by planning staff, reviewed by line managers, and decided upon either by the CEO or at meetings with department executives. While planning committees and project teams are involved in both countries, they are more involved in all three stages in German banks.

Organizational Unit	Prepare US	Prepare German	Review US	Review German	Decide US	Decide German
Planning department (staff)	64%	85%	92%	59%	22%	22%
Line department	94%	48%	75%	70%	33%	30%
Corporate staff department	47%	15%	64%	19%	22%	15%
Strategic planning committee	18%	37%	59%	44%	44%	15%
Task force or project team	31%	52%	34%	48%	9%	15%
Meeting of CEO and department executives	6%	11%	78%	67%	81%	48%
CEO by him/herself	0%	0%	31%	33%	50%	52%
A committee of board of directors	0%	0%	23%	19%	14%	22%
The board of directors	0%	0%	31%	15%	37%	25%
other	0%	4%	1%	7%	0%	1%

(n = 40 for US; n = 31 for German)

Table 8.3 Subunits Involved in Planning (US vs. Germany Top 300)

The next section of the questionnaire was concerned with <u>reasons</u> for strategic planning. Examining basic problems of the company, thinking about future changes and improving resource allocation were of very high concern for both German and US banks, while learning from past performance, improving short-range planning, integrate and control departments were of lesser importance. Significant differences between the two countries appeared on seven of the sixteen items tested. The single most important reason for German banks to plan strategically was the concern with future changes, while for US banks the clarification of goals and policies to have a guideline was of ultimate importance. German banks were significantly more concerned about the basic problems of the company, with learning from past performance, with taking action at early stages and thinking about future changes than US banks. For the latter, improved resource allocation and the concern to have a plan that guides the bank in the future was significantly higher than for German banks. In general, German banks stressed more external motives for their planning activities, while US banks stressed more internal reasons.

Variables	Mean		
	US	GER	Alpha
Problems	3,5	4,2	,02
Learn from Past	2,9	3,6	,03
Decide	2,9	3,7	,02
Act early	3,8	4,2	,10
Anticipate Change	4,2	4,7	,01
Improve Budget	2,9	2,8	n.s.
Avoid Uncertainty	2,7	3,8	n.s.
Collect Ideas	3,2	3,4	n.s.
Have a Guide	4,4	3,6	,01
Improve Communication	3,6	3,5	n.s.
Coordinate Projects	3,3	3,6	n.s.
Change Managers	3,4	3,5	n.s.
Integrate	2,7	2,8	n.s.
Resource Allocation	4,0	3,3	,03
Clarify Goals	4,4	4,0	n.s.
Control	2,1	2,6	n.s.

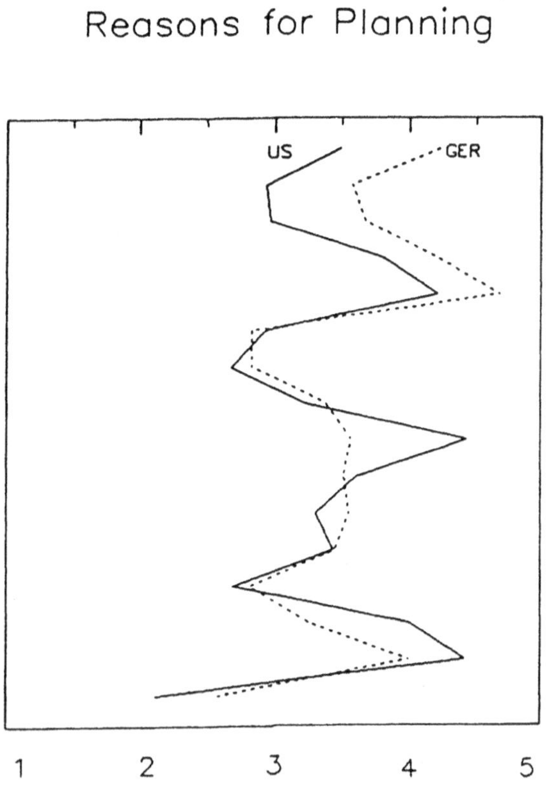

Figure 8.2 Reasons for Planning (US vs. German Top 300)

Although there were similarities on several items, US and German banks in the sample differ in the time frame of their strategic plans, the tasks line and staff managers perform have during planning, and in the reasons for strategic planning. The hypothesis of different planning systems is therefore supported.

8.22 US vs. German Planning Processes

The strategic planning process was depicted by its characteristics and activities performed. Both German and US banks put more emphasis on identifying the real future issues than on solving problems during the planning process, progress stepwise and not continuously, update the plans regularly, and regard planning as an opportunity for advancement and an element of variety on the job. German banks, however, are significantly more quantitative oriented during planning, with plans prepared by planning staff. US banks are significantly more dedicated to action and change during the planning process, the plans are prepared by line managers, intuition and reviews play a more important role, and managers derive individual bonuses from long-term bank performance. Eight out of 20 items show significant differences.

Variables	Mean US	Mean GER	Alpha
Define Issues	4,3	4,4	n.s.
Solve Problems	2,6	2,9	n.s.
Quantitative	2,1	2,8	,05
Project Oriented	2,7	3,2	n.s.
Action Oriented	4,1	3,5	,05
Change Oriented	3,9	3,4	,05
SW before OT	3,5	3,8	n.s.
OT before SW	3,8	4,0	n.s.
Consultants Solve	1,9	1,9	n.s.
Consultants Frame	2,2	1,7	n.s.
Bonus Plan	3,9	3,1	,03
No Updates	1,6	1,7	n.s.
Annual Cycle	4,3	3,8	,07
Staff Plans	1,6	3,4	,00
Line Plans	4,1	2,4	,00
Intuition	3,7	1,9	,03
Incremental	3,3	3,4	n.s.
Career	2,9	2,6	n.s.
Variety	3,3	3,1	n.s.
Well-Defined	2,1	2,6	n.s.

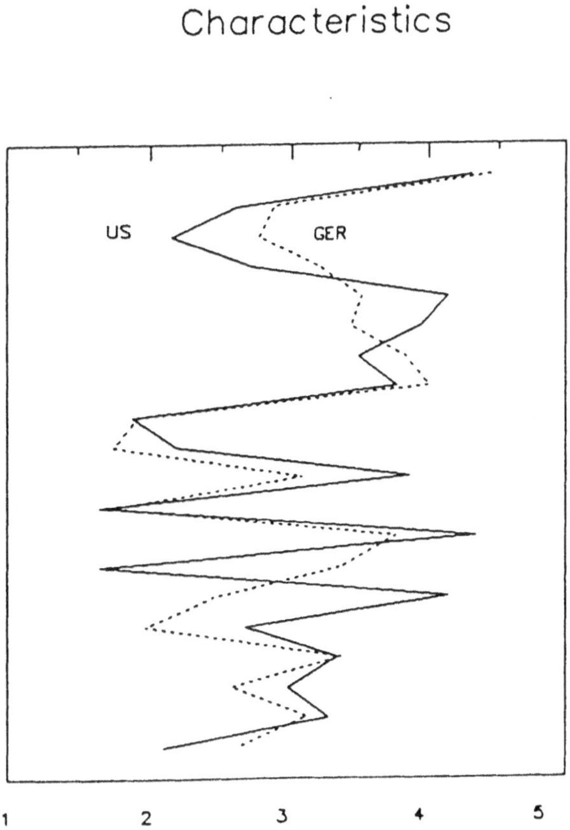

Figure 8.3 Process Characteristics (US vs German Top 300)

Environmental forecasting, analyzing strengths and weaknesses as well as problems and opportunities, developing new markets and addressing unresolved problems were the most important activities reported by both US and German bank managers. While mergers and acquisitions are important activities during strategic planning for US bank managers, they are significantly less undertaken by German bank managers. German banks conduct significantly more performance reviews against financial goals, and put more emphasis on forecasting the future of the bank under the present strategy than US banks.

Variables	Mean US	Mean GER	Alpha
Environmt. Forecasts	3,9	4,1	n.s.
SW-Analysis	4,3	4,6	n.s.
Extrapolate	3,5	4,5	,00
Issues	4,3	e,5	n.s.
Product Ventures	3,3	3,5	n.s.
M & As	3,9	2,3	,00
New Markets	3,9	3,7	n.s.
Tackle Problems	4,0	3,7	n.s.
Contingency	3,1	3,2	n.s.
Project Reviews	3,2	3,1	n.s.
Performance Reviews	3,2	4,0	,02

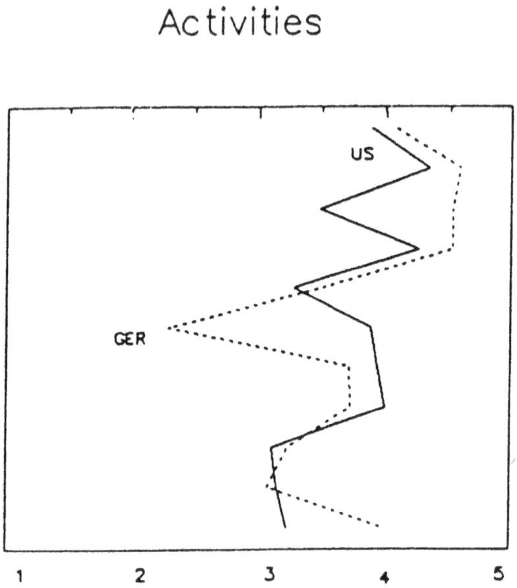

Figure 8.4 Process Activities (US vs. German Top 300)

The findings on planning process are mixed. Planning process characteristics and activities are similar in German and US banks. However, planning processes at German banks are significantly more quantitative, forecasting-driven, financial review-driven. US banks, on the other hand, also stress the importance of intuition and general reviews. In German banks, planning is a staff activity, while it is a line activity in US banks. Planning at US banks are more action-oriented, with individual bonuses tied to strategic accomplishments. The hypotheses of different planning processes is therefore supported.

8.23 US vs. German Planning Heuristics

In general, both German and US banks did not report major behavioral problems that arise from their strategic planning efforts. US banks were on both T-tests and Chi-Square tests significantly more concerned with managers who consider the purpose of planning to be the plan itself. Padding plans to avoid supervision, short-term orientation, and boredom with planning were more of a problem for US than for German banks; however, these items were only significant on the Chi-square tests.

Only one of 14 items on planning heuristics is significant on both t-tests and Chi-Square tests. The hypothesis with regard to differences in planning heuristics is therefore rejected.

Variables	Mean US	Mean GER	Alpha
Projections	2,8	3,3	n.s.
Bargaining	2,9	3,1	n.s.
Padding	3,2	2,6	* n.s.,06
Plan = End	3,1	2,3	,03
Resist Discipline	3,3	3,0	n.s.
Resist Change	3,3	3,1	n.s
Fear	2,8	2,9	n.s
Day-to-Day	3,4	2,9	* n.s.,04
Department	3,0	3,1	n.s
Expectation	3,0	3,2	n.s.
Compliance	2,9	2,9	n.s.
File	3,2	3,2	n.s.
Bored	2,9	2,7	* n.s.,07
Credibility	3,2	3,0	n.s.

* not significant with t-test; however, significant with X2-test.

Behavior/Heuristics

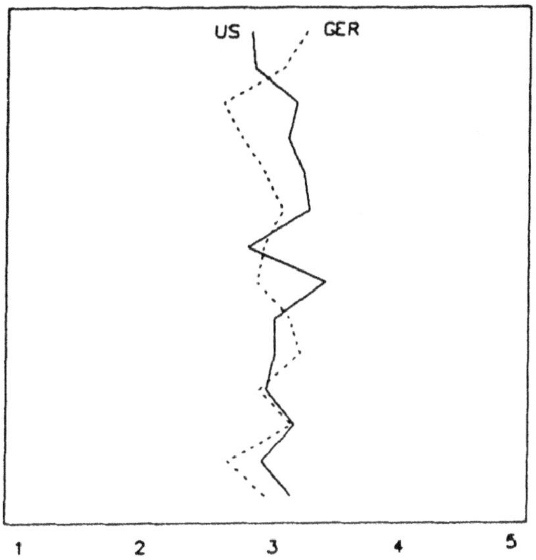

Figure 8.5 Planning Heuristics (US vs. German Top 300)

8.24 Summary

Questionnaire responses of German and US banks among the top 300 of the world were analyzed. While the hypotheses of different planning systems (time frames, reasons) and processes (characteristics, acts) were supported, this was not the case for the hypothesis on heuristics. Holding industry, size, and economic environment constant, it was however shown that planning systems and processes vary among cultures.

German bank planning systems are characterized by a higher concern for details, leaving planning to specialists (high uncertainty avoidance; Hofstede 1980:384). However, they apply longer time frames. In both countries, planning is a participative activity, either through joint decisions in executive meetings (USA) or through project teams (Germany), which refers to low power distance. US banks place emphasis on individual rewards and supervision (Individualism). US banks allow for intuition, and stress the broad clarification of goals, while German banks stress more objective, financial information sources (Organizational Learning). Findings on this dimension are contradictory to what was expected. Therefore, in general the culture-planning model was supported. The influence of planning heuristics and the organizational learning-dimension need additional specification, modeling and research.

Findings of a two-country comparison were reported above. Next, questionnaire items that showed significant differences are tested with a larger database to reconfirm the findings.

8.3 Ten-Country Group Comparison of Strategic Planning

In this section 286 responses from ten groups of countries are analyzed to learn if the variance between the country groups is larger than within the country groups. Less stringent non-parametric Kruskal-Wallis analysis of variance is cross-checked with more powerful f-test analysis of variance. Included are those items that showed significant in the above comparison of German/US responses among the top 300.

While some of the sample includes single country data (Austria, Italy, Japan, Canada), for the remaining countries regroupings were necessary. As was explained in the methodology chapter, country clusters were formed on the basis of cultural and economic considerations, holding constant for uncertainty avoidance, power distance, individualism, inflation rate, and gross national product per capita. This approach proved to be useful by Hofstede (1983b:49). Thereby, the following clusters were formed: France/Belgium, Britain/Ireland, Spain/Portugal, Australia/New Zealand, LatAm1 (responses from high inflation, middle power distance, middle individualism Latin American countries), and LatAm2 (middle inflation, high PD, low IDV).

8.31 Planning Systems

Banks in all ten country groups[59] prepare short-term plans. Most of them also have mid-term plans, with Canadian and British banks less prevalent. However, only 1/3 of the Italian, 1/2 of the Latin American and 2/3 of the Japanese banks in the sample prepare strategic plans, while about 85% of the banks in the other six countries do so.

Types of Plans	AUT	FRA/BEL	GBR/IRE	ITA	SPA/POR	AUL/NZL	JAP	LatAm1	LatAm2	CDN
Long-Range plan	77,3%	81,8%	89,5%	33,3%	88,2%	78,6%	61,5%	57,1%	50,0%	87,5%
Medium Range Plan	86,4%	100,0%	73,3%	93,8%	92,3%	93,3%	90,9%	95,2%	90,9%	76,9%
Short Term Plan	100,0%	100,0%	100,0%	95,2%	100,0%	100,0%	100,0%	100,0%	97,2%	100,0%

Table 8.4 Types of Plans Prepared (Ten-Country Comparison)

Short-term plans cover generally one year, with Japanese banks using half-year time horizons. With regard to medium range plans, these cover usually a time horizon of three years, while for Austrian and Italian banks the responses show four years. The time horizon of Japanese bank's plans is only about four years and thereby much shorter than at Austrian, Canadian, and British banks (5-7 years).

---

[59] For convenience, 'Country' is used for 'country cluster'.

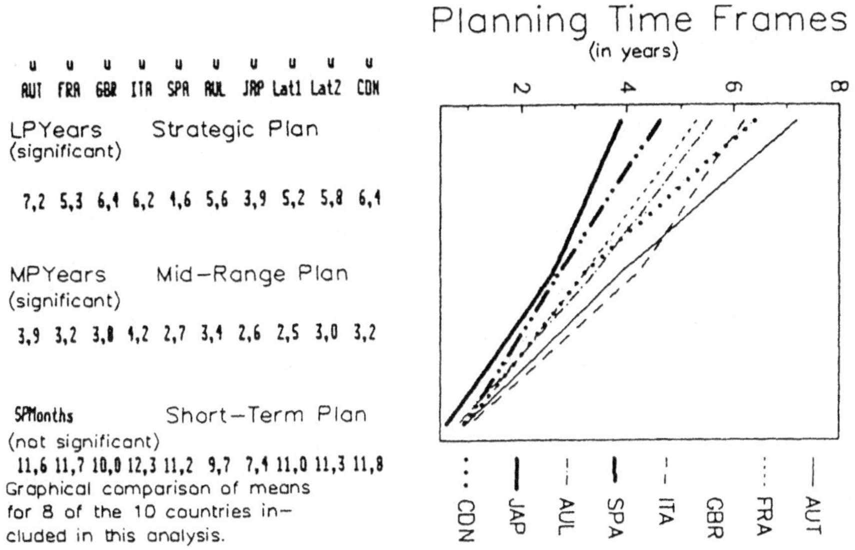

Figure 8.6 Plan's Time Frames (Ten-Country Comparison;[60]

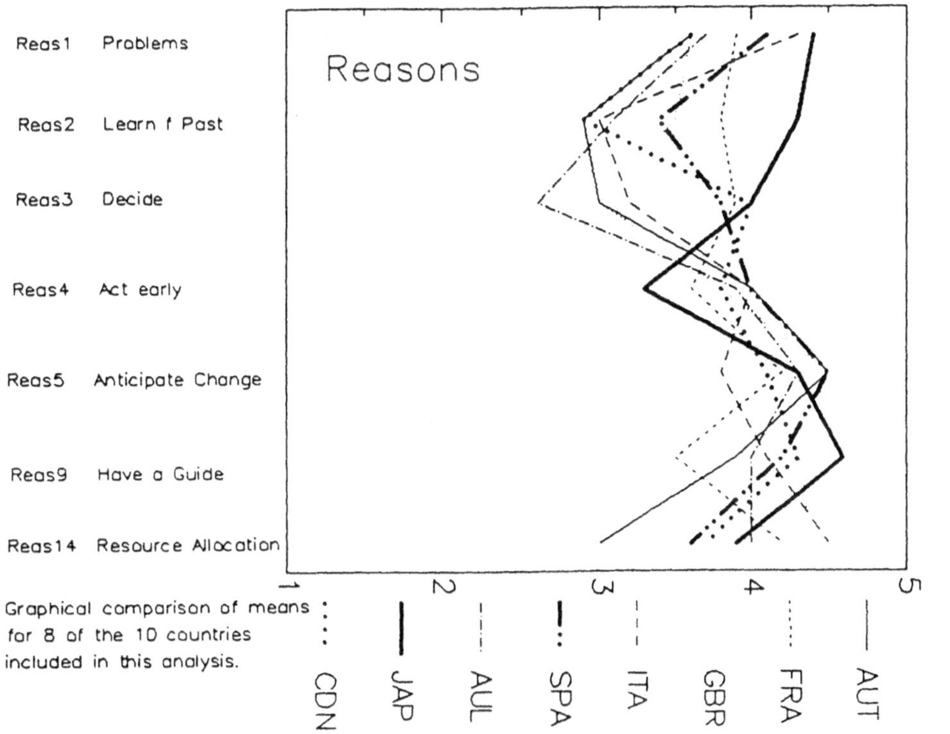

Figure 8.7 Reasons for Planning (Ten-Country Comparison)

[60] Due to technical limitations, for only eight of the ten countries the graphs are shown here.

All items on the reason-section in the questionnaire that were significant in the US/German comparison also were significant in this ten-country comparison. While learning from the past is not a very important reason to plan strategically for Canadian, Austrian and Italian banks, this is emphasized by French and especially by Japanese banks. Japanese, Canadian, French and Spanish banks stressed forecast-based decisions as reasons for planning. While taking actions at early stages in general is an important reason, this is not the case for Japanese banks. Anticipating change was no important reason for Italian banks, but for most banks in other countries. Having a plan as a guideline for the future was more important for Japanese than for other (especially the French) banks. While for Italian and British banks resource allocation is a major reasons, this is not the case for Austrian banks.

In general, the hypotheses that banks in different cultural environments create different planning systems is supported by the above data.

8.32 Planning Processes

Japanese and Italian banks are very much quantitatively oriented in their planning processes, while Spanish banks are not. British, Austrian, Canadian and Spanish banks are less action-oriented in

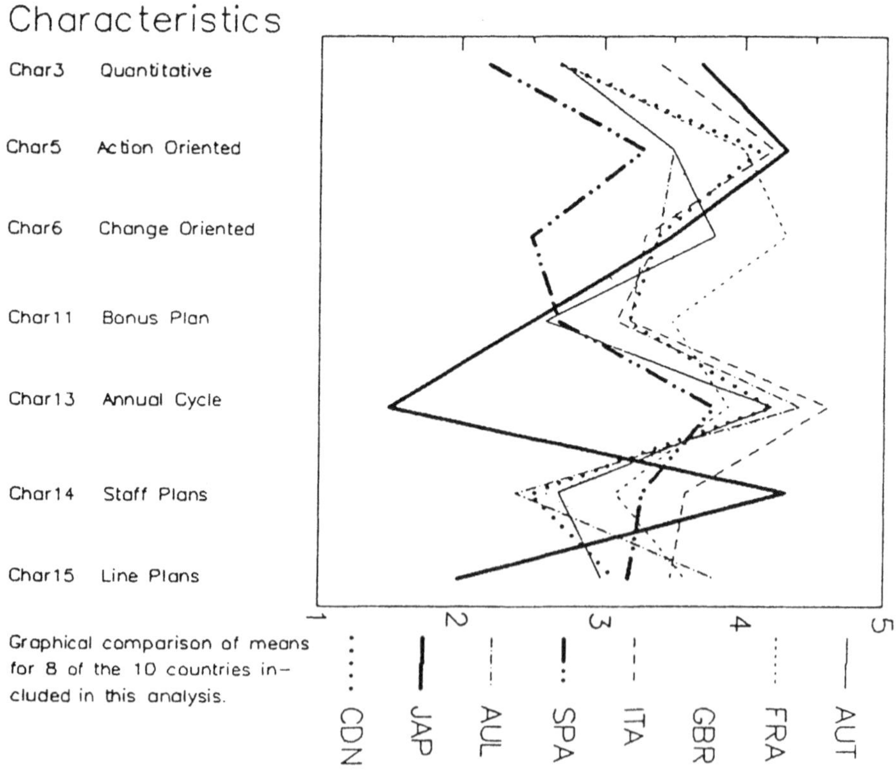

Figure 8.8 Planning Characteristics (Ten-Country Comparison)

the planning process than the other banks. French banks emphasizeand Latin American banks tie planning efforts to individual bonus change to a much larger extent than Spanish. While French, Britishplans, this is done less frequently at other banks. While most banks use annual planning cycles, the Japanese banks strongly rejected such annual revision. In Japanese and Latin American banks, planning is a staff function, not a line function. Spanish and Italian banks stress the involvement of both line and planning staff people. In Australian and British banks, planning is a line function, not performed by planning staff.

With regard to <u>activities</u>, Australian, British and Latin American banks stress the importance of forecasts in their planning efforts, while this is a lesser important activity for Italian banks. For Australian and British banks, mergers and acquisitions are part of the planning activities, while this is not the case for Austrian, Spanish and Canadian banks. For Japanese, Italian, Latin American and Austrian banks, performance reviews are important during the planning process. The hypotheses about the influence of culture on planning processes is therefore supported for both the process characteristics and the process activities.

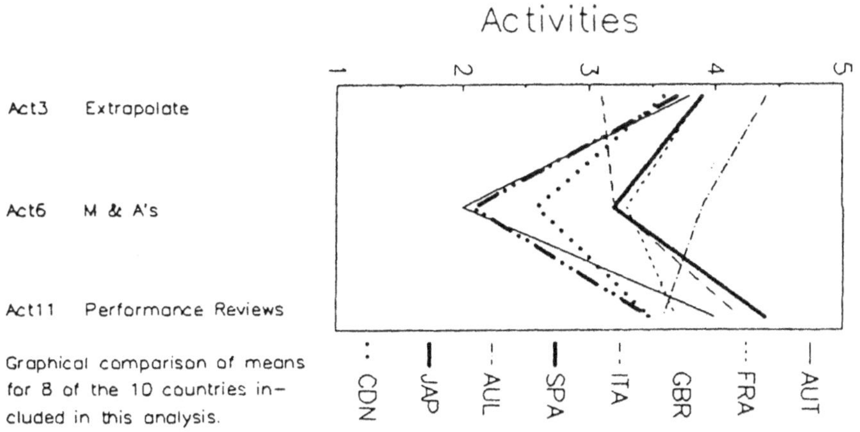

Figure 8.9 Planning Activities (Ten-Country Comparison)

8.33 Planning Heuristics

Japanese, Latin American and Italian banks were very much concerned with managers padding plans, while this was of lesser importance for other banks. Japanese, Spanish, Italian and Latin American banks had problems with managers that avoid thinking beyond short-run, operational activities, while this did not concern very much British, French, and Austrian banks. Managers being fed up with planning are of no concern to Austrian banks, while Italian, Spanish and Japanese report these heuristics.

The larger sample showed no significant difference on one of the items that were significant in the US/German comparison (Behav4, considering the purpose of planning to be the plan itself).

However, the other items were again significant. Therefore, there is some evidence supporting the hypothesis on cultural influences on heuristics.

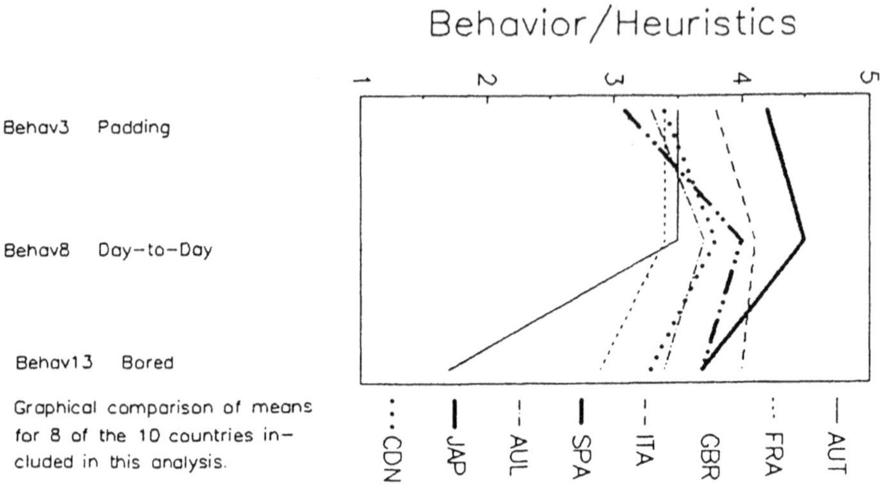

Figure 8.10 Planning Heuristics (Ten-Country Comparison)

8.34 Summary

In this section, the items that showed significant differences in the US/German comparison were cross-checked with a larger sample and a larger number of countries. All but three of the items which were significant in the US/German comparison again showed significant differences. Therefore, there is further support for the hypotheses of cultural influences on planning systems, heuristics, and processes.

8.4 Potential Contributions

While the above sections reported the findings from the empirical research that was undertaken, the following sections reviews the implications of the findings, the theoretical models that were developed and the practical descriptions of planning processes with regard to theory, methodology, and managerial practice.

8.41 Implications to Theory

Througout the preceding chapters, concepts of strategic planning were critically reviewed. Cultural metaphors that underly strategy and planning conceptions were explained and linked with general cultural influences on decision processes. Literature reviews with regard to the development and evolution of the concepts of strategy, planning, and decision making were provided and definitions that can serve as a basis for comparative planning studies were developed. Categorizations of strategic planning systems found in the literature were put in a comprehensive framework. Underlying cultural metaphors were emphasized and five archetypes of strategic planning systems were delineated. Thereby, testable propositions of the link between cultural dimensions and planning approaches were developed for further research, for example through giving direction to the interaction of dimensions and approaches as suggested below.

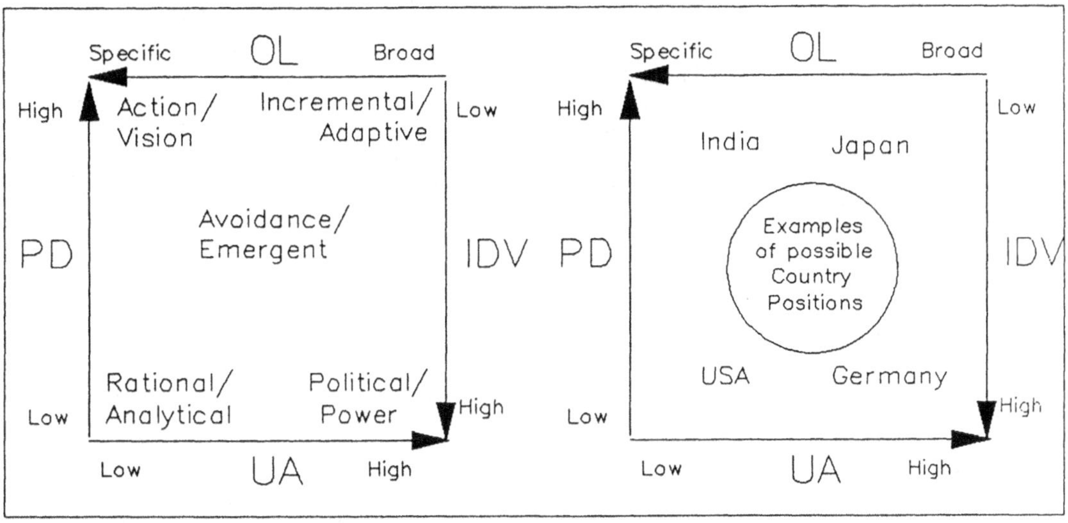

The figures above show suggested ways of interaction of cultural dimensions and planning approaches. Rankings of the countries were adapted from: Hofstede (1980); Sullivan/Nonaka (1986); Suzuki (1986); Orpen (1984); Horovitz (1980); Kagona et al (1986); Snodgrass et al (1984, 1986).

	USA	Japan	Germany	India
UA	Low	High	High	Low
PD	Low	High	Low	High
IDV	High	Low	High	Low
OL	Specific	Broad	Broad	Specific

Figure 8.11 Possible Links of Culture and Planning Approaches

Links were also established between cultural dimensions and planning heuristics. The interaction between societal culture and corporate culture was discussed. A number of testable hypotheses for further research can be derived from these concepts.

A link between contextual factors and planning practices was developed. Industry, economic, technical, legal, political and cultural influences on planning practices were discussed. Industry paradigms were reviewed and industry influences on planning practices were delineated. A link between a company's core product and influences on the planning process was developed.

A comprehensive model linking cultural dimensions (uncertainty avoidance, power distance, organizational learning, and individualism) and planning systems (time frames, reasons), heuristics, and processes (characteristics, acts) was developed and empirically tested. The review of alternative models linking culture and planning practices found in the literature as well as the combination of concepts from the fields of behavioral science and comparative research in the development of the Culture-

Planning Model here enriches the knowledge in both fields. The review of empirical studies on cultural influences on planning practices together with the research undertaken here and the theoretical models developed here serve as rich input for the further development of theoretical models and further empirical research. An empirical link could be established between culture and planning frameworks. So far only broad links between culture and management practices were established. Here an empirical link of culture with one single managerial task is established. This helps in crystallizing thoughts about the transferability of management practices from one culture to another, and in further research. It is argued, that planning systems and processes must fit to the societal culture in which a companies strategic planning efforts are embedded. Therefore, the transfer of strategic planning frameworks from one culture to another (e.g. from the US to Latin Amerika, or from Japan to Europe) has its limitations, if cultural fit is not considered.

8.42 Implications to Methodology

The methodological rigor of studies found in the literature about industry and cultural influences on planning systems was reviewed. Classification of such studies was developed that can be used for further methodological comparisons. Strengths and weaknesses of previous studies were shown. An empirical study of cultural influences on strategic planning practices was undertaken with careful attention to methodological rigor. A large database was created. Contextual factors (industry, size of the company, economic environment) were controlled for. Less stringent statistical tests (e.g. Chi-square) were always cross-checked with more powerful statistical tests (e.g. t-tests) to ensure for appropriate measurement. Concepts used were always operationalized and the direction of links between them was established. Thereby, a rich framework for further empirical research was developed.

8.43 Implications to Practice

Differences in militaristic and management concepts of strategy were characterized. It was argued that strategies can both be created deliberately, but can also gradually evolve. This is important to practicing managers in implementing strategic planning systems that fit to both the societal and corporate culture. The definitions that were developed for planning, strategy, and what planning canb't be, can assist practitioners in setting up planning systems. The evolutionary aspect of planning that was shown draws attention to the historical development of planning practices. The categorization of approaches towards planning systems that was developed can serve as a guideline for rethinking the adequacy of current planning practices. Both are important if practitioners want to change or redirect planning frameworks at their companies. Awareness about what can go wrong in planning, and knowledge about the underlying psychological and sociological reasons for planning problems and heuristics can aid in setting up and running planning systems.

The review of industry influences on planning practices will help bank managers to rethink the industry-wide accepted assumptions. The reviews of bank planning studies found in the literature can help practicing bank managers to evaluate their respective planning systems. The rich description of planning practices found in interviews with US banks can help practitioners to compare different approaches, systems and views. They thereby can learn how to improve their respective planning frameworks.

The link between culture and planning frameworks that was empirically proven draws awareness on the side of the manager to the transferability of planning systems from one culture to another and in that way can increase the effectiveness of planning and decrease the level of frustration with unfitted planning systems.

8.5 Summary and Conclusion

Before summing up this research, it is critical to clarify its philosophy. Emphasizing the cultural element in planning is no attempt to reduce all dissimilarities across companies to culture. However, the study questions the position of universal applicability and transferability of planning systems.

Chapter one introduces the reader to the combination of issues that are discussed throughout the book and explains its rationale. Chapter two highlights normative and empirical views of the planning process, while reviewing conceptualizations of "planning" and "strategy." The conclusion was drawn that military conceptions of strategy are culture-bound, that "strategy" should be seen as "pattern in the stream of actions and decisions," that planning is "a frame of action and decision making," and that the concept of "planning" itself is culture-bound.

In chapter three, the Culture-Planning Model was proposed to categorize planning process approaches. The goal was to describe the underlying cultural dimensions. The conclusion was drawn that Uncertainty Avoidance (UA), Organizational Learning (OL), Power Distance (PD), and Individualism (IDV) are useful discriminators to categorize planning approaches into Action/Vision, Avoidance/ Emergent, Incremental/Adaptive, Rational/Analytical, and Political/Power-models. It was argued that the adequacy of these approaches depends on the relative magnitude of the four cultural dimensions.

In chapter four, relevant heuristical influences on strategic decision processes and their sources were identified. The Culture-Planning Model was proposed to specify underlying characteristics and the influence of societal culture. The conclusion was drawn that heuristics are a natural part of planning, and that rationality and therefore heuristics are culture-bound. Depending on the relative magnitude of OL, IDV, PD, and UA, specific heuristics are more prone to take place during planning than others.

The specific goal of chapter fiver was to discuss to environmental influences on planning other than culture and to explore industry influences. Therefore, environmental constructs were reviewed. The banking industry was depicted by the characteristics of its services. Literature reviews were presented about influences of industry, company size, and economic, legal and technological environemts on planning. Specific attention was given to evidence from the banking industry. The conclusion was drawn that it is necessary to hold these factors constant in empirical research on planning practices. The core product and the service characteristics of banks were argued to influence planning. In the studies reviewed it was claimed that in comparison to other industries, bank planning still seems to be short-term; that banks have functional or departmental plans and lack truly strategic plans; that banks are more concerned with regulatory (accountancy) than customer issues, and that traditional (corporate) bank culture does not foster strategic thinking. However, due to methodological shortcomings, no coherent picture of bank planning emerged from the studies reviewed. Specifically, there is a lack of international comparisons of bank planning.

The goal of <u>chapter six</u> was to develop a framework for the examination of the impact of culture on the planning process. Cultural dimensions and constructs that are frequently used in the literature to describe cultural influences on managerial practices were reviewed. The conclusion was drawn that value and information processing dimensions can be integrated into Hofstede's (1980) definition of culture which was used here. From the review of theoretical conceptualizations of cultural influences on planning, the conclusion was drawn that a model is needed which is not restricted to either the control, implementation or formulation aspects of strategic planning; a model that does not rely on the phase theorem and is based on both organizational theory and findings from comparative management; one that includes both cultural values, cognition, and information processing perceptions and behavior; a model that uses an empirically derived framework and integrates theoretical concepts.

The Culture-Planning Model as developed throughout the chapters was summarized and explained. Three types of empirical studies on cultural influences on planning were reviewed: case studies, large-scale studies at multinational companies and in countries on different levels of development, and comparative planning studies in developed countries. The conclusion was drawn that for comparative planning studies the country level of development should be kept stable, that companies should be compared in their respective home countries, and that it is necessary to control for market, industry, economic, legal, and political influences. In general, the findings of the comparative studies reviewed reconfirm the propositions developed in the Culture-Planning model.

<u>Chapter seven</u> described research design and methodology. Survey instruments, as well as sample population were discussed. For the questionnaires, data handling and chosen statistical procedures and tools were explained. Methodological problems were raised.

<u>Chapter eight</u> reported the findings from the empirical studies.

From the interviews with US banks the conclusion was drawn that the distinction between planning systems (time frame, reasons), heuristics (behavior) and processes (characteristics, acts) proved quite useful to describe and analyze planning practices. The planning frameworks of the 14 banks interviewed were split between those resembling high uncertainty avoidance (formal, highly structured activities, short time horizons, staff-driven, past/present-orientation etc.), and those resembling low uncertainty avoidance (issue-oriented, informal, line-driven). In general, power distance was low (decentralization, two-way communication, bottom-up planning). However, planning was also frequently used for supervisory purposes. Emphasis is put on tasks and individual initiative (high individualism). The use of quantitative, specific and objective information sources with a clear focus on relevant issues was prevalent (specific organizational learning).

A comparison of questionnaire responses from US and German banks, holding constant bank size and environmental facets, constituted the second part of the final chapter. The hypotheses of cultural influences on strategic planning systems (time frames, reasons) and processes (characteristics, activities) were supported, while no significant cultural influence on planning heuristics was found. The same conclusions were drawn from a ten-country-comparison. Holding industry, company size, level of economic development, and level of regulatory changes constant, it was shown that planning systems and process do vary among cultures. Finally, potential contributions to theory and practice were explored. Recommendations for further research were established.

JOURNAL ABBREVIATIONS

AME	Academy of Management Executive
AMJ	Academy of Management Journal
AMR	Academy of Management Review
APJM	Asia Pacific Journal of Management
ASQ	Administrative Science Quarterly
BMM	Bankers Monthly Magazine
HBR	Harvard Business Review
ISMO	International Studies of Management & Organization
JCCP	Journal of Cross-Cultural Psychology
JIBS	Journal of International Business Studies
JBR	Journal of Bank Research
JBS	Journal of Business Strategy
JRB	Journal of Retail Banking
JM	Journal of Management
JMS	Journal of Management Studies
LRP	Long Range Planning
MIR	Management International Review
MP	Managerial Planning
MS	Management Science
ÖBA	Österreichisches Bank-Archiv
SMJ	Strategic Management Journal

REFERENCES

Ackoff, Russel (1971): Towards a System of Systems Concepts. In: MS, 17, 2, pp. 661-671.

Ackoff, Russel (1974): Redesigning the Future. Wiley, New York.

Ackoff, Russel (1981): On the Use of Models in Corporate Planning. In: SMJ, 2, pp. 353-359.

Adler, Nancy (1983): A Typology of Management Studies Involving Culture. In: JIBS, 14, 3, pp. 29-47.

Adler, Nancy (1984): Understanding the Ways of Understanding. Cross-Cultural Management Methodology Reviewd. In: Farmer, Richard (ed): Advances in International Comparative Management, vol 1. JAI Press, Greenwich, CT 1984, pp. 31-67.

Adler, Nancy (1986): International Dimensions of Organizational Behavior. Kent Publ., Boston, MA 1986.

Adler, Nancy / Doktor, Robert / Redding, Gordon (1986): From the Atlantic to the Pacific Century: Cross-Cultural Management Reviewed. In: JM, 3, pp. 75-68.

Adler, Nancy / Selnicek, M. (1986): Is 'Organizational Culture' Culture Bound? In: Human Resources Management, 25, 1, pp. 73-90.

Ajiferuke, M. / Boddewyn, James (1970): Culture and Other 'Explanatory' Variables in Comparative Management Studies. In: AMJ, 12, 2, pp. 153-163.

Al-Bazzaz, Shawki / Grinyer, Peter (1980): How Planning Works in Practice - A Survey of 48 U.K. Companies. In: LRP, 13, 4, pp. 30-42.

Albrecht, Karl / Zemke, Ron (1985): Service America. Dow Jones-Irwin, Homewood, IL 1985.

Aldrich, Howard (1979): Organizations and Environments. Prentice-Hall, Englewood Cliffs, NJ 1979.

Allen, Gordon (1981): The Japanese Economy. St. Martin's Press, New York 1981.

Allison, Graham (1971): Essence of Decision. Little, Brown & Co., Boston, MA, 1971.

Amey, Lloyd (1986): Corporate Planning. A Systems View. Praeger, NY 1986.

Anderson, Carl / Paine, Frank (1975): Managerial Perceptions and Strategic Behavior. In: AMJ, 17, pp. 811-823.

Andrews, Kenneth (1980): The Concept of Corporate Strategy., Irwin, Homewood, IL, revised ed, 1980.

Ansoff, Igor (1969): Toward a Strategic Theory of the Firm. In Ansoff, Igor (ed): Business Strategy. Penguin Books, Harmondsworth, Middlesex, GB 1969, pp. 7-40.

Ansoff, Igor (1977): The State of Practice in Planning Systems. In: Sloan Management Review, 18, 2, pp. 1-24.

Ansoff, Igor (1979): Strategic Management. John Wiley & Sons, New York 1979.

Ansoff, Igor (1980): Strategic Issue Management. In: SMJ, 1, 2, pp. 131-148.

Ansoff, Igor (1983): Corporate Capability for Managing Change. In: Advances in Strategic Management, vol 2. JAI Press, New York 1983.

Ansoff, Igor (1984): Implanting Strategic Management. Prentice Hall, Englewood Cliffs, NJ 1984.

Anthony, Roger (1965): Planning and Control Systems, Division Research, Harvard Business School, Boston, MA 1965.
Argyris, Chris (1977): Double Loop Learning in Organizations. In: HBR, 55, 5, pp. 75-86.
Argyris, Chris (1985): Strategy, Change, and Defensive Routines. Pitman, Boston, MA 1985.
Argyris, Chris / Schön, D.A. (1978): Organizational Learning. Addison-Welsley, Reading, MA, 1978.
Agryris, Chris / Schön, D.A. (1980): Theory in Practice: Increasing Professional Effectiveness. Jossey-Bass, San Francisco, CA 1980.
Armstrong, James (1982): The Value of Formal Planning for Strategic Decisions. Review of Emperical Research. In: SMJ, 3, pp. 197-211.
Arndt, H.W. (1988): Comparative Advantage in Trade in Financial Services. In: Banca Nazionale del Lavoro Quarterly Review, 164, 1, pp. 61-78.
Aron, Rene (1976): Penser la Guerre, Clausewitz. Gallimard, Paris, France 1976.
Aronson, Elliot (1984): The Social Animal. Freeman & Co, New York, 4th ed. 1984.
Astley, Graham / Fombrun, Charles (1983): Collective Strategy: Social Ecology of Organizational Environments. In: AMR, 8, 4, pp. 576-587.
Axelrod, R. (1976): Structure of Decision: The Cognitive Maps of Political Elites. Princeton Univ. Press., Princeton, NJ, 1976.
Ayal, Igal / Hornik, Jacob (1986): Foreign Source Effects on Response Behavior in Cross-National Mail Surveys. In: International Journal of Research in Marketing, 3, 3, pp. 157-167.
Baird, Ina / Thomas, Howard (1985): Towad a Contingency Model of Strategic Risk Taking. In: AMR, 10, 2, pp. 230-243.
Bamberger, Ines (1977): Grundprobleme und Forschungsansätze der langfristigen Zielplanung. In: Zeitschrift für Organisation, 46, 3, pp. 91-99.
Die Bank (1987): Die 50 grössten Institutsgruppen. In: Die Bank, 11/1987, pp. 637-639.
The Banker (1986a): Top 500 by Country. In: The Banker (London), Blanden, Michael / Jones, Colin (researchers), 136, 727, pp. 85-112.
The Banker (1986b): Top 100 Latin American Banks by Country. In: The Banker (London). Nisse, Jason (researcher), 136, 730, pp. 89-91.
The Banker (1987a): Top 500 by Country. In: The Banker (London), Blanden, Michael / Jones, Colin (researchers), 137, 732, pp. 81-109.
The Banker (1987b): Top 100 Latin American Banks by Country. In: The Banker (London). No researcher given, 137, 742, pp. 61-64.
The Banker (1987c): Top 200 Asian Banks by Country. In: The Banker (London). Colin Jones (researcher). 137, 741, pp. 103-107.
The Banker (1988a): Top 500 by Country. In: The Banker (London), Blanden, Michael/ Jones, Colin (researchers), 138, 749, pp. 113-130.
The Banker (1988b): Top 500 by Country. US Bank Mergers 1987. In: The Banker (London), 138, 749, p. 111.

The Banker (1988c): Latin America - Top 100. Lyon, Simon (Researcher). In: The Banker (London), 138, 752, pp. 125-132.
The Banker (1988d): Europe - Top 300. Jones, Colin (Researcher). In: The Banker (London), 138, 752, pp. 59-77.
The Banker (1988e): Asia - Top 200. McDougall, Rosamund (Researcher). In: The Banker (London), 138, 751, pp. 73-98.
The Banker (1988f): Top 100 Japanese Banks. Lyon, Simon (Researcher). In: The Banker (London), 138, 745, pp. 57-61.
Bankers' Almanac (1985a): The Bankers' Almanac World Ranking. Thomas Skinner Directories, West Sussex, GB, 1st ed. 1985.
Bankers' Almanac (1985b): The Bankers' Almanac and Yearbook 1985. Vol 1, Banks. Thomas Skinner Directories, Business Press Int'l, GB.
Bankers' Almanac (1988): The Bankers' Almanac World Ranking 1988. Thomas Skinner Directories, West Sussex, GB.
Barnes, James (1984): Cognitive Biases and Their Impact on Strategic Planning. In: SMJ, 5, pp. 129-137.
Bartlett, Sarah (1986): Bank Scoreboard. A Solid Year, with Regionals Leading the Way. In: Business Week, US edition, April 7, 1986, pp. 65-73.
Bauer, Ron / Gergen, Kirk (1968): The Study of Policy Formation. Free Press, New York 1968.
Baumol, William (1959): Business Behavior, Value and Growth. Harcourt Jovanovich, New York 1959.
Bazerman, Max (1986): Judgment in Managerial Decision Making. John Wiley & Sons, New York 1986.
Bazzaz, Shawki / Grinyer, Peter (1981): Corporate Planning in the U.K.: The State of the Art in the 70s. In: SMJ, 2, pp. 155-168.
Beach, Lee Roy / Smith, Barbara / Lundell, James / Mitchell, Terence (1988): Image Theory: Descriptive Sufficiency of a Simple Rule for the Compatibility Test. In: Journal of Behavioral Decision Making, 1, 1, pp. 17-28.
Beck, Robert (1987): Visions, Values, and Strategies: Changing Attitudes and Culture. In: AME, 1, 1, pp. 33-41.
Bent, Barbara / Halliday, Lisa / Swain, Alan (1987): The World's Largest Banks. In: Institutional Investor, July 1987, pp. 143-170.
Bertalanffy, Ludwig von (1950): The Theory of Open Systems in Physics and Biology. In: Science, pp. 23-29.
Berthel, Jürgen / Möws, Dieter (1970): Information und Planung in industriellen Unternehmenungen. Eine empirische Studie. Department for Industrial Research, Berlin Free University, FRG 1970.
Bettinger, Cass (1986): The Elements of Effective Planning. In: The Bankers Magazine, 169, 2, pp. 17-24.
Bhagat, Rabi (1977): Cognitive Complexity, Temporal Orientation and Managerial Effectiveness. A Theoretical and Empirical Investigation. Unpublished Ph.D. dissertation, University of Illinois at Urbana-Champaign, U.S.A., 1977.
Bhide, Amar (1986): Hustle as Strategy. In: HBR, 64, 5, pp. 59-65.
Bienkowski, John (1985): The Banks That Manage Technology. In: Bankers Monthly Magazine, May 15, 1985, pp. 3-29.
Bigler, William (1986): The Strategy-Culture Linkage: A Procedural Guide. Paper, presented at the 1986 Annual Meeting of the Academy of Management, Chicago, Aug. 1986.

Birnbaum, Philipp / Wong, Gilbert (1985): Organizational Structure of Multinational Banks in Hong Kong from a Culture-Free Perspective. In: ASQ, 30, pp. 267-277.

Blanden, Michael (1987): The Risen Sun, Top 500 Country Tables. In: The Banker (London), 137, 739, pp. 74-78.

Blandenl, Michael (1988): Long Live the Regionals. In: The Banker (London), 138, 751, p. 107.

Blanden, Michael / Jones, Colin (1988): Top 500 Banks. Down, But By No Means Out. In: The Banker (London), 138, 751, pp. 56-61.

Blank, Jonas / Gustke, Constance (1988): The 100 Biggest Banks. In: Fortune International, 118, 3, pp. D41-D45.

Bologna, Jack (1980): Why Managers Resist Planning. In: MP, 28, 4, pp. 23-25.

Bonelli, Robert (1987): Corporate Planning: A Growing Role Among The Regionals. In: The Bankers Magazine, July-Aug. 1987, pp. 43-49.

Bosland, Nico (1985): An Evaluation of Replication Studies Using the Value Survey Module. IRIC Institute for Research on Intercultural Cooperation, Working Paper 85-2, June 1985.

Boulding, K.E. (1956): General Systems Theory - The Skeleton of Science. In: MS, 2, pp. 197-208.

Boulton, William / Lindsay, William / Franklin, Stephen / Rue, Leslie (1982a): Strategic Planning: Determining the Impact of Environmental Characteristics and Uncertainty. In: AMJ, 25, 3, pp. 500-509.

Boulton, William / Lindsay, William / Franklin, Stephen / Rue, Leslie (1982b): How Are Companies Planning Now - A Survey. In: LRP, 15, 1, pp. 82-86.

Bourgeois, L.J. (1980): Strategy and Environment: A Conceptual Integration. In: AMR, 5, pp. 25-39.

Bourgeois, L.J. (1984): Strategic Management and Determinism. In: AMR, 9, 4, pp. 586-596.

Bourgeois, L.J. / Brodwin, David (1984): Strategic Implementation: Five Approaches to an Elusive Phenomenon. In: SMJ, 5, pp. 241-264.

Bracker, Jeffrey (1980): The Historical Development of the Strategic Management Concept. In: AMR, 5, 2, pp. 219-224.

Bradley, J.W. / Korn, D.H. Korn (1984): Constituencies, Conflict, and Cost-Benefit Analysis as Factors in Acquisition Strategy. In: Hax, A. (ed): Readings on Strategic Management. Ballinger Publ. Co., Cambridge, MA 1984, pp. 203-216.

Brislin, Richard (1980): Translation and Content Analysis of Oral and Written Material. In: Triandis, Harry / Berry, J.W. (1980): Handbook of Cross-Cultural Psychology. vol. 2,, Allyn & Bacon, Boston, MA, pp. 389-444.

Brockner, Joel / Rubin, Jeffrey / Land, Elaine (1981): Face-Saving and Entrapment. In: Journal of Experimental Social Psychology, 17, pp. 68-79.

Bröker, Günther (1986): Strukturwandel im Bankwesen - ein internationaler Ueberblick. In: ÖBA, March 1986, pp. 67-82.

Brunsson, Nils (1982): The Irrationality of Actions and Action Rationality: Decisions, Ideologies and Organizational Actions. In: JMS, 19, 1, 1982, pp. 29-44.

Buchholz, Rogene (1986): Business. Implications for Management and Strategy Formulation. Prentice Hall, Englewood-Cliffs, NJ, 2nd ed 1986.

Burgelman, Robert (1983): Corporate Entrepreneurship and Strategic Management: Insights from a process Study. In: MS, 29, pp. 1349-1364.
Burgelman, Robert (1985): Applying the Methodology of Grounded Theorizing in Strategic Management: A Summary of Recent Findings and Their Implications. In: Advances in Strategic Management, Vol 3, JAI Press, 1985, pp. 83-99,
Burr, Lawrence (1987): Australian Banking. The Foreigners Grab Market Share. In: Australian Business, Sept. 2, 1987, pp. 79-81.
Business Week (1977): A Painful Job: Turning Bankers Into Managers. In: Business Week, US ed., March 7, 1977, pp. 49-50.
Business Week (1984): The New Breed of Strategic Planner. Number-Crunching Professionals are Giving Way to Line Managers. Cover Story. In: Business Week, US ed., Sept 17, 1984, pp. 62-66.
Business Week (1988a): The Top 1000 U.S. Companies Ranked by Industry. In: Business Week, special issue, US ed., April 15, 1988, pp. 234-238.
Business Week (1988b): The Worlds' Top 200 Banks. Glasgall, William (Researcher). In: Business Week, International Ed., June 27, 1988, pp. 58-65.
Business Week (1988c): Bank Scoreboard. Miller, Frederick (Researcher). In: Business Week, US ed., April 4, 1988, pp. 92-99.
Butler, Richard / Astley, Graham / Hickson, David / Malloroy, Geoffrey / Wilson, David (1979): Strategic Decision-Making: Concepts of Content and Process. In: ISMO, 9, 4, pp. 5-36.
Buzzel, Robert / Gale, Bradley (1987): The PIMS Principles. Linking Strategy to Performance. Free Press, New York 1987.
Camillus, John (1975): Evaluating the Benefits of Formal Planning Systems. In: LRP, June, pp. 33-40.
Camillus, John (1982): Reconciling Logical Incrementalism and Synoptic Formalism - An Integrated Approach to Designing Strategic Planning Processes. In: SMJ, 3, pp. 277-283.
Campbell, Donald (1988): Task Complexity: A Review and Analysis. In: AMR, 13, 1, pp. 40-52.
Candell, Gregory / Hulin, Charles (1986): Cross-Language and Cross-Cultural Comparisions in Scale Translations. Independent Sources of Information About Item Nonequivalence. In: JCCP, 17, 4, pp. 417-440.
Canon, Thomas (1968): Business Strategy and Policy. Harcourt Brace Jovanovich, New York 1968.
Capon, Neol / Christodolou, Chris / Farley, John / Hulbert, James (1984): A Comparison of Corporate Planning Practice in American and Australian Manufacturing Companies. In: JIBS, 15, 2, pp. 41-55.
Capon, Noel / Christodolou, Chris / Farlye, John / Hulbert, James (1987): A Comparative Analysis of The Strategy and Structure of United States and Australian Corporations. In: JIBS, 18, 1, pp. 51-74.
Capon, Noel / Farley, John / Hulbert, James (1980): International Diffusion of Corporate and Strategic Planning Practices. In: Columbia Journal of World Business, 15, 3, pp. 5-13.
Carman, James / Langeard, Eric (1980): Growth Strategies for Service Firms. In: SMJ, 1, pp. 7-22.

Cauwenbergh, Andre van / Cool, Karel (1982): Strategic Management in a New Framwork. In: SMJ, 3, pp. 245-264.
Chaffee, Ellen (1985): Three Models of Strategy. In: AMR, 10, 1, 1985, pp. 89-98.
Chakravarthy, Belaji (1986): Measuring Strategic Performance. In: SMJ, 7, pp. 437-458.
Chakravarthy, Belaji / Lorange, Peter (1984): Managing Strategic Adaption: Options in Administrative Systems Design. In: Hax, A. (ed): Readings in Strategic Management. Ballinger Publ, Co., Cambridge, MA 1984, pp. 35-48.
Chandler, Alfred (1962): Strategy and Structure: Chapters in the History of American Industrial Enterprise, The MIT Press, Cambridge, MA 1962.
Channon, Derek (1977): Strategy Formulation As An Analytical Process. In: ISMO. 2, pp. 41-57.
Channon, Derek (1986): Bank Strategic Management and Marketing. J. Wiley & Sons, Chichester, GB 1986.
Chase, Richard / Erikson, Warren (1988): The Service Factory. In: AME, 2, 3, pp. 191-196.
Child, John (1972): Organizational Structure, Environment and Performance: The Role of Strategic Choice. In: Sociology, 6, pp. 2-22.
Child, John (1981): Culture, Contingency and Capitalism in the Cross-National Study of Organizations. In: Cummings, L.L. / Staw, B.M. (eds): Research in Organizational Behavior. JAI Press, Greenwich, CT 1981, pp. 303-356.
Child, John / Francis, Arthur (1977): Strategy Formulation as a Structured Process. In: ISMO, 7, 2, Summer 1977, pp. 110-126.
Chinn, Warren / Murasawa, Yoshihisa / Vandenbrink, John (1986): Strategic Planning: A View From Japan. In: Gardner, James / Rachlin, Robert / Seeny, Allen (eds): Handbook of Strategic Planning. John Wiley, NY 1986, pp. 7.1-7.17.
Chinta, Ravi / Jenster, Per / King, William (1987): Functions for Strategic Planners. In: King, William / Clelland David (1987, eds.): Strategic Planning and Management Handbook. Van Nostrand Reinhold Co., NY 1987.
Christodolou, Chris (1984): Strategic Planning by Selected Australian Organizations. Published doctoral dissertation, Monash University, Australia, 1984.
Christodolou, Chris (1986): The Impact of Home Office Culture on Subsidiary Strategic Planning. Paper, presented at the 6th Annual Strategic Management Society Conference, Singapore, Oct. 1986.
Christodolou, Chris (1988): Australian Industry: Sophisticated Planning and Weak R & D? In: LRP, 21, 1, pp. 82-89.
Churchman, C.W. (1971): The Design of Inquiry Systems. Basic Books, New York.
Churchill, Gilbert (1987): Marketing Research. Dryden Press, Chicago, IL, 4th ed. 1987.
Clausewitz, Claus von (1918): On War. Dutton, London, GB 1918; German reprint (1980): Vom Kriege. Reinbeck, FRG 1980.
Clement, Werner / Lukesch, D. (1981): Allgemeine Wirtschaftspolitik. Vol. 1, HWU, Vienna University of Economics, Vienna, Austria, reprint, 1981.
Cohen, Kalman / Cyert, Richard (1973): Strategy Formulation, Implementation and Monitoring. In: Journal of Business, July 1973, pp. 349-367.

Cohen, Michael / March, James / Olsen, Johan (1972): A Gargage Can Model of Organizational Choice. In: ASQ, 17, pp. 1-25.
Conlon, Edward / Leatherwood, Marya (1986): Sunk Costs and Financial Decision Making: A Review of the Behavioral Literature. BEBR Faculty Working Paper No. 1287, University of Illinois at Urbana-Champaign, USA, Sept. 1986.
Corrigan, Gerald (1987): A Perspective on the Globalization of Financial Markets and Institutions. In: Quarterly Review of the Federal Reserve Bank of New York, 12, Spring 1987, pp. 1-9.
Cowan, David (1986): Developing a Process Model of Problem Recognition. In: AMR, 11, 4, pp, 763-776.
Csath, Magdolna (1989): Corporate Planning in Hungarian Companies. In: LRP, 22, 116, pp. 89-98.
Cyert, Richard / March, James (1963): A Behavioral Theory of the Firm. Englewood Cliffs, NJ 1963.
Daft, Richard / Weick, Karl (1984): Toward a Model Organizations as Interpretation Systems. In: AMR, 9, 2, pp. 284-295.
Daft, Richard / Steers, Richard (1986): Organizations. A Micro/ Macro Approach, Scott. Foresman & Co., Glenview, IL, 1986.
Dalby, Homer (1986): Planning on Both Sides of the Atlantic. In: The Bankers Magazine, 169, 2, pp. 33-46.
Daneke, Gegory / Steiss, Alan (1979): Policy Analysis: The Undisciplined Discipline. In: International Journal of Public Administration, 1, 1, pp. 95-113.
Das, Hari (1983): Qualitative Research in Organizational Behavior. In: JMS, 20, 3, pp. 301-314.
Das, T.K. (1987): Strategic Planning and Individual Temporal Orientation. In: SMJ, 8, pp. 203-209.
Davidson, William (1982): Global Strategic Management. Wiley, New York 1982.
Davis, Steven (1985): Excellence in Banking. MacMillan, New York 1985.
Deal, Terrence / Kennedy, Allen (1982): Corporate Cultures. Addison-Wesley, Reading, MA, 1982.
Degenhart, Heinrich (1983): Strategische Unternehmensführung in Kreditinstituten: Schlüssel zur Zukunftsbewältigung? In: ÖBA, 31, 7, pp. 251-265.
Denning, B.W. (1971): Corporate Planning, McGraw Hill, London, GB 1971.
Denzin, Norman (1978): The Research Act. Mc Graw Hill, N.Y, 2nd ed. 1978.
Dess, Gregory / Beard, Donald (1984): Dimensions of Organizational Task Environments. In: ASQ, 29, pp. 52-73.
Dess, Gregory / Davis, Peter (1984): Porter's (1980) Generic Strategies as Determinants of Strategic Group Membership and Organizational Performance. In: AMJ, 27, 3, pp, 467-488.
Dewey, John (1933): How We Think. D.C. Heath, Boston, MA, new ed. 1933.
Diller, Hermann (1980): Marketingplanung. Vahlen Verlag, Munich, FRG 1980.
DiMaggio, Paul / Powell, Walter (1983): The Iron Cage Revisited: Institutional Isomorphism and Collective Rationality in Organizational Fields. In: American Sociaological Review, 48, pp. 147-160.

Doktor, Robert (1983): Some Tentative Comments on Japanese and American Decison Making. In: Decision Sciences, 14, 4, pp. 607-615.
Donnelly, James / Berry, Leonard / Thomphson, Thomas (1985): Marketing Financial Services. A Strategic Vision. Dow Jones Irwin, Homewood, IL 1985.
Downey, Kirk / Ireland, Duane (1979): Quantitative Versus Qualitative: Environmental Assessment in Organizational Studies. In: ASQ, 14, pp. 630-637.
Downs, Anthony (1967): The Life Cycle of Bureaus. Reprinted in: Shafritz, Jay / Hyde, Albert (1978, eds): Classics of Public Administration. Moore Publ. Co., Oak Park, IL 1978.
Doz, Yves (1980): Strategic Management in Multinational Companies. In: Sloan Management Review. Winter 1980, pp. 27-46.
Drucker, Peter (1971): What We Can Learn From Japanese Management. In: HBR, 49, 3, pp. 110-122.
Duhaime, Irene / Grant, John (1984): Factors Influencing Divestment Decison-Making: Evidence from a Field Study. In: SMJ, 5, pp. 301-318.
Duhaime, Irene / Schwenk, Charles (1985): Conjectures on Cognitive Simplification in Acquisition and Divestment Decision Making. In: AMR, 10, 2, pp. 287-295.
Dunbar, Roger / Dutton, John (1986): Policy-Making Perspectives: Contrasts Between Problem-Setting and Problem-Solving. Paper presented at the 1986 Annual Meeting of the Academy of Management, Chicago, Aug. 1986.
Duncan, Robert / Weiss, Andrew (1979): Organizational Learning: Implications for Organizational Design. In Staw, B. (ed), Research in Organizational Behavior. Vol. 1, JAI Press, Greenwich, CT, 1979, pp. 75-123.
Dunphy, Dexter (1987): Convergence/Divergence: A Temporal Review of the Japanese Enterprise and Its Management. In: AMR, 12, 3, pp. 445-459.
Durstberger, Herbert (1985): Die Strategische Planung bei US-Banken. In: Die Bank, 2/1985, pp. 69-72.
Durstberger, Herbert (1987): Die Strategische Planung bei US-Banken. In: Congena (ed): Bank-Entwicklung, Gabler, Wiesbaden, FRG 1987, pp. 121-132.
Dutton, Jane / Fahey, Liam / Narayanan, V. K. (1983): Toward Understanding Strategic Issue Diagnosis. In: SMJ, 4, pp. 307-323.
Dutton, Jane / Ottensmeyer, Edward (1987): Strategic Issue Management Systems: Forms, Functions, and Contexts. In: AMR, 12, 2, pp. 355-365.
Earl, Peter (1984): The Corporate Imagination. Sharpe Inc., New York, 1984.
Eckhardt, Arndt (1979): Strategien der organisatorischen Gestaltung. Konzeptionelle und empirische Grundlagen der Gestaltungstheorie, Frankfurt, FRG 1979.
Le Nouvel Economiste (1987): Etablissements de Credit. In: Le Nouvel Economiste Special 5000, Novembre 1987, pp. 272-273.
Economist Intelligence Service (1988): International Economic Appraisal Service. Level 1 Country Tables Statistical Information. Economist Intelligence Service, London, GB,Feb. 1988.

Edwards, John (1977): Strategy Formulation as a Stylistic Process. In: ISMO, 7, 2, pp. 13-27.
Edwards, Raoul (1987): Measuring Performance. In: The United States Banker, 38, 7, July 1987, pp. 34-56.
Eilon, Samuel (1985): Editorial. Structuring Unstructured Decisions. In: Omega, 13, 5, pp. 369-377.
Einhorn, Hillel / Hogarth, Robin (1981): Behavioral Decision Theory: Processes of Judgment and Choice. In: Annual Review of Psychology, 32, pp. 53-88.
Einhorn, Hillel / Hogarth, Robin (1987): Decision Making: Going Forward in Reverse. In: HBR, 65, 1, pp. 66-70.
Elbing, Alvar (1978): Behavioral Decisions in Organizations. Scott & Foresman, Glenview, IL, 2nd ed. 1978.
Emory, William (1985): Business Research Methods. Irwin, Homewood, IL, 3rd ed. 1985.
England, George (1983): Japanese and American Management: Theory Z and Beyond. In: JIBS, 14, 4, pp. 131-141.
England, George / Negandhi, Anant (1979): Organizational Functioning in a Cross-Cultural Perspective. Comparative Administration Research Institute, Kent, OH 1979.
Enz, Cathy (1986): New Directives for Cross-Cultural Studies: Linking Organizational and Societal Cultures. In: Farmer, Richard (ed): Advances in International Comparative Management, vol. 2. JAI Press, Greenwich, CT 1986, pp. 173-189.
Euromoney (1987): The Euromoney 500. The Ups and Downs of Banking. In: Euromoney. Houldsworth, Anne / Irvine, Laura / Matarezzo, Domenico / Martinez, Jose / Bagy, Laura /Schafer, Catherine /Faulkes, Louise (researchers), June 1987, pp. 121-224.
Euromoney (1988): The Euromoney 500. Grizzly Time for North America - But Watch Out Japan and Europe. In: Euromoney. Paparatto, Thomas / Hamilton, Lisa (researchers), June 1988, pp. 75-135.
Evered, Roger (1983): So What is Strategy? In: LRP, 16, 3, pp. 57-72.
Fahey, Liam (1981): On Strategic Management Decision Processes. In: SMJ, 2, 3, pp. 43-60.
Farmer, Richard / Richman, Barry (1964): A Model for Research in Comparative Management. In: California Management Review, 7, 2, pp. 55-68.
Faucheux, Claude (1977): Strategy Formulation as a Cultural Process. In: ISMO. 7, 2, pp. 127-138.
Fayol, Henri (1972): General and Industrial Management. 1st published in 1949: Administration Industrielle et Generale; reprint, Pitman Publ., NY 1972.
Fidler, Stephen (1989): Financal Sector Worried Over Questions of Principle. In: Financial Times, Oct. 31, 1989, p. 29.
Fiegenbaum, Avi / McGee, John / Thomas, Howard (1986): Exploring the Linkage Between Strategic Groups and Competitive Strategy. In: BEBR Faculty Working Paper # 1238, University of Illinois at Urbana-Champaign, USA, April 1986.
Fiegenbaum, Avi / Thomas, Howard (1988): Attitudes Toward Risk and The Risk-Return Paradox: Prospect Theory Explanations. In: AMJ, 31, 1, pp. 85-106.
Fiol, Marlene / Lyles, Marjorie (1985): Organiyational Learning. In: AMR, 10, 4, pp. 803-813.

Fischhoff, Baruch (1975): Hindsight =/ Foresight: The Effect of Outcome Knowledge on Judgment under Uncertainty. In: Journal of Experimental Psychology. Human Perception and Performance. 1, 3, pp. 288-299.
Fischhoff, Baruch / Goitein, Bernard (1984): The Informal Use of Formal Models. In: AMR, 9, 3, pp. 505-512.
Fombrun, Charles / Astley, Graham (1983): Strategies of Collective Action: The Case of the Financial Services Industry. In: Advances in Strategic Management, vol. 2. JAI Press, New York 1983, pp. 125-139.
Fombrun, Charles / Zajac, Edward (1987): Structural and Perceptual Influences on Intraindustry Stratification. In: AMJ, 20, 1, pp. 33-50.
Foster, M.J. (1986): The Value of Formal Planning for Strategic Decisions. In: SMJ, 7, pp. 179-182.
Fredrick, Glenn (1983): The State of Private Sector Strategic Planning in Canada. In: LRP, 16, 3, pp, 40-46.
Frederickson, James (1983): Strategic Process Research: Questions and Recommendations. In: AMR, 8, 3,pp. 565-575.
Fredrickson, James (1984): The Comprehensiveness of Strategic Decision Processes: Extension, Observations, Future Directions. In: AMJ, 27, 3, pp. 445-466.
Fredrickson, James (1986a): An Exploratory Approach to measuring Perceptions of Strategic Decision Process Constructs. In: SMJ, 7, pp. 473-483.
Fredrickson, James (1986b): The Strategic Decision Process and Organizational Structure. In: AMR, 11, pp. 280-297.
Fredrickson, James / Iaquinto, Anthony (1988): The Comprehensiveness of Strategic Decision Processes: Differences Across Environments. Paper, presented at the Annual Meeting of the Academy of Management, Anaheim, CA 1988.
Fredrickson, James / Mitchell, T.R.(1984): Strategic Decision Processes: Comprehensiveness and Performance in an Industry With an Unstable Environment. In: AMJ, 27, pp. 399-423.
Freeman, Edward / Lorange, Peter (1985): Theory Building in Strategic Management. In: Advances in Strategic Management, vol. 3. JAI Press, New York 1985, pp. 9-38.
Feeman, R.E. (1984): Strategic Management: A Stakeholder Approach. Pitman, Boston, 1984.
Friedman, Joel / Wurzburg, Richard / Pihl, Waino / Reene, Michael (1983): New Dimensions in Banking: Managing the Strategic Position. Arthur Anderson & Co. & Bank Administration Institute. USA 1984.
Friedrichs, Jürgen (1981): Methoden Empirischer Sozialforschung. Westdeutscher Verlag, Ogladen, FRG 1981.
Gaitanides, Michael (1986): Strategic Planning and Structuring of Organization. In: Macharzina, Klaus / Stähle, Wolfgang (eds): European Approaches to International Management. Walter de Gruyter, Berlin, FRG 1986.
Gälweiler, Aloys (1980): Determinanten des Zeithorizontes in der Unternehmensplanung. In: Hand, D. / Taylor, B. (eds): Strategische Unternehmensplanung. Physica, Würzburg FRG 1980; reprinted from: Angewandte Planung, 1, 1977, pp. 95-106.
Gälweiler, Aloys (1986): Unternehmensplanung: Grundlagen und Praxis. Campus Verlag, Frankfurt, FRG 1986.
Gälweiler, Aloys (1987): Strategische Unternehmensführung. Campus Verlag, Frankfurt, FRG 1987.

Gamm, Larry (1976): Planning in Administration. In: Policy Studies Journal, 5, 4, pp. 70-73.

Gardner, David / Thomas, Howard (1985): Strategic Marketing: History, Issues, and Emergent Themes. In: Thomas, H. / Gardner, D. (eds): Strategic Marketing and Management. Wiley, New York 1985, pp. 17-39.

Garland, John / Farmer, Richard (1986): International Dimensions of Business Policy and Strategy. Kent. Publ. Co., Boston, MA 1986.

Garreau, Joe (1981): The Nine Nations of North America. Houghton Miffin Company, NY 1981.

Gibson, James / Ivancevich, John / Donnelly, James (1985): Organizations. Business Publications, Plano, TX, 5th ed. 1985.

Ginsberg, Avi / Venkatraman, N. (1985): Contingency Perspectives of Organizational Strategy: A Critical Review of the Empirical Research. AMR, 10, 3, pp. 421-434.

Ginter, Peter / Rucks, Andrew / Duncan, Jack (1985): Planners' Perceptions of the Strategic Management Process. In: JMS, 22, 6, pp.581-596.

Ginter, Peter / White, Donald (1982): A Social Learning Approach to Strategic Management: Toward a Theoretical Foundation. In: AMR, 7, 2, pp. 253-261.

Giroux, Gary (1980): A Survey of Forecasting Techniques Used by Commercial Banks. In: JBR, 11, 1, pp. 51-56.

Giroux, Gary (1981): Financial Forecasting in Banking. UMI Research Press, Ann Arbor, MI 1981.

Giroux, Gary / Rose, Peter (1984): An Update of Bank Planning Systems: Results of a Nationwide Survey of Large U.S. Banks. In: JBR, 15, 3, pp. 136-147.

Glaser, Barney / Strauss, Anselma (1967): Discovery of Grounded Theory: Strategies for Qualitative Research. Aldine, Chicago.

Glasgall, William (1988): The World's Top 200 Banks. In: Business Week, June 27, 1988, pp. 53-59.

Glass, Gene / Hopkins, Kenneth (1984): Statistical Methods in Education and Psychology. Prentice-Hall, Englewood Cliffs, New Jersey, 2nd ed. 1984.

Glenn, E. (1981): Man and Mankind: Conflicts and Communication Between Cultures. Ablex, Norwood, NJ 1981.

Gluck, Frederick (1986): Strategic Planning in a New Key. In: The McKinsey Quarterly, Winter 1986, pp. 18-41.

Gluck, Frederick / Kaufman, Stephen / Walleck, Steven (1982): The Four Phases of Strategic Management. In: JBS, 2, 3, pp. 9-21.

Glueck, William (1976): Business Policy. McGraw Hill, NY, 2nd ed., 1976.

Glueck, William (1980): Business Policy and Strategic Management. McGaw hill, Ny, 3rd ed. 1980.

Godse, V.T. (1986): Planning for Banking - The Indian Experience. in: LRP, 19, 1, pp. 105-112.

Golling, Hans-Joachim (1977): Berücksichtigung von Unsicherheiten bei Unternehmensentscheidungen. Ergebnisse einer empirischen Untersuchung. Working Paper, Department of Business Administration, Berlin Technical University, FRG 1977.

Golvan, Yves Le (1986): La Planification Marketing au sein des Résaux d'Agences. In: La Revue Banque, 461, 5, pp. 455-461.

Goodman, Robert / Newell, Stephanie (1989): Industry Wisdom: An Aid to Formulating Strategy or Harmful to Firm Performance? Paper, presented at the 9th annual Strategic Management Society Conference, Oct. 11-13, 1989, San Francisco.
Gordon, George (1985): The Relationship of Corporate Culture to Industry Sector and Corporate Performance. In: Kilman, Ralph / Saxton, Mary / Serpa, Roy (eds): Gaining Control of the Corporate Culture. Jossey-Bass, San Francisco, CA 1985.
Gordon, Raymond (1980): Interviewing. Strategy, Techniques, and Tactics. Dorsey Press, Homewood, IL, 3rd ed. 1980.
Gordon, Woods (1985): The Acquisition Decision. National Association of Accountants, Montvale, NJ, 1985.
Goy, Michel (1978): Strategic Decision Making in Large European Firms. In: LRP, 11, 3, pp. 41-48.
Graddy, Duane / Spencer, Austin / Brunsen, William (1985): Commercial Banking and the Financial Services Industry. Reston Publ., Reston, VA, 1985.
Grant, John (1987): The Corporate Strategic Process: A Synthesizing Framework for General Management. In: King, William / Clelland, David (eds): Strategic Planning and Management Handboook. Van Nostrand Reinhold Co., New York 1987.
Gray, Daniel (1986): Uses and Misuses of Strategic Planning. In: HBR, 64, 1, pp. 89-97.
Greenly, Gordon (1986): Does Strategic Planning Improve Company Performance? In: LRP, 19, 2, pp. 101-109.
Greipel, Peter (1988): Strategie und Kultur. Doctoral Dissertation, University of Wuppertal/Switzerland. Verlag Paul Haupt, Bern.
Griggs, Steve (1987): Analyzing Qualitative Data. In: Journal of the Market Research Society, 29, 1, pp. 15-34.
Grinyer, Peter / Al-Bazzaz, Shawki / Yasai-Arekani, M. (1986): Towards a Contingency Theory of Corporate Planning: Findings in 48 Companies. In: SMJ, 7, pp. 3-28.
Gup, Benton (1980): Guide to Strategic Planning. McGraw-Hill, New York, 1980.
Gup, Benton / Whitehead, David (1983): Shifting the Game Plan: Strategic Planning in Financial Institutions. In: Economic Review of the Federal Reserve Bank of Atlanta, Dec. 1983, pp. 22-33.
Guth, William / MacMillan, Ian (1986): Strategy Implementation Versus Middle Management Self-interest. In: SMJ, 7, pp. 313-327.
Guttentag, Jack / Herring, Richard (1986): Strategic Planning by International Banks to cope With Uncertainty. In: Savona, Paul / Sutija, George (eds): Strategic Planning In International Banking. McMillan, London, GB 1986.
Gzuk, Roland (1975): Messung der Effizienz von Entscheidungen. Mohr Siebek Verlag, Tübingen, FRG 1975.
Haas, Peter / Wemple, Barent (1985): Profile. Strategic Planning at First Fidelity. In: The Bankers Magazine, 168, 2, pp. 64-66.
Hage, James (1980): Theories of Organizations. Form, Process, and Transformation. Wiley Interscience, N.Y, 1980.
Hahn, David / Taylor, Bernd (1980): Srategische Unternehmensplanung. Physica Verlag, Wien, Austria 1980.

Haire, M. / Ghiselli, E.E. / Porter, L.W. (1966): Managerial Thinking, an International Study. Wiley, NY 1966.
Haiss, Peter (1983): Interne Revision im Mittelbetrieb am Beispiel einer Verkaufs-Verwaltungs-Abteilung eines österreichischen Mittelbetriebes. Unpublished Master's Thesis, University of Economics and Business Administration, Vienna, Austria, 1983.
Haiss, Peter (1988): Restructuring the US Banking Industry. In: Der Markt, 27, 107, pp. 173-179.
Haiss, Peter (1989a): Cultural Influences on Strategic Planning in the Banking Industry. Doctoral Dissertation, Vienna University of Economics, Vienna, Austria, June 1989. UMI United Microfilms International, Ann Arbor, USA.
Haiss, Peter (1989b): Bank Rankings: Comparing Like with Alike? In: ÖBA, 37, 12, pp. 1170-1182.
Hambrick Donald / Lei, David (1985): Toward an Empirical Prioritization of Contingency Variables for Business Strategy. In: AMJ, 28, 4, pp. 763-788.
Hambro Euromoney (1985): The Hambro Euromoney Directory 1985. Swanton, Ian (ed). Euromoney Publications Ltd and Hambros Bank Ltd, London, GB 1985.
Hannan, Michael / Freeman, John (1977): The Population Ecology of Organizations. American Journal of Sociology, 82, 3, pp. 929-964.
Hare, Paul (1985): Planning the British Economy. McMillan, London, GB 1985.
Harper, Ian (1986): Why Financial Deregulation? In: Australian Economic Review, 73, 3, pp. 37-49.
Haspeslagh, Paul (1982): Portfolio Planning: Use and Limits. HBR, 60, 1, pp. 58-73.
Hax, Arnoldo (1984, ed): Readings on Strategic Management. Ballinger Publishing Co., Cambridge, MA 1984.
Hax, Arnoldo / Majluf, Nicolas (1984): Strategic Management: An Integrative Perspective. Prentice Hall, Englewood Cliffs, NJ 1984.
Hax, Arnoldo / Majluf, Nicolas (1988): The Concept of Strategy and the Strategy Formation Process. In: Interfaces, 13, 3, pp. 99-109.
Hayashi, Kichiro (1978): Corporate Planning Practices in Japanese Multinationals. In: AMJ, 21, 2, pp. 211-226.
Hayes, Robert (1985): Strategic Planning - Forward in Reverse? In: HBR, 63, 6, pp. 111-119.
Heckhausen, Heinz (1981): Entwicklung und Sozialisation. In: Weinert, Franz / Graumann, Carl / Heckhausen, Heinz / Hofer, Manfred (eds): Pädagogische Psychologie. Fischer, vol. 1. 1981, pp. 83-97.
Hector, Gary (1988): How Banking Will Shake Out. In: Fortune International, 117, 9, pp. 89-100.
Hedberg, Bo (1981): How Organizations Learn and Unlearn. In: Nystrom, Paul / Starbuck, William (eds): Handbook of Organizational Design, vol. 1. Oxford University Presss, Oxford, GB 1981, pp. 1-27.
Hedberg, Bo / Jönsson, Sten (1977): Strategy Formulation as a Discontinuous Process. In: ISMO, 7, 2, pp. 88-109.
Hegarty, Harvey / Hoffman, Richard (1987): Who Influences Strategic Decisions? In: LRP, 20, 2, pp. 76-85.

Henderson, Bruce (1983): Understanding the Forces of Strategic and Natural Competition. In: Kerin, Roger / Peterson, Robert (eds): Perspectives on Strategic Marketing Management. Allyn and Bacon, Boston, MA, 2nd ed 1983, pp. 42-47.
Herper, Jan (1986): Why Financial Deregulation:" In: Australian Economic Review, 73, 3, pp. 37-49.
Hertz, David / Thomas, Howard (1983): Decision and Risk Analysis in a New Product and Facilities Planning Problem. In: Sloan Management Review, 24, 2, pp. 17-31.
Heskett, James (1987): Lessons in the Service Sector. In: HBR, 65, 3, pp. 118-126.
Hessling, Pjotr (1973): Studies in Cross-Cultural Organization. In: Columbia Journal of World Business, 8, 4, pp. 120-134.
Higgins, John (1980): Strategic and Operational Planning Systems. Prentice-Hall, London, GB 1980.
Higgins, John (1984): Strategy. Formulation, Implementation, and Control. Dryden Press, Chicago, IL 1984.
Higgins, John / Finn, R. (1977): The Organization and Practice of Corporate Planning in the U.K. In: LRP, 10, 4, pp. 88-92.
Higgins, R. B. (1981): Long-Range Planning in the Mature Coroporation. In: SMJ, 1, pp. 235-250.
Higgs, Malcolm (1988): Management Development Strategy in the Financial Sector. MacMillan Press, London, GB 1988.
Hirsch, Paul (1972): Processing Fads and Fashions: An Organization-Set Analysis of Cultural Industry Systems. In: American Journal of Sociology, 77, 1, pp. 639-659.
Hirsch, Paul (1975): Organizational Effectiveness and the Institutional Environment. In: ASQ, 20, 9, pp. 327-342.
Hofer, Charles (1976): Research on Strategic Planning: A Survey of Past Studies and Suggestions for Future Efforts. In: Journal of Economics and Business, 28, 3, pp. 261-287.
Hofer, Charles / Schendel, Dan (1978): Strategy Formulations: Analytical Concepts. West Publishing Company, St. Paul, Minnesota 1978.
Hofer, Charles / Murray, Edwin / Charan, Ram / Pitts, A. (1980): Strategic Management: A Casebook in Buiness Policy and Planning. West Publ. Co., N.Y. 1980.
Hofstede, Geert (1977): Cultural Determinants of the Exercise of Power in a Hierarchy. Working Paper 77-8. Brussels: European Institute for Advanced Studies in Management, 1977.
Hofstede, Geert (1980): Culture's Consequences. Vol. 5, Cross-Cultural Research and Methodology Series. Sage Publications, Beverly Hills, CA 1980.
Hofstede, Geert (1983a): The Cultural Relativity of the Quality of Organizational Practice and Theory. In: JIBS, 14, 2, pp. 75-89.
Hofstede, Geert (1983b): National Cultures in Four Dimensions. A Research-based Theory of Cultural Differences Among Nations. In: ISMO. 13, 1-2, pp. 46-74.
Hofstede, Geert (1984a): Cultural Dimensions in Management and Planning. In: APJM, 1, 1, pp. 81-99.
Hofstede, Geert (1984b): The Cultural Relativity of the Quality of Life Concept. In: AMR, 9, 3, pp. 389-398.
Hofstede, Geert (1986): Cultural Differences in Teaching and Learning. In: International Journal of Intercultural Relations, 10, pp. 301-320.

Hogarth, Robin / Makridakis, Spyros (1981): Forecasting and Planning: An Evaluation. In: MS, 27, 2, pp. 115-134.
Holmberg, Steven / Baker, Kent (1982): The CEO'r Role in Strategic Planning. In: JBR, 12, 4, pp. 219-227.
Holsti, O. (1968): Content Analysis. In: Lindsey, G. / Aronson, E. (eds): Handbook of Social Psychology, vol. 2, Addison-Wesley, Reading, mass., 2nd ed. 1968, pp.596-692.
Holzmüller, Hartmut (1986): Zur Strukturierung der grenzüberschreitenden Konsumentenforschung und spezifischen Methodenproblemen in der Datengewinnung. In: Jahrbuch der Absatz- und Verbrauchsforschung. Gfk-Nürnberg, FRG (eds). Duncker & Humbolt, Berlin 1986, pp. 42-70.
Horovitz, Jacques (1980): Top Management Control in Europe. St. Martin's Press, New York 1980.
Horovitz, Jacques / Thietart, R.A. (1982): Strategy, Management Design and Firm Performance. In: SMJ, 3, pp. 67-76.
Horváth, Dezsö / McMillan, Charles (1979): Strategic Choice and the Structure of Decision Processes. In: ISMO, 9, 3, pp. 87-112.
Houldsworth, Anne / Irvine, Laura / Matarezzo, Domenico / Martinez, Jose / Bagy, Laura /Schafer, Catherine /Faulkes, Louise (1987): The Euromoney 500. Mergers and Acquisitions in 1986, 1987. In: Euromoney, June 1987, p. 121-122.
Howe, Stewart (1986): Corporate Strategy. MacMillan, London, GB 1986.
Hrebiniak, Lawrence / Joyce, William (1985): Organizational Adaptation: Strategic Choice and Environmental Determinism. In: ASQ, 30, pp. 336-349.
Hrbeniak, Lawrence / Snow, Charles (1980): Industry Differences in Environmental Uncertainty and Organizational Characteristics Related To Uncertainty. In: AMJ, 23, 4, pp. 750-759.
Huber, G.P. / Power, D.(1985): Retrospective Reports of Strategic Level Managers: Guidelines for Increasing Their Accuracy. In: SMJ, 6, pp. 173-179.
Huff, Anne (1982): Industry Influences on Strategy Reformulation. In: SMJ 3, pp. 119-131.
Huff, Anne / Reger, Rhonda (1987): A Review of Strategic Process Research. In: JM, 13, 2, pp. 211-236.
Hui, Cynthia / Triandis, Harry (1985): Measurement in Cross-Cultural Psychology. In: JCCP, 16, 2, pp. 131-152.
Hulbert, James / Brandt, William (1980): Managing the Multinational Subsidiary. Holt, Rineyart & Winston, NY 1980.
Hulin, Charles (1987): A Psychometric Theory of Evaluations of Item and Scale Translations. Fidelity Across Languages. In: JCCP, 18, 2, pp. 115-142.
Hunt, James (1981): Applying American Behavioral Science: Some Cross-Cultural Implications. In: Organizational Dynamics, 10, 1, pp. 55-62.
Hunt, M.S. (1972): Competition in the Major Home Appliance Industry, 1960-1070. Unpublished Ph.D. Dissertation, Harvard University, Cambridge, MA 1972.
Hussey, David (1985): Introducing Corporate Planning. Oxford, GB, 3rd ed. 1985.
Hutt, Michael / Reingen, Peter / Ronchetto, John (1988): Tracing Emergent Processes in Marketing Strategy Formation. In: Journal of Marketing. 52, 1, pp. 4-19.

Institutional Investor (1987): The World's Largest Banks. In: Institutional Invester. Bent, Barbara / Halliday, Lisa / Swain, Christie (researchers), July 1987, pp. 143-170.

International Economic Appraisal Service (1988): Level 1 Statistical Information. Country Tables. Economist Intelligence Service, London, GB, February 1988.

Isenberg, Daniel (1984): How Senior Managers Think. In: HBR, 62, 8, pp. 81-90.

Jaccard, James / Wan, Choi (1986): Cross-Cultural Methods for the Study of Behavioral Decision Making. In: JCCP, 17, 2, pp. 123-149.

Jackofsky, Ellen / Slocum, John / McQuaid, Sara (1988): Cultural Values and the CEO: Alluring Comparisons? In: AME, 2, 1, pp. 39-49.

Jackson, Susan / Dutton, Jane (1986): The Labeling of Strategic Issues as Threats and Opportunities: Implications for Process and Action. Paper presented at the Annual Meeting of the Academy of Management, Chicago, 1986.

Jacob, Adolf-Friedrich (1986): Strategische Planung in Banken. Fritz Knapp Verlag, Frankfurt, FRG 1986.

Jaeger, Alfred (1986): Organizational Development and National Culture: Where's the Fit? In: AMR, 11, 1, pp. 179-190.

Jaeger, Alfred / Baliga, B.R. (1985): Control Systems and Strategic Adaptation. In: SMJ, 6, 2, pp. 115-134.

Jahoda, Gustaf (1984): Do we Need A Concept of Culture? In: JCCP, 15, 2, pp. 139-151.

Janis, Irving (1973): Victims of Groupthink: A Psychological Study of Foreign Policy Decisions and Fiascos. Houghton Mifflin, Boston, 1973.

Jauch, Lawrence (1984): An Inventory of Selected Academic Research on Strategic Management. In: Advancves in Strategic Management, vol. 2, pp. 141-175, JAI Press, Greenwich Associates, CN 1984.

Jauch, Lawrence / Osborn, R.N. (1981): Toward an Integrated Theory of Strategy. In: AMR, 6, pp. 491-498.

Jauch, Lawrence / Kraft, Kenneth (1986): Strategic Management of Uncertainty. In: AMR, 11, 4, pp. 777-790.

Javidan, Mansour (1984): The Impact of Environmental Uncertainty on Long-range Planning Practices of the U.S. Savings and Loan Industry. In: SMJ, 5, 4, pp. 381-392.

Javidan, Mansour (1985): Where Planning Fails - An Executive Survey. In: LRP, 18, 5, pp, 89-96.

Jemison, David / Sitkin, Sim (1986): Corporate Acquisitions: A Process Perspective. In: AMR, 11, 1, pp. 145-163.

Jick, Todd (1979): Mixing Qualitative and Quantitative Methods: Triangulation in Action. In: ASQ, 24, 12, pp. 602-611.

Johnson, Gerry (1988): Rethinking Incrementalism. In: SMJ, 9, pp. 75-91.

Johnson, Herbert (1973): Strategic Planning for Banks. In: JBR, 4, 2, pp. 79-83.

Kagono, Tadao / Nonaka, Ikujiro / Sakakibara, Kiyonori / Okumura, Akihiro / Sakamoto, Shiori / Johansson, Johny (1985): Strategic vs. Evolutionary Management. A U.S.-Japan Comparison of Strategy and Organization. North-Holland, New York 1985.

Kahneman, Daniel / Slovic, Paul / Tversky, Amos (1982): Judgment Under Uncertainty: Heuristics and Biases. Cambridge University Press, Cambridge, GB, 1982.
Kallmann, E.A. / Shapiro, J.J. (1978): The Motor Fright Industry A Case Against Planning. In: LRP, 11, 1, pp. 81-86.
Kantona, George (1969): Rational Behavior and Economic Behavior." In: Enis, B.M. / Cox, K.K. (1969, eds.): Marketing Classics, Boston 1969, pp. 91-106.
Kassarjian, Harold (1977): Content Analysis in Consumer Research. In: Journal of Consumer Research, 4, 3, pp. 8-18.
Katz, Daniel / Kahn, Robert (1966): The Social Psychology of Organizations. Wiley, New York 1966.
King, William / Clelland, David (1978): Strategic Planning and Policy. Van Nostrand Reinhold Co., N.Y. 1978.
Kirsch, W. / Esser, W.M. / Bamberger, I. / Börsig, C / Du Voitel,R.D. / Esser, W.M. Keppler, W. / Knopf, R. (1975): Planung und Organisation in Unternehmen - Bericht aus einem empirischen Foschungsprojekt. Munich University, Munich, FRG 1975.
Klein, Hans (1977): Impact of Long Range Planning on Profit and Growth in Selected Segments of Commercial Banks. DBA Dissertation, University of Kentucky, Lexington, KY 1977.
Klein, Hans (1979): Growth, Profit, and Long Range Planning in Banks. UMI Research Press, Ann Arbor, MI 1979.
Klein, Hans (1980): How Well Does Your Banker Plan for the Future? In: MP, 30, 4, pp. 17-20.
Klein, Hans (1981): The Impact of Planning on Growth and Profit. In: JBR, 12, 1, pp.105-109.
Kluckhohn, F.R. / Strodtbeck, F.L. (1961): Variations in Value Orientations. Greenwood Press, Westport, CN 1961.
Köhler, Richard / Übele, Herbert (1986): Planning Techniques: Conditions for Their Application and Acceptance. In: Witte, Eberhard / Zimmermann, Hans-Jürgen (eds.) Empirical Research on Organizational Decision-Making. Elevier Science Publishers, N.Y. 1986.
Kono, Toyohiro (1976): Long Range Planning - Japan-USA - A Comparative Study. In: LRP, 9, 5, pp. 61-71.
Kono, Toyohiro (1984): Long Range Planning of U.K. And Japanese Corporations - A Comparative Study. In: LRP, 17, 2, pp. 58-76.
Kotler, Philipp (1980): Principles of Marketing. Prentice Hall, Englewood-Cliffs, NJ 1980.
Kotler, Philipp (1983): Marketing Warfare in the 1980s. In: Kerin, Roger / Peterson, Robert (1983, eds): Perspectives on Strategic Marketing Management.Allyon & Bacon, Inc., Boston, MA 1983, pp. 67-81. Reprinted from: Kotler, Philipp (1980): Marketing Warfare in the 1980s. In: Journal of Business Strategy, Fall 1980.
Kotler, Philipp (1984): Marketing Management. Analysis, Planning, and Control. Prentice-Hall, Englewood Cliffs, NJ, 5th ed 1984.
Kotter, John / Schlesinger, Leonard (1979): Choosing Strategies for Change. In: HBR, 57, 3, pp. 106-114.
Kotter, John (1982): What Effective General Managers Really Do. In: HBR, 60, 8, pp. 157-167.

Kroeber, A. / Kluckhohn, F.R. (1952): Culture: A Critical Review of Concepts and Definitions. Peapody Museum Papers, 47, 1, Harvard University Campridge, MA; quoted from: Negandhi, Anant (1983:25): Cross-Cultural Research: Trend and Future Directions. In: JIBS, Fall 1983, pp. 17-28; and from: Adler, Nancy (1986b:8): International Dimensions of Organizational Behavior. Kent Publ., Boston, MA 1986.

Krümmel, Hans-J. (1987): Bankwirtschaftliche Perspektiven fuer die 80er Jahre. In: Krümmel, Hans-J./Rudoph, Bernd (1987, eds.): Bankenmanagement fuer neue Maerkte. Fritz Knapp Verlag, Frankfurt, FRG 1987, pp. 13-30.

Kudla, Ronald (1978): The Components of Strategic Planning. In: LRP, 11, 12, pp. 48-52.

Kudla, Ronald (1981): Strategic Planning and Risk. In: Review of Business and Economic Research. 17, 1, pp. 1-14.

Kudla, Ronald (1982): The Current Practice of Bank Long-Range Planning. In: LRP, 15, 3, pp. 132-138.

Kühn, Richard (1985): Grundzüge eines heuristischen Verfahrens zur Erarbeitung von Planungskonzeptionen. In: Die Betriebswirtschaft, 45, 5, pp. 531-543.

Kumar, Parmanand (1978): Long-Range Planning Practices By U.S. Companies. In: MP, 26, 4, pp. 31-38.

Kumon, S. (1984): Some Principles Governing the Thought and Behavior of Japanists. In: Journal of Japanese Studies, 8, pp. 5-28.

LaForge, Lawrence / Wood, Robley (1980): The Use of Operations Research in the Planning Activities of Large U.S. Banks. In: JBR, 11, 3, pp. 179-181.

Lammers, Cornelis / Hickson, David (1979a): Organizations Alike and Unlike: International and Interinstitutional Studies in the Sociology of Organizations. Rougledge & Kegan Paul, London, GB 1979.

Lammers, Cornelius / Hickson, David (1979b): Are Organizations Culture-Boud? In: Lammers, C.J. / Hickson, D.J. (eds): Organizations Alike and Unlike. Routledge & Kegan Paul, London, GB 1979, pp. 402-419.

Langer, Ellen (1975): The Illusion of Control. In: Journal of Personality and Social Psychology, 32, 6, pp. 311-325.

Larwood, Laurie / Whittaker, William (1977): Managerial Myopia: Self-Serving Biases in Organizational Planning. In: Journal of Applied Psychology, 6, 2, pp. 194-198.

Lassere, Philippe (1983): Strategic Planning in South-East Asia: Does it Work? In: Euro-Asia Business Review, 2, 2, pp. 37-41.

Laurie, Samantha (1988): More Than Money. In: The Banker, May 1988, pp. 42-44.

Lawrence, Paul (1981): The Harvard Organization and Environmt Research Program. In: Van de Ven, A./ Joyce, E. (eds): Perspectives on Organization Design and Behavior. Wiley Interscience, N.Y., 1981, pp. 311-337.

Lawrence, Paul / Lorsch, Jay (1967): Organization and Environment. Harvard University Presss, Boston 1967.

Lawrence, Paul / Lorsch, Jay (1969): Organization and Environment: Managing Differentiation and Integration. Harvard University, Graduate School of Business Administration, Boston, MA 1967.

Lazarsfeld, Paul (1967): Methodische Probleme der empirischen Sozialforschung. In: Hartmann, Hans (1967): Moderne amerikanische Soziologie. Stuttgart, FRG, pp. 95-117.
Leatherwood, Marya / Colon, Edward (1986): The Impact of Diffusibility of Blame on Subsequent Persistence in a Project. BEBR Faculty Working Paper # 1286, University of Illinois at Urbana-Champaign, Sept. 1986.
Leblebici, Husey / Salancik, Gerald (1981): Effects of Environmental Uncertainty on Information and Decision Processes in Banks. In: ASQ, 26, pp. 578-596.
Lenway, Stefanie (1985): The Politics of U.S. International Trade. Protection, Expansion and Excape. Pitman Publishing, Marshfiled, MA 1985.
Lenz, Robert (1981): 'Determinants' of Organizational Performance: an Inderdisciplinary Review. in: SMJ, 2, pp. 131-154.
Lenz, Robert / Engledow, Jack (1986): Environmental Analysis: The Applicability of Current Theory. In: SMJ, 7, pp. 329-436.
Lenz, Robert / Lyles, Marjorie (1984): Tackling the Human Problems in Planning. In: LRP, 17, 3, pp. 31-45.
Lenz, Robert / Lyles, Marjorie (1985): Paralysis by Analysis: Is Your Planning System Becoming Too Rational? In: LRP, 18, 4, pp. 64-72.
Lenz, Robert / Lyles, Marjorie (1986): Managing Human Problems in Strategic Planning Systems. In: JBS 6, 4, pp. 57-66.
Leontiades, Milton (1986): Managing the Unmanageable. Strategies for Success within the Conglomerate. Addison-Wesley Publ. Co., Reading, MA 1986.
Levitt, Theodore (1986) Production-Line Approach to Service. In: Classic Advice on Managing Systems, HBR Review on Management, reprinted from: HBR, Harper & Row Publ, NY 1986, pp. 379-396.
Liddell-Hall, Basil (1967): Strategy. Praeger Publishing, New York 1967.
Lilienthal, David (1944): Planning and Planners. Reprinted in: Shafritz, Jay / Hyde, Altert (1978): Classics of Public Administration. Moore Publ. Co., Oak Park, IL, 1978, pp. 95-101.
Lindblom, Charles (1968): The Policy Making Process. Prentice Hall, Englewood Cliffs, NJ 1968.
Lindsay, William / Rue, Leslie (1980): Impact of the Organization Environment on the Long-Range Planning Process: A Contingency View. In: AMJ, 23, 5, pp. 385-404.
Litschert, Robert (1968): Some Characteristics of Long-Range Planning: An Industry Study. In: Academy of Management, Sept. 1968.
Litschert, Robert (1971): The Structure of Long-Range Planning Groups. In: AMJ, 14, pp. 33-43.
Litschert, Robert / Nicholson, Edward (1973): Formal Long-Range Planning Groups: Their Evolutionary nature. In: Journal of Economics and Business, 25, pp. 45-52.
Litschert, Robert / Nicholson, Edward (1974): Corporate Long-Range-Planning Groups - Some Different Approaches. In: LRP, 7, 8, pp. 62-66.
Lorange, Peter (1979): Formal Planning Systems: their Role in Strategy Impleementation. In: Schendel, Dan / Hover, Charles (eds) Strategic management: A New Role of Business Policy and Planning. Little, Brown & Co., Boston, MA 1979.

Lorange, Peter (1986): Tailormaking of Strategic management Systems Design: Matching Systems Capabilities to Strategic Needs. In: Advances in Strategic Management, 4, pp, 59-79, JAI Press, New York, 1986.
Lorange, Peter / Vancil, Richard (1976): How to Design a Strategic Planning System. In: HBR, 54, 3, pp. 75-81.
Lorange, Peter / Vancil, Richard (1977): Strategic Planning Systems. Prentice-Hall, Englewood Cliffs, NJ 1977.
Lusser, Markus (1987): Rahmenbedingungen und ihre Bedeutung für die Attraktivität eines Finanzplatzes - einige Überlegungen am Beispiel der Schweiz. In: Süchting, Joachim / Hooven, Eckart van (eds): Handbuch des Bankmarketing. Gabler, Wiesbaden, FRG 1987, pp. 37-58.
Lyles, Marjorie (1980): Organizational Problem Formulation: An Empirical Study. In: ASQ, 25, pp. 102-119.
Lyles, Marjorie (1981): Formulating Strategic Problems: Empirical Analysis and Model Development. In: SMJ, 2, pp. 61-75.
Lyles, Marjorie / Mitroff, Ian (1980): Organizational Problem Formulation: An Empirical Study. In: ASQ, 25, pp. 102-119.
Lyles, Marjorie / Lenz, Robert (1982): Managing the Planning Process: A Field Study of the Human Side of Planning. In: SMJ, 3, pp. 105-118.
Lyles, Marjorie / Thomas, Howard (1986): Problem Formulation and Organizational Decision-Making: Biases and Assumptions Underlying Alternative Models of Strategic Problem Formulation. In: JMS, 3, 4, pp. 51-63.
McClintock, Charles / Brannan, Diane / Maynard-Moody, Steven (1979): Applying the Logic of Sample Surveys to Qualitative Case Studies: The Case Cluster Method. In: ASQ, 24, pp. 612-629.
McNamee, Patrick (1985): Tools and Techniques for Strategic Planning. Pergamon Press, Oxford, GB, 1985.
Mahon, John / Murray, Edwin (1981): Strategic Planning for Regulated Companies. In: SMJ, 2, pp. 251-262
Makridakis, Spyros / Héau, Dominique (1987): The Evolution of Strategic Planning and Management. In: King, William / Cleland, David (eds): Strategic Planning and Management Handbook. Van Nostrand Reinhold, New York 1987.
Malmstrom, Carl (1986): Strategic Planning for Financial Services Companies. In: Gardner, James / Rachlin, Robert / Sweeny, Allen (eds): Handbook of Strategic Planning. John Wiley, New York 1986.
Mans, G. (1973): Stand und Entwcklung von Planungssystemen in der BRD. Analyse einer empirischen Untersuchung. In: Grochla, Erwin / Szyperski, Norbert (eds): Modell- und Computer-gestützte Unternehmensplanung. Vahlen, Wiesbaden 1973, pp. 41-63.
March, James (1978): Bounded Rationality, Ambiguity, and the Engeneering of Choice. In: Bell Journal of Economics, 9, pp. 587-608.
March, James (1979): Ambiguity and the Engineering of Choice. In: ISMO, 9, 3, pp. 9-39.
March, James (1981): Footnotes ot Organizational Change. In: ASQ, 26, pp. 563-577.
March, James / Simon, Herbert (1958): Organizations. John Wiley, New York 1958.

Marin, Gerardo / Betancourt, Hector / Kashima, Yoshihisa (1983): Ethnic Affirmation versus Social Desirability. Explaining Diescrepancies in Bilinguals' Responses to a Questionnaire. In: JCCP, 14, 2, Jue 1983, pp. 173-186.
Martin, Joanne / Siehl, Caren (1983): Organizational culture and Counterculture: An Uneasy Symbiosis. In: Organizational Dynamics, Autumn 1983, pp. 52-64.
Maslow, A.H. (1943): A Theory of Human Motivation. In: Psychological Review, July 1943, pp. 370-396.
Mason, Richard / Mitroff, Ian (1981): Challenging Strategic Planning Assumptions. Wiley, New York, 1981.
Mason, Richard / Mitroff, Ian (1983): A Teleological Power-Oriented Theory of Strategy. In: Advances in Strategic Management, vol. 2, JAI Press, New York 1983.
Mazzolini, Renato (1979): Government Controlled Enterprises. Wiley, NY 1979.
Mazzolini, Renato (1981): How Strategic Decisions are Made. In: LRP, 14, 3, pp. 85-96.
Meffert, Heribert (1979): Marketing. Gabler, Wiesbaden, FRG, 4th ed. 1979.
Mergers & Acquisitions (1985): Almanac & Index 1985. In: Mergers & Acquisitions, 19, 5, pp. 36-38.
Metzger, Robert / Rau, Susan (1982): Strategic Planning for Future Bank Growth. In: Bankers Magazine, 165, 4, pp. 57-65.
Michael, Donald (1973): On Learning to Plan - And Planning to Learn. Jossey-Bass, San Francisco, CA, 1973.
Miketta, Eckhard (1987): Aspekte der Bankentwicklung. In: Congena (ed): Bank Entwicklung. Gabler, Wiesbaden, FRG 1987.
Miles, Anthony (1985): Reintegrating Strategy. In: Boston Consulting Group (eds): Perspectives. The Strategy Development Process. BCG, Boston, MA 1985, pp. 1-6.
Miles, Matthew / Huberman, Michael (1984): Qualitative Data Analysis. Sage Publications, Beverly Hills, CA 1984.
Miles, Raymond / Snow, Charles (1978): Structure and Process. McGraw-Hill, NY 1978.
Miles, Raymond / Snow, Charles / Meyer, Alan / Coleman, Henry (1978): Organizational Strategy, Structure, and Process. In: AMR, 3,3, pp. 546-562.
Miller, Danny (1987): The Structural and Environmental Correlates of Business Strategy. In: SMJ, 8, pp. 55-76.
Miller, Danny / Friesen, Peter (1980): Archetypes of Organizational Transition. In: ASQ, 25, pp. 268-299.
Miller, Danny / Friesen, Peter (1983): Strategy Making and The Environment. In: SMJ, 4, pp. 221-235.
Miller, Edwin (1984): Comparative Management Conceptualization. In: Farmer, Richard (ed, 1984): Advances in Strategic Management, vol. 1, pp. 69-82.
Miner, John (1984): Participation and Management. In: Welpert, Bernd / Sorge, Arndt (eds): International Perspectives on Organizational Democracy. Wiley, New York, pp. 183-196.
Mintzberg, Henry (1973): The Nature of Managerial Work. Harper & Row, New York 1973.
Mintzberg, Henry (1973a): A New Look at the Chief Executives Job. In: Organizational Dynamics, Winter 1973b, reprinted in: Glueck, W.F. (1976, ed): Business Policy, Strategy Formulation and Management Action. McGraw Hill, New York, 2nd ed. 1976, pp. 36-45.

Mintzberg, Henry (1973b): Strategy-Making in Three Modes. In: California Management Review, 16, 2, pp. 45-60.
Mintzberg, Henry (1975): The Manager's Job: Folklore and Fact. In: HBR, 53, 4, pp. 49-61.
Mintzberg, Henry (1976): Planning on the Left Side and Managing on the Right. In: HBR, 54, 4, pp. 49-58.
Mintzberg, Henry (1977): Strategy Formulation as a Historical Process. In: ISMO, 7, 2, pp. 28-40.
Mintzberg, Henry (1978): Patterns in Strategy Formation. In: MS, 24, 9, pp. 934-948.
Mintzberg, Henry (1979a): An Emerging Strategy of 'Direct' Research. In: ASQ, 24, pp. 582-589.
Mintzberg, Henry (1979b): The Structuring of Organizations. Prentice Hall, Englewood Cliffs, NJ 1979.
Mintzberg, Henry (1980): Beyond Implementation: An Analysis of the Resistance to Policy Analysis. In: Infor, 18, 2, 1980.
Mintzberg, Henry (1981): What is Planning Anyway? In: SMJ, 2, pp. 319-324.
Mintzberg, Henry (1985): Of Strategies, Deliberate and Emergent. In: SMJ, 5, pp. 257-272.
Mintzberg, Henry (1987): Crafting Strategy. In: HBR, 65,4, pp. 66-75.
Mintzberg, Herny / Raisinghani, Duru / Théorêt, André (1976): The Structure of 'Unstructured' Decision Processes. In: ASQ, 21, 2, pp. 246-275.
Mintzberg, Henry / Waters, James (1982): Tracking Strategy in an Entrepreneurial Firm. In: AMJ, 25, 3, pp. 454-499.
Mintzberg, Henry / Waters, James (1985): Of Strategies, Deliberate and Emergent. In: SMJ, 6, pp. 257-272.
Misumi, Jyuji (1984): Decision-making in Japanese Groups and Organizations. In: Wilpert, Bernd / Sorge, Arndt (eds): International Perspectives on Organizational Democracy. John Wiley & Sons, NY 1984, pp. 530-539.
Mitchell, William (1986): Selected Financial Centres. Summary of Banking and Tax Regulations. Price Waterhouse, Canada 1986.
Mitroff, Ian / Emshoff, James (1979): On Strategic Assumption Making: A Dialectical Approach to Policy and Planning. In: AMR, 4, pp. 1-12.
Mitroff, Ian / Featheringham, T.R. (1974): On Systematic Problem Solving and Error of the Third Kind. In: Behavioral Science, 19, pp. 383-393.
Mitroff, Ian / Mason, Richard (1980): Structuring Ill-Structured Policy Issues: Further Explorations in a Methodology for Messy Problems. In: SMJ, 1, pp. 331-342.
Moag, Joseph (1973): Strategic Planning in Banks- A Behavioral Science Perspective. In: JBR, 4, 2, pp, 84-92.
Montebelle, Michel / Buignes, Pierre (1982): How French Industry Plans. In: LRP, 15, 3, pp. 116-121.
Moormann, Jürgen (1988a): Zum Stand der strategischen Planung in Geschäftsbanken des deutschsprachigen Raumes - Ergebnisse einer Umfrage. Working Paper No. 206, Department of Business Administration, University Kiel, FRG, March 1988.
Moormann, Jürgen (1988b): Strategische Planung in Geschaefts-banken: Ergebnis einer Umfrage. In: Die Bank, 6/1988, pp. 309-315.

Morgan, George / Martin, John (1986): A Rationale for Planning: Implications form the Economic Theory of the Firm. In: Managerial and Decision Economics, 7, 4, pp. 219-228.
Mrema, Elisante (1987): Strategic Planning in Tanzania. In: LRP, 20, 3, pp. 105-110.
Mulder, M. (1971): Power Equalization Through Participation? In: ASQ, 16, pp. 31-38.
Murray, John (1978): Toward a Contingency Model of Strategic Management. In: ISMO, 8, 4, pp. 7-34.
Nath, Raghu (1968): A Methodological Review of Cross-Cultural Management Research. In: Social Science Journal, 20, 1, pp. 35-62.
Naylor, Thomas / Schauland, Horst (1976): A Survey of Users of Corporate Planning Models. In: MS, 22, 9, pp. 927-937.
Negandhi, Anant (1973): Management and Economic Development in Taiwan. Martin Nijhoff, The Hague 1973.
Negandhi, Anant (1975a): Organization Theory in an Open System. A Study of Transferring Advances Management Practices to Developing Nations. Dunellen, NY 1975.
Negandhi, Anant (1975b): Comparative Management and Organizational Theory: A Marriage Needed. In: AMJ, 18, 2, pp. 223-243.
Negandhi, Anant (1983a): Management in the Third World. In: APJM, 14, 2, pp. 15-25.
Negandhi, Anant (1983b): Cross-Cultural Management Research: Trends and Future Directions. In: JIBS, 14, 2, pp. 17-28.
Negandhi, Anant (1985): Management Strategies and Policies of American, German and Japanese Multinational Corporations. In: Management Japan, 18, 1, pp. 12-20.
Negandhi, Anant (1986): Managerial Effectiveness in Singapore and Indonesia: A Neo-Classical Extension of the Farmer-Richman Model. In: Working paper #85-4651, University of Illinois at Urbana-Champaign.
Negandhi, Anant (1987): International Management. Allyn & Bacon, Boston, MA 1987.
Negandhi, Anant / Baliga, B.R. (1981): The Tables are Turning. German and Japanese Multinational Companies in the United States. Oelschlager, Gunn & Main, Cambridge, MA 1981.
Negandhi, Anand / Prasad, Benjamin (1971): Comparative Management. Appleton-Century Corfts, New York 1971.
Negandhi, Anant / Welge, Martin (1984): Beyond Theory Z: Global Rationalization Strategies of American, German and Japanese Multinational Companies. JAI Press, Greenwich, CT 1984.
Nicholson, Edward / Litschert, Robert (1973): Long-Range Planning in Banking: Ten Case Studies. In: JBR, Spring 1973, pp. 31-40.
Norusis, Marija (1986): SPSS/PC+. SPSS Inc., Chicago, IL, 1986.
Nutt, Paul (1984a): Types of Organizational Decision Processes. In: ASQ, 29, pp. 414-450.
Nutt, Paul (1984b): Planning Process Archetypes And Their Effectiveness. In: Decision Sciences, 15, 2, pp. 221-238.
Ohmae, Kenichi (1982): The Mind of the Strategist. Penguin Books, New York 1982.
Orbach, William (1984): Japanese vs. American Strategic Management. Paper, presented ath the Organizational Policy & Development Conference, University of Louisville, Louisville, KY, April 1984.

Orihata, Motokazu (1985): The Essence of Corporate Change. In: Boston Consulting Group (ed): Perspectives: The Strategy Development Process. Boston Consulting Group, Boston, MA 1985, pp. 15-18.
Orpen, Christopher (1984): Long-Range Planning in Large Corporations: A Cross-National Survey. In: MP, 33, 3, pp. 18-22.
Ouchi, William (1980): Markets, Bureaucracies, and Clans. In: ASQ, 25, 1, pp. 124-141.
Ouchi, William (1981): Theory Z. Addison-Wesley Publ., Reading, MA 1981.
Ouchi, William / Jaeger, Alfred (1978): Type Z Organization: Stability in the Midst of Mobility. In: AMR, 3, 2, pp. 305-314.
Paine, Frank / Naumes, W. (1982): Organizational Strategy and Policy. Dryden Press, Hinsdale, IL, 3rd ed. 1982.
Paparetto, Thomas / Hamilton, Lisa (1988): The Euromoney 500. Grizzly Time for North America - But Watch Out Japan and Europe. In: Euromoney, June 1988, pp. 75-135.
Parsons, Talcott (1951): The Social System. Routledge and Kegan Paul, London, GB 1951.
Parsons, Talcott (1961): Theories of Society. Free Press, New York 1961.
Pascale, Richard (1978): Communicationand Decision Making Accross Cultues: Japanese and American Comparisons. In: ASQ, 23, 1, pp. 91-110.
Pascale, Richard / Athos, Anthony (1981): The Art of Japanese Management. Warner Books, New York 1981.
Paul, Ronald / Donavan, Neil / Taylor, James (1978): The Reality Gap in Strategic Planning. In: HBR, 56, 3, pp. 124-130.
Pearce, John / Freeman, Elizabeth / Robinson, Richard (1987): The Tenuous Link Between Formal Strategic Planning and Financial Performance. In: AMR, 12, 4, pp. 658-675.
Pearce, John / Herron, Lawrence (1987): A Consulting Tool for Service Sector Business Planning. Paper, presented at the Annual Conference of the Academy of Management, New Orleans, Aug. 1987.
Perrow, Charles (1967): A Framework for the Comparative Analysis of Organizations. In: American Sociological Review, 32, 2, pp. 94-108.
Perrow, Charles (1970): Organizational Analysis: A Socialogical Perspective. Wadsworth Publishing, Belmont, CA 1970.
Peters, Tom / Waterman, Robert (1982): In Search of Excellence. Lessons from Americas Best-Run Companies. Warner Books, New York 1982.
Peters, Tom (1987): A World Turned Uside Down. In: AME, 1, 3, pp. 233-243.
Pettigrew, Andrew (1977): Strategy Formulation as a Political Process. In: ISMO, 7, 2, pp. 78-87.
Pettway, Samuel (1986): Fourth Annual Banking Survey of Chief Executive Officers. Egon Zehnder International, Feb. 1986.
Pfeffer, Jeffrey / Salanzik, Gerald (1978): The External Control of Organizations: A Resource Dependence Perspective. Harper & Row, New York 1978.
Phillips, Margaret (1986): An Exploratory Investigation Into the Existence of Industry Culture. Paper, presented at the Sixth Annual Strategic Management Societey Conference, Singapore, October 1986.

Piore, Michael (1979): Qualitative Research Techniques in Economics. In: ASQ, 24, 4, pp. 560-569.
Poensgen, Otto / Hort, Helmut (1986): Situative Influences on Corporate Planning. In: Witte, E. / Zimmermann, H.-J. (eds): Empirical Research on Organizational Decision-Making. North-Holland, New York 1986, pp. 269-299.
Pohlman, Jerry (1982): Strategic Planning for Savings and Loans in a Volatile Economic Environment. In: Federal Home Loan Bank of San Francisco (ed): Proceeedings of the Eight Annual Conference, Strategic Planning for Economc & Technolgical Change in the Financial Services Industry, San Francisco, CA 1982.
Polk's (1986a): Polk's World Bank Directory. United States Edition, Midyear 1986 Issue, R.L. Plk & Co., Nasville, TE 1986.
Polk's (1986b): Polk's World Bank Directory. Int'l Edition, Mid-Year 1986 Issue, R.L. Polk & Co., Nasville, TE 1986.
Pondy, Louis / Mitroff, Ian (1981): Beyond Open System Models of Organization. In: Cummings, L./Staw, Bern (eds): Research in Organizational Behavior, vol. 1. JAI Press, Greenwich, CT 1981, pp. 3-39.
Porac, Joseph / Thomas, Howard / Emme, Bethany (1985): Cognitieve Taxonomies in a Retailer's Understanding of the Competitive Environment. In: BEBR Faculty Working Paper # 1215 , University of Illinois at Urbana-Champaign, Dec. 1985.
Porter, Michael (1980): Competitive Strategy. Free Press, New York 1980.
Porter, Michael (1981): The Contributions of Industrial Organization To Strategic Management. In: AMR, 6, 4, pp. 609-620.
Porter, Michael (1985): Competitive Advantage. Free Press, New York 1985.
Porter, Lyman / Steers, Richard / Mowday, Richard / Bouldin, Agnes (1974): Organizational Commitment, Job Satisfaction, and Turnover Among Psychiatric Technicians. In: Journal of Applied Psychology, 59, pp. 603-609.
Prasad, Benjamin (1984): The Paradox of Planning in Banks. In: The Bankers Magazine, 167, 3, pp. 77-81.
Price, James / Mueller, Charles (1986): Handbook of Organizational Measurement. Wiley, New York 1986.
Priewasser, Erich (1977): Die Implementierung von bankbetrieblichen Planungs- und Entscheidungsmodellen. In: Mueller-Merbach, H. (ed): Quantitative Ansätze in der BWL, Vahlen, Munich 1977, pp.301-314.
Priewasser, Erich (1979): Bankbetriebliche Planungs- und Entscheidungsmodelle. In: Controller Magazin, 2/79, pp. 67-72.
Pugh, Derk / Hickson, David (1976): Organizational Structure in Context: The Aston Programme. Saxon House, London, GB 1976.
Quinn, James (1978): Strategic Change: 'Logical Incrementalism.' In: Sloan Management Review, 29, 1, pp. 7-21.
Quinn, James (1980): Strategies for Change: Logical Incrementalism. Irvin, Homewood, IL 1980.
Quinn, James (1983): Formulating Strategy One Step at a Time. In: Kerin, Roger / Peterson, Robert (eds): Perspectives on Strategic Marketing Management. Allyn & Bacon, Boston, MA 1983, pp. 455-483.

Quinn, Robert / Cameron, Kim (1983): Organizational Life Cycles and Shifting Criteria of Effectiveness: Some Preliminary Evidence. In: MS, 29, 1, Jan. 1983, pp. 33-51.
Quinn, Robert / McGrath, Michael (1985): The Transformation of Organizational Culture. In: Frost, Peter / Moore, L.F. /Louise, M.R. / Martin, J. (eds): Organizational Culture. Sage Publications, Beverly Hills, CA 1985, pp. 315-334.
Raffée, Hans (1974): Grundprobleme der Betriebswirtschaftslehre. Vandenhoeck & Ruprecht, Gütlingen, FRG 1974.
Ramamurti, Ravi (1986): Strategic Planning in Government-dependent Businesses. In: LRP, 19, 3, pp. 62-71.
Ramanujam, Vasudevan / Camillus, John / Venkatraman, N. (1984): The Design and Use of Strategic Planning Systems: Some Key Issues for the Eighties. No publishing company given. Cleveland, OH 1984.
Ramanujam, Vasudevan / Camillus, John / Venkatraman, N. (1987): Trends in Strategic Planning. In: King, William / Clelanc, David (eds): Strategic Planning and Management Handbook. Van Nostrand Reinhold, New York 1987, ppl 611-628.
Ramanujam, Vasudevan / Venktatraman, N. (1985): Eight Half-Truths of Strategic Planning: A Fresh Look. In: Planning Review, 12, 1, pp. 22-27.
Ramanujam, Vasudevan / Venkatraman, N. (1986): Planning System Characteristics and Planning Effectiveness. Paper, presened at the TIMS/ORSA meetings at Boston, May 1985. Revised edition, March 1986.
Ramunajam Vasudevan / Venkantraman, N. / Camillus, John (1986a): Objective-Based Efaluation of Strategic Planning Systems. In: Omega, 14, 4, pp. 299-306.
Ramanujam, Vasudevan / Venkatraman, N. / Camillus, John (1986b): Multi-Objective Assessment of Effectiveness of Strategic Planning: A Discriminant Analysis Approach. In: AMJ, 29, 2, pp. 347-372.
Rand McNally (1982): Rand McNally International Bankers Directory. Rand McNally, New York, Final Edition 1982.
Raphael, David (1986): Betting The Bank on Technology - Technology Strategic Planning at Bank of America. In: LRP, 19, 2, pp. 23-30.
Rau, Susan (1988): Why Planning Ain't What it Used to Be. In: The Bankers Magazine, 71, 1, pp. 62-66.
Redding, Gordon (1980): Cognition as an Aspect of Culture And Its Relation To Management Proceses: An Exploratory View Of The Chinese Case. In: JMS, 17, pp. 127-148.
Redding, Gordon / Maryin-Johns, T.A. (1979): Paradigm Differences and Their Relation to Management, with Reference to South-East Asia. In: England, G.W. / Negnadhi, A. / Wilpert, B. (eds): Organizational Functioning in a Cross-Cultural Perspective. Comparative Administration Research Insitutite, Kent, OH 1979, pp. 103-125.
Regli, Jürg (1983): Bankmarketing. Doctoral Dissertation, Institut für Bankwissenschaft an der Hochschule St. Gallen, Suisse. Reprinted in: Kilgus, Ernst / Schuster, Leo (eds): Bankwissenschaftliche Forschungen, 1983.
Reidenbach, Eric (1986): Bank Marketing. A Guide to Strategic Planning. Reston Publ., Prentice-Hall, NJ 1986.
Revell, Jack (1980): Costs and Margins in Banking. An International Survey. OECD-Publications, Paris, France 1980.

Revell, Jack (1985a): Bank Profitability. Statistical Supplement, Financial Statements of Banks 1982-1986. OECD Publications, Paris, France 1985.
Revell, Jack (1985b): International Comparisons of Bank Costs and Profits. In: The Banker (London), 134, 707, pp. 25-30.
Revell, Jack (1988): Bank Profitability. Statistical Supplement, Financial Statements of Banks 1982-1986. OECD-Publications, Paris 1988.
Rhenman, E. (1973): Organization Theory for Long Range Planning. Wiley, NY 1973.
Rhyne, Lawrence (1986): The Relationship of Strategic Planning to Financial Performance. In: SMJ, 7, pp. 423-436.
Rhyne, Lawrence (1987): Information System Support: A Prerequisite for Effective Planning. In: King, William / Cleland, David (eds): Strategic Planning and Management Handbook, Van Nostrand Reinhold Co., New York 1987, pp. 210-225.
Rieger, Fritz / Wong-Rieger, Durhane (1984): The Influence of National Culture on Strategy. Paper, presented at the Annual Meeting of the Academy of Management, San Diege, August 1985.
Rieger, Fritz / Wong-Rieger, Durhane (1986): Competitive Strategies and Culture: European and Asian Approaches Compared. Paper, presented at the Annual Meeting of the Strategic Management Society, Sigapore, October 1986.
Ringbakk, K.A. (1969): Organized Planning in Major U.S. Companies. In: LRP, 2, 2, pp. 46-57.
Robinson, Richard (1983): Measures of Small firm Effectiveness for Strategic Planning Research. In: Journal of Small Business Management, 21, 2, April 1983, pp. 22-29.
Robinson, Richard / Pearce, John (1983): The Impact of Formalized Strategic Planning on Financial Performance in Small Organizations. In: SMJ, 4, 3, pp. 197-207.
Rockart, J.F. / Morton, Scott (1984): Implications of Changes in Information Technology for Corporate Strategy. In: Hax, Arnoldo (ed): Readings on Strategic Management. Ballinger, Cambridge, MA 1984, pp. 133-144.
Rudolph, Bernd (1987): Aufbau und Ablauf der strategischen Bankplanung. In: Congena (ed): Bank-Entwicklung. Gabler, Wiesbaden, FRG 1987, pp. 111-120.
Rue, Leslie (1973): How and Who of Long Range Planning. In: Business Horizons, 16, 4, pp. 23-30.
Rue, Leslie (1973a): Theoretical and Operational Implications of Long-Range Planning On Selected Measures of Financial Performance in U.S. Industry. Ph.D. Dissertation, Georgia State University, GA 1973.
Rule, John / Sedgwick, Mark (1986): The Next Ten Years in Banking: European and American Views. In: JRB, 8, 1/2, pp. 41-47.
Rust, Holger (1983): Inhaltsanalyse. Urban & Schwarzenberg, Vienna 1983.
Rutland, Peter (1985): The Myth of the Plan. Hutchinson & Co., London, GB 1985.
Said, Kamal / Seiler, Robert (1979): An Empirical Study of Long-Range Planning Systems: Strengths-Weaknesses-Outlook. In: MP, 28, 1, pp. 24-28.
Sais, Maurice / Montebello, Michel (1980): Strategic Management in Western Europe. In: Glueck, William(ed): Business Policy and Strategic Management. McGraw Hill, New York, 3rd ed. 1980.

Salancik, Gerald (1977): Commitment is Too Easy. In: Organizational Dynamics, 6, 1, pp. 62-80.
Salancik, Gerald / Pfeffer, Jeffry (1977): Who Gets Power - And How They Hold on to It. In: Organizational Dynamics, 6, 4, pp. 3-21.
Salter, Malcolm / Weinhold, Wolf (1982): What Lies Ahead for Merger Activities in the 1980s. In: JBS 2, 4, pp. 66-95.
Sapp, Richard (1980): Bank Look Ahead: A Survey of Bank Planning. In: Magazine of Bank Administration, pp. 33-40.
Sapp, Richard / Seiler, Robert (1981): The Relationship Between Long-Range Planning and Financial Performance of U.S. Commercial Banks. In: MP, 30, 2, pp. 32-36.
Sapp, Richard / Smith, Roger (1984): Strategic Management for Bankers. The Planning Forum, Oxford, OH 1984.
Sarrazin, J. (1977): Decentralized Planning in a Large French Company: An Interpretative Study. In: ISMO, 7, pp. 37-59.
Sawyer, George (1983): Corporate Planning as a Creative Process. Planning Executives Institute, Oxford, OH 1983.
Schein, E. (1985): Organizational Culture and Leadership. Jossey-Bass, San Francisco, CA 1985.
Schendel, Dan / Hofer, Charles (1979): Strategic Management: A New View of Business Policy and Planning., Little, Brown & Co., Boston, MA 1979.
Scheuch, Fritz (1982): Dienstleistungsmarketing. Vahlen, Munich, FRG 1982.
Scheuck, Fritz / Hasenauer, Rainer (1981): Entscheidungen im Marketing. Service Fachverlag WU Wien, Vienna, Austria, 2nd ed. 1981.
Schierenbeck, Henner (1987): Ertragsorientiertes Bankmanagement. Controlling in Kreditinstituten. Gabler, Wiesbaden, FRG, 2nd ed. 1987.
Schmid, Robert / Eber-Schmid, Barbara (1982): Planning in Financial Institutions: The Case for Awareness. In: MP, 31, 1, pp. 13-20.
Schneider, Susan (1987): Strategy Formulation: The Impact of National Culture. Working Paper No. 87/38, INSEAD, Fonainebleau, France, 1987.
Schneider, Susan (1989): Strategy Formulation: The Impact of National Culture. Organization Studies, 10, 2, pp. 149-168.
Scholz, Christian (1984): Planning Procedures in German Companies - Findings and Consequences. In: LRP, 17, 6, pp. 94-103.
Scholz, Christian (1987): Strategisches Management. Walter de Gruyter, New York 1987.
Schwenk, Charles (1984): Cognitive Simplification Processes in Strategic Decision-Making. In: SMJ, 5, pp. 111-128.
Schwenk, Charles (1985a): Management Illusions and Biases: Their Impact on Strategic Decisions. In: LRP, 18, 5, pp. 74-80.
Schwenk, Charles (1985b): Information, Cognitive Biases, and Commitment to a Course of Action. In: AMR, 11, 1, pp. 198-310.
Schwenk, Charles (1988): The Essence of Strategic Decision Making. Lexington Books, Lexington, MA 1988.
Schwenk, Charles / Cosier, R.A. (1985): Effects of the Expert, Devil's Advocate, and Dialectical Inquiry Methods on Prediction Performance. In: Organizational Behavior and Human Performance, 26, pp. 409-424.

Scott, Richard (1981): Organizations. Rational, Natural and Open Systems. Prentice Hall, Englewood-Cliffs, NJ 1981.
Scott, Richard (1983): The Organization of Environments: Network, Cultural, and Historical Elements. In: Meyer, John / Scott, Richard (eds): Organizational Environments. Sage Publ, London, GB 1983.
Seeger, John / Shuman, Jeffrey / Teebagy, Nicholas (1986): Measuring Strategic Planning Behaviors in Different Cultures. Paper, presented at the 6h Annual Strategic Management Society Conference, Singapore, Oct. 1986.
Seeger, John / Shuman, Jeffrey / Teebagy, Nicholas (1987): Culture-Related Differences in Entrepreneurs' Planning Behavior. Paper, presented at the 32nd Annual World Conferences of The International Council for Small Business, Vancouver, BC, Canada.
Sekaran, Uma (1986): Mapping Bank Emlopyee Perceptions of Organizational Stimuli in Two Countries. In: JM, 12, 1, pp. 19-30.
Sekaran, Uma / Snodgrass, Carol (1986a): A Model for Examining Effectiveness Cross-Culturally. In: Farmer, Richard (ed): Advances in International Comparative Management, vol. 2, JAI Press, Greenwich, CT 1986, pp. 211-232.
Sekaran, Uma / Snodgrass, Coral (1986b): Impact of Culture on Strategic Choices Governing Organizations' Relationships with the External Environment. Paper, presented at the Annual Meeting of the Academy of Management, Chicago, August 1986.
Sekaran, Uma / Snodgrass, Carol (1987): Impact of Culture on Organisation Members' Styles of Interaction with the External Environment. In: APJM, 5, 1, pp. 38-51.
Selltiz, Claire / Wrightsman, Lawrence / Cook, Stuart (1976): Research Methods in Social Relations. Holt, Rinehart & Winston, N.Y., 3rd ed 1976.
Sethi, Narendra (1987): Strategic Planning Processes in a Global Context. In: King, William / Cleland, David (1987): Strategic Planning and Management Handbook. Van Nostrand Reinhold, New York 1987, pp. 117-128.
Shank, John (1973): Long Range Planning Systems: Achieving Both 'Realism' and 'Reach.' In: JBR, 4, 3, pp. 185-193.
Shank, John / Niblock, Edward / Sandalls, William (1973): Balance 'Creativity' and 'Practicality' in Formal Planning. In: HBR, 51, 1, pp. 87-95.
Sheth, Jagdish / Sethi, Prakash (1981): A Theory of Cross-Cultural Behavior. In: Woodside/Sheth/Bennet (eds): Consumer and Industrial Buying Behavior, pp. 369-386.
Shipper, Frank / White, Charles (1983): Linking Organizational Effectiveness and Environmental Change. In: LRP, 16, 3, pp. 99-106.
Shrader, Charles / Taylor, Lew / Dalton, Dan (1984): Strategic Planning and Organizational Performance: A Critical Appraisal. In: JM, 10, 2, pp. 149-171.
Shrivastava, Paul (1983): A Typology of Organizational Learning Systems. In: JMS, 20, pp. 7-28.
Shrivastava, Paul (1985): Integrating Strategy Formulation with Organizational Culture. In: JBS, 5, 3, pp. 103-111.
Shrivastava, Paul (1987): Rigor and Practical Usefulness of Research in Strategic Management. In: SMJ, 8, pp. 77-92.

Shrivastava, Paul / Grant, John (1985): Empirically Derived Models of Strategic Decision-Making. In: SMJ, 6, pp. 97-113.

Shrivastava, Paul / Mitroff, Ian (1983): Frames of References Managers Use: A Study in Appolied Sociology of Knowledge. In: Advances in Strategic Management, vol. 1, JAI Press, New York 1983, pp. 161-182.

Siller, Helmut (1985): Grundsätze des ordnungsgemaessen strategischen Controllings. Doctoral Dissertation, University of Economics and Business Administration, Vienna, Austria, Schriftenreihe des oesterreichischen Controller-Institutes, vol. 1, Service Fachverlag an der WU Wien, Wien 1985.

Sim, A.B. (1977): Decentralized Management of Subsidiaries and Their Performance. In: MIR, 2, pp. 45-50.

Simon, Herbert (1957): Models of Man: Social and National. Wiley, New York 1957.

Simon, Herbert (1959): Theories of Decision-Making in Economics and Behavioral Science. In: American Economic Review, 49, pp. 223-83.

Simon, Herbert (1976): Administrative Behavior. The Free Press, New York, 3rd ed 1976.

Slovic, Paul / Fischhoff, Baruch / Lichtenstein, Sarah (1977): Behavioral Decision Theory. In: Annual Review of Psychology, 28, pp. 1-39.

Smircich, Linda (1983): Concepts of Culture and Organizational Analysis. In: ASQ, 28, 3, pp. 339-358.

Smith, Howard (1975): Strategies of Social Research: The Methodological Imagination. Prentice-Hall, Englewood Cliffs, NJ 1975.

Snodgrass, Carol (1984): Cultural Influences on Strategic Control System Requirements. Unpublished Ph.D. Thesis, University of Pittsburgh, PA 1984.

Snodgrass, Coral / Grant, John (1986): Cultural Influences on Strategic Planning and Control Systems. In: Farmer, Richard (ed): Advances in Strategic Management, vol. 4. JAI Press, Greenwich, CN 1986, pp. 205-228.

Snodgrass, Carol / Grant, John / Kreder, Martina (1986): The Impact of National Culture on Strategic Control Systems: A Tri-Country Study. Paper, presented at the 6th Annual Strategic Management Society Conference, Singapore, Oct. 1986.

Sorge, Arndt (1983): Review: 'Culture's Consequences.' In: ASQ, 28, 4, pp. 625-629.

Spekman, R.E. / Stern, L.W. (1979): Environmental Uncertainty and Buying Group Structure: an Emperical Investigation. In: Journal of Marketing, 43, 1, pp. 54-64.

Spender, J.C. (1980): Strategy-Making in Business. Unpublished Ph.D. Dissertation, Mancherster University, GB 1980.

Spooner, Lisa (1985a): Cultural Revolution Calls For Revamped Marketing mindset. In: Savings Institutions, March 1985, pp. 106-109.

Spooner, Lisa (1985b): Savers Survey sets the Stage for Strategic Planning. In: Savings Institutions, May 1985, pp. 72-79.

Staw, Barry (1981): The Escalation of Commitment to a Course of Action. In: AMR, 6, pp. 577-587.

Staw, Barry / Fox, Fredrick (1977): Escalation: The Determinants of Commitment to a Chosen Course of Action. In: Human Relations, 5, pp. 431-450.

Steinbruner, J.D. (1974): The Cybernetic Theory of Decision, Princeton University Press, Princeton, NJ 1974.
Steiner, George (1972): Pitfalls in Comprehensive Long Range Planning. Planning Executives Institute, Oxford, OH 1972.
Steiner, George (1979): Top Management Planning. Collier-McMillan London, GB 1979.
Steiner, George / Miner, John (1982): Management Policy and Strategy. MacMillan Publishing, New York, 2nd ed. 1982.
Steiner, George / Miner, John / Gray, Edard (1982): Management Policy and Strategy. MacMillan Publ. Co., New York, 2nd ed. 1982.
Steiner, George / Schollhammer, Hans (1975): Pitfalls in Multinational Long Range Planning. In: LRP, 8, 2, pp. 2-12. Reprinted in: Husey, David (ed.): The Truth About Corporate Planning. Pergamon Press, New York 1983, pp. 387-409.
Stevenson, Merril (1986): International Banking Survey. Wooing the Customer. In: The Economist, March 22, 1986, pp. 5-65.
Stubbard, Charles (1986a): Uncertainty, Complexity, Conflicts of Interest, Emotional Involment, and the Quality of Crisis Thinking. BEBR Faculty Working Paper No. 1289, University of Illinois at Urbana-Champaign, USA 1986.
Stubbard, Charles (1986b): Designing Strategic Planning Systems: Cognitive Elaboration, Cognitive Reduction, and the Quality of Strategic Thinking under Conditions of Uncertainty, Complexity, Conflicting Interests, and Emotional Involvement. In: BEBR Faculty Working Paper No. 1295, University of Illinois at Urbana-Champaign, USA 1986.
Süchting, Joachim (1987): Bankmanagement. Poeschl, Stuttgart, FRG, 2nd ed. 1987.
Sudman, Seymour / Bradburn, Michael (1982): Asking Questions, San Francisco, CA, Jossey Bass Publ., 1982
Sullivan, Jermiah / Nonaka, Ikujiro (1986): The Application of Organizational Learning Theory to Japanese and American Management. In: JIBS, 17, 3, pp. 127-147.
Sullivan, Jeremiah / Nonaka, Ikujiro (1988): Culture and Strategic Issue Categorization Theory. In: MIR, 28, 3, pp. 6-10.
Suzuki, Norihiko (1986): A Strategic Profile of Engineering and Nonengineering Ceo-Led Companies: The United States and Japan. in: Farmer, Richard (ed): Advances in International Comparative Management, vol. 2. JAI Press, NY 1986, pp. 69-83.
Szyperski, Norbert (1974): Entscheidungstheorie. Poeschl, Stuttgart, FRG 1974.
Szyperski, Norbert / Müller-Böling (1986): Organizational Structure of Planning Systems in Different Environments. In: Witte, E. / Zimmermann, H.-J. (eds): Empirical Research on Organizational Decision-Making. North-Holland, Wiesbaden, FRG 1986.
Szyperski, Norbert / Schünemann, Jörg (1973): Planungsteoretische Grundlagen der Unternehmensplanung. In: Grochla, E. / Szyperski, N. (eds)): Modell- und Computergestützte Unternehmensplanung. Wiesbaden, FRG 1973, pp. 197-202.
Takahashi, Nobuo / Takayangi, Satoru (1985): Decision Procedure Models and Empirical Research: The Japanese Experience. In: Human Relations, 38, 8, pp. 767-780.

Taylor, Bernard (1987): An Overview of Strategic Planning Styles. In: King, William / Cleland, David (eds): Strategic Planning and Management Handbook. Van Nostrand Reinhold co., New York, 1987.

Taylor, Bernard / Irving, Paul (1971): Organized Planning in Major U.K. Companies. In: LRP, 3, 4, 1971.

Taylor, Edward (1871): Primitive Culture. John Murray, London, GB 1871.

Thomas, Christopher (1986): First Banking and Finance Industry Survey of Australian Chief Executives. Egon Zehnder Int'l, July 1986.

Thomas, Howard (1984): Strategic Decision Analysis: Applied Decision Analysis and Its Role in the Strategic Management Process. In: SMJ, 5, pp. 139-156.

Thompson, Arthur / Strickland, A.J. (1983): Strategy Formulation and Implementation. Business Publications, Inc., Plano, TX, revised ed. 1983.

Thompson, James (1967): Organizations in Action. McGraw Hill, New York 1967.

Tilston, Donald / Wightman, David / McRae, Donald (1985): Innovative Success in the Retail Financial Market. PA Consulting Group & Lafferty Publications, London, GB 1985.

Töpfer, Armin (1976): Planungs- und Kontrollsysteme industrieller Unternehmungen. Eine theoretische, technologische und empirische Analyse. Duncker & Humboldt, Berlin, FRG 1976.

Tosi, Henry / Slocum, John (1984): Contingency Theory: Some Suggested Directions. In: JM, 10, 1, pp. 9-26.

Triandis, Harry (1972): The Analysis of Subjective Culture. Wiley, NY 1972.

Triandis, Harry (1977): Interpersonal Behavior. Brooks/Cole, Monetery, CA 1977.

Triandis, Harry (1982): Review of Culture's Consequences: International Differences in Work-Related Values. In: Human Organization, 41, 1, pp. 86-90.

Triandis, Harry (1983): Dimensions of Cultural Variation as Parametes of Organizational Theories. In: ISMO, 12, 4, pp. 139-169.

Triandis, Harry (1984): A Theoretical Framework for the more Efficient Construction of Culture Assimilators. In: International Journal of Intercultural Relations, 8, 3, pp. 310-330.

Triandis, Harry / Berry, J.W. (1980): Handbook of Cross-Cultural Psychology, vol. 2, Methodology. Booz, Allyn & Bacon, Boston, MA 1980.

Trice, Harrison / Beyer, Janice (1984): Studying Organizational Cultures Through Rites and Ceremonials. In: AMR, 9, 4, pp. 653-669.

Tsurumi, Yoshi (1976): The Japanese Are Coming. Balling Publishing, Cambridge, MA 1976.

Tull, Charles (1979): A New Look at Bank Planning. In: MP, 28, 6, pp. 37-39.

Turillo, Michael (1985): A National Study shows the appeal of service and delivery system mixes. In: Savings Institutions, March 1985, pp. 90-96.

Tushman, Michael / Romanelli, Elaine (1985): Organizational Evolution: A Metomorphosis Model of Convergence and Reorientation. In: Cummings, L.L. / Staw, B. (eds): Research in Organizational Behavior, Vol. 7. JAI Press, Greenwich, CT, 1985, pp. 171-222.

Tversky, Amos / Kahneman, Daniel (1974): Judgment under Uncertainty: Heuristics and Biases. In: Science, 185, 4157, pp. 1124-1131.

Twomey, Daniel / Scherr, Frederick / Hunt, Walter (1988): Configuration of a Functional Department: A Study of Contextual and Structural Variables. In: Journal of Organizational Behavior, 9, 1, pp. 61-75.

Tzu, Sun (1963): The Art of War. Translated reprint. Oxford University Press, Oxford, GB 1963.

Ulvila, Jacob / Brown, Rex (1982): Decision Analysis Comes of Age. In: HBR, 60, 5, pp. 130-140.

Ungson, Gerardo / Braunstein, Daniel / Hall, Phillip (1981): Managerial Information Processing: A Research Review. In: ASQ, 26, 2, pp. 116-134.

Unterman, Israel (1973): Strategic Planning in Banks. In: Bankers Magazine, 156, pp. 57-65.

U.S. Office of Management and Budget (1987): Standard Industrial Classification Manual. Executive Office of the President, Washington, DC, U.S. Government Printing Office, 1987.

Uyterhoeven, Hugo (1972): General Managers in the Middle. In: HBR, 50, 2, pp. 75-86.

Venkatraman, N. / Grant, John (1986): Construct Measurement in Organizational Strategy Research: A Critique and Proposal. In: AMR, 11, 1, pp. 71-87.

Vernon, Raymond (1977): Storm over the Multinationals. Harvard University Press, Cambridge, MA 1977.

Vittas, Dimitri (1978): Public Ownership in Banking: A Survey of Seven Countries. In: Issues in Bank Regulation, 2, 2, pp. 7-22.

Volkema, Roger (1986): Problem Formulation as a Pusposive Activity. In: SMJ, 7, pp. 267-179.

Wabitsch, F. (1977): Eine empirische Untersuchung der Planung in österreichischen Kreditinstituten unter besonderer Berücksichtigung von Informationsgesichtspunkten. Unpublished Doctoral Dissertation, University of Economics and Business Administration, Vienna, Austria 1977.

Waite, David (1982): Deregulation and the Banking Industry. In: Bankers Magazine, Jan/Feb. 1982, pp. 26-35.

Wakolbinger, Rosemarie (1980): Statistik 2. Service Fachverlag, Univeristy of Economics, Vienna, Austria, 6th edition, 1980.

Walsh, James (1985): Cognition and Strategy: The Effects of Schematic Information Processign on Strategy Making. Paper, presented at the Annual Meeting of the Academy of Management, San Diego, 1985.

Ward's (1983): Ward's Directory of 51.000 Largest Companies, Information Access Company, Belmont, CA 1983.

Ward's (1985): Ward`s Business Directory. Major International Companies, vol. 3, 25th aniversary edition. Information Access Company, Belmont, CA 1985.

Weber, Max (1946): Bureaucracy. In: Shafritz, Jay / Hyde, Albert (eds, 1978): Classics of Public Administration. Moore Publ., Oak Park, IL 1978, pp. 23-29.

Webster, Fredrick / Wind, Yoram (1972): A General Model for Understanding Organizational Buying Behavior. In: Journal of Marketing, 36, April 1972, pp. 12-19.

Weick, Karl (1969): The Social Psychology of Organizing. Addison-Wesley, Reading, MA 1969.

Weick, Karl (1977): Enactment Processes in Organization. In: Staw, B / Salancik G. (eds): New Directions in Organizational Behavior. St. Clair, Chicago, IL 1977, pp. 267-300.

Weick, Karl (1979a): The Social Psychology of Organizations. 2nd ed., Addison-Wesley, Reading, MA 1979.

Weick, Karl (1979b): Cognitive Processes in Organizations. In: Staw, B. (ed): Research in Organizational Behavior, Vol. 1. JAI Presss, Greenwich, CT 1979, pp. 41-74.

Weigele, Otmar (1983): Strategische Unternehmensplanung in Universalbanken. Schriftenreihe des Instituts für Kredit- und Versicherungswirtschaft, Abteilung Bankbetriebslehre. Bühler, W. (ed). Doctoral Dissertation, University of Economics and Business Administration, Vienna, Austria, Service Fachverlag, Vienna, Austria 1983.

Wells, Louis (1972): The Product Life Cycle and International Trade. Harvard University Press, Boston, MA 1972.

Westwood, Robert / Everett, James (1987): Culture's Consequences: A Methodology for Comparative Management Studies in Southeast Asia? In: APJM, 4, 3, pp. 187-202.

Wheelen, Thomas / Hunger, David (1984): Strategic Management. Addison-Wesley, Reading, MA 1984.

Whetten, David (1980): Organizational Decline: A Neglected Topic in Organizational Science. In: AMR, 5, 4, pp. 577-588.

White, Donald / Jensen, Thomas (1987): Redefining Cross National Comparison: The Case for Subcultural Analysis. Paper, presented at the 1987 Annual Meeting of the Academy of Management, New Orleans, August 10, 1987.

Wilson, J.G. (1986): Banking Policy and Structure: A comparative Analysis. Croom Helm, Breckenham, Kent, GB 1986.

Witte, Eberhard (1971): Das Informationsverhalten in Informationssytemen - Die These der unvollkommenen Informationsnachfrage. In: Grochla, E. / Szyperski, N. (eds): MIS - Management-Informationssysteme. Wiesbaden, FRG 1971, pp. 831-842.

Witte, Eberhard (1972): Field Research on Complex Decision Making. The Phase Theorem. In: ISMO, 59, pp. 156-182.

Wood, Robley (1980): Long Range Planning in Large United States Banks. In: LRP, 13, 3, pp. 91-98.

Wood, Robley / LaForge, Lawrence (1979): The Impact of Comprehensive Planning on Financial Performance. In: AMJ, 22, pp. 516-526.

Wood, Robley /LaForge, Lawrence (1980): The Evolution and Current State of Development of Profit Planning Systems in Large U.S. Banks. In: MP, 28, 6, pp. 26-31.

Wood, Robley / LaForge, Lawrence (1981): Toward the Development of a Planning Scale: An Example from the Banking Industry. In: SMJ, 2, pp. 209-216.

Woodward, Joan (1958): Management and Technology. Her Majesty's Stationery Office, London 1958.

Woodward, Joan (1962): Industrial Organizations. Oxford University Press, London, GB 1962.

Wrapp, Edward (1984): Good Managers Don't Make Policy Decisions. In: HBR, 62, 4, pp. 8-21.

Wright, David (1982): New Zealand - A Newcomer to Planning. In: LRP, 15, 3, pp. 122-131.

Wright, Don (1985): The Effective Bank Director. Reston Publishing, Reston, VA 1985.

Wright, George / Phillips, Lawrence (1980): Cultural Variations in Probabalistic Thinking/ Alternative Was of Dealing with Uncertainty. In: International Journal of Psychology, 15, 4, pp. 239-251.

Wright, Norman (1982): Southern Banking Survey of Critical Issues Facing Chief Executive Officers. Egon Zehnder International, Nov. 1982.

Wright, Norman (1986): Second Survey of Bank Chief Executives in Asia. Egon Zehnder International, Nov. 1986.

Wright, Norman (1987): Third Survey of Bank Chief Executives in Asia. Egon Zehnder International, 1987.

Wright, Richard / Pauli, Gunter (1988): Die Zweite Welle. Orac, Vienna, Austria 1988.

Yalif, Anat (1982): Strategic Planning Techniques. In: The Magazine of Bank Administration, April 1982, pp. 22-26.

Yamaguchi, Tamotsu (1988): The Challenge of Internationalization: Japan's Kokusaika. In: AME, 22, 1, pp. 33-36.

Yang, Charles (1984): Demystifying Japanese Mangement Principles. In: HBR, 62, 6, pp. 172-182.

Zaltman, Gerald / Wallendor, Melanie (1982): Consumer Behavior: Basic Findings and Management Implications. John Wiley & Sons, 2nd ed 1982.

Zapotocky, Stefan / Malzer, Michael (1984): Anmerkungen zur Unternehmensplanung im Bankbetrieb. In: ÖBA, 32, 9, pp. 307-319.

Zehetner, Franz (1988): Die europäische Herausforderung für österreichische Banken. In: ÖBA, 33, 3, pp. 195-211.

Zutshi, Ravinder (1981): Strategic Planning Systems Evaluation Methodology: A Systems Approach. Ph.D. Thesis, University of Pittsburgh, University Microfilms Int'l, Ann Arbor, MI 1981.

Appendix 1: US vs. German Top 300 Test Statistics

T-Test Variable	Label	Mean u US	Mean u GER	Std Dev s US	Std Dev s GER	t-Value	DF	Alpha	Original 1-5 Likert X2	DF	Alpha	Variable
LPY	LPYears	4,8	6,2	1,3	2,3	-2,51	29,80	0,018	15,222	7	0,033	LPY
MPY	MPYears	2,9	3,3	0,8	1,7	-0,82	18,45	0,422	6,773	5	0,238	MPY
SPM	SPMonths	12,2	12,0	0,9	0,0	n.a.	n.a.	n.a.	0,775	1	1,000	SPM

T-Test Variable	Label	Mean u US	Mean u GER	Std Dev s US	Std Dev s GER	t Value	DF	Alpha	Recoded 1-3 Likert X2	DF	Alpha	Variable
Reas1	Problems	3,49	4,22	1,27	1,04	-2,40	53,11	0,020	4,871	2	0,087	Reas1
Reas2	Learn f Past	2,94	3,58	1,22	1,07	-2,17	57,73	0,034	3,584	2	0,166	Reas2
Reas3	Decide	2,97	3,68	1,30	1,07	-2,33	57,19	0,024	3,728	2	0,155	Reas3
Reas4	Act early	3,81	4,20	0,92	0,91	-1,65	52,05	0,104	1,000	2	0,606	Reas4
Reas5	Antpte Chage	4,21	4,68	0,81	0,63	-2,54	56,80	0,014	1,436	2	0,487	Reas5
Reas6	Imprve Budgt	2,94	2,83	1,33	1,30	0,33	52,60	0,743	0,465	2	0,792	Reas6
Reas7	Avoid Uncert	2,68	2,83	1,11	1,07	-0,50	48,37	0,622	0,444	2	0,801	Reas7
Reas8	Colect Ideas	3,22	3,38	1,20	1,10	-0,51	52,39	0,613	0,077	2	0,962	Reas8
Reas9	Have Guide	4,43	3,57	0,82	1,41	2,66	31,74	0,012	7,329	2	0,025	Reas9
Reas10	Imprv Connct	3,61	3,52	1,15	1,09	0,31	53,76	0,754	0,054	2	0,973	Reas10
Reas11	Coord Projct	3,31	3,56	1,19	1,19	-0,82	51,72	0,416	0,229	2	0,891	Reas11
Reas12	Chge Alterns	3,44	3,45	1,21	1,29	-0,04	42,66	0,969	3,873	2	0,144	Reas12
Reas13	Integrate	2,69	2,82	1,03	1,22	-0,41	40,09	0,683	0,102	2	0,951	Reas13
Reas14	Rsurce Allct	4,00	3,25	1,12	1,29	- 2,32	44,47	0,025	6,019	2	0,049	Reas14
Reas15	Clarify Goal	4,42	4,00	0,81	1,32	-- 1,40	36,32	0,169	3,523	2	0,172	Reas15
Reas16	Control	2,12	2,58	1,01	1,41	-1,39	39,01	0,174	4,609	2	0,099	Reas16

T-Test Variable	Label	Mean u US	Mean u GER	Std Dev s US	Std Dev s GER	t Value	DF	Alpha	Recoded 1-3 Likert X2	DF	Alpha	Variable
Char1	Defin Issues	4,31	4,44	0,82	0,82	-0,63	51,83	0,532	0,208	2	0,901	Char1
Char2	Solve Probln	2,61	2,88	1,08	1,23	-0,86	44,89	0,396	0,528	2	0,768	Char2
Char3	Quantitative	2,14	2,77	1,01	1,31	-2,05	45,52	0,046	3,103	2	0,212	Char3
Char4	Project Ortd	2,72	3,20	1,21	1,29	-1,46	49,56	0,151	3,497	2	0,174	Char4
Char5	Action Ortd	4,14	3,52	1,05	1,26	2,02	45,29	0,050	6,344	2	0,041	Char5
Char6	Change Ortd	3,94	3,44	0,89	1,04	1,97	46,36	0,055	2,073	2	0,355	Char6
Char7	SU -> OI	3,50	3,83	1,08	1,13	-1,14	47,97	0,260	1,726	2	0,422	Char7
Char8	OI -> SU	3,77	4,00	1,00	1,10	-0,81	46,36	0,422	1,499	2	0,472	Char8
Char9	Cons Solve	1,87	1,91	1,20	1,37	-0,13	43,67	0,898	0,279	2	0,869	Char9
Char10	Cons Frame	2,17	1,74	1,45	1,25	1,14	50,35	0,258	3,962	2	0,137	Char10
Char11	Bonus Plan	3,86	3,08	1,12	1,41	2,29	43,99	0,027	8,677	2	0,013	Char11
Char12	No Updates	1,64	1,72	0,99	1,14	-0,29	46,99	0,774	0,960	2	0,618	Char12
Char13	Annual Cycle	4,34	3,76	1,16	1,20	1,88	50,81	0,066	6,883	2	0,032	Char13
Char14	Staff Plans	1,64	3,38	0,83	1,56	-5,01	31,88	0,000	26,100	2	0,000	Char14
Char15	Line Plans	4,14	2,44	1,02	1,45	5,07	40,13	0,000	21,233	2	0,000	Char15
Char16	Intuition	2,67	1,96	1,17	1,16	2,31	49,77	0,025	7,802	2	0,020	Char16
Char17	Incremental	3,34	3,37	1,16	1,02	-1,09	46,74	0,280	2,545	2	0,280	Char17
Char18	Career	2,97	2,57	1,08	1,27	1,27	41,44	0,212	1,911	2	0,385	Char18
Char19	Variety	3,27	3,11	1,13	1,19	0,50	35,78	0,623	2,556	2	0,279	Char19
Char20	Well-Defined	2,08	2,60	1,23	1,39	-1,39	35,39	0,174	1,170	2	0,557	Char20

u = Mean; s = Standard Deviation; DF = Degrees of Freedom; alpha = significance level; X2 = Chi-Square.

USTop300 vs GermanTop300 Test

T-Test		Mean		Std Dev		t	DF	Alpha	Recoded 1-3 Likert			
Variable	Label	u US	u GER	s US	s GER	Value			X2	DF	Alpha	Variable
Act1	Env Forecast	3,89	4,08	1,08	1,15	-0,66	49,71	0,511	0,067	2	0,967	Act1
Act2	SW-Analysis	4,34	4,58	0,64	0,70	-1,34	51,00	0,187	3,610	2	0,164	Act2
Act3	Extrapolate	3,49	4,52	1,17	0,82	-4,02	57,99	0,000	8,811	2	0,012	Act3
Act4	Issues	4,26	4,52	0,78	0,77	-1,30	52,25	0,201	1,088	2	0,580	Act4
Act5	Prod Venturs	3,29	3,52	1,23	1,01	-0,81	56,83	0,421	5,917	2	0,051	Act5
Act6	M&A's	3,89	2,30	1,18	1,29	4,71	44,15	0,000	15,050	2	0,001	Act6
Act7	New Markets	3,94	3,72	0,84	1,17	0,81	40,85	0,421	2,086	2	0,352	Act7
Act8	Tackl Probln	4,00	3,73	0,77	1,15	1,03	40,940	0,307	5,773	2	0,056	Act8
Act9	Contigency P	3,11	3,24	1,08	1,49	-0,38	43,34	0,708	0,355	2	0,837	Act9
Act10	Project Revs	3,15	3,08	1,17	1,14	0,20	50,37	0,846	1,073	2	0,585	Act10
Act11	Perfnce Revs	3,23	4,00	1,37	1,09	-2,44	58,66	0,018	7,113	2	0,029	Act11

T-Test		Mean		Std Dev		t	DF	Alpha	Recoded 1-3 Likert			
Variable	Label	u US	u GER	s US	s GER	Value			X2	DF	Alpha	Variable
Behav1	Projections	2,84	3,27	1,04	1,05	-1,40	37,93	0,170	3,236	2	0,198	Behav1
Behav2	Bargaining	2,86	3,09	1,17	1,26	-0,62	40,37	0,536	3,068	2	0,216	Behav2
Behav3	Padding	3,20	2,63	1,04	1,31	1,48	26,83	0,150	5,787	2	0,055	Behav3
Behav4	Plan * End	3,13	2,27	1,25	1,28	2,27	42,82	0,028	6,873	2	0,032	Behav4
Behav5	Rsist Discpl	3,25	2,95	0,97	1,20	0,93	37,55	0,358	1,876	2	0,391	Behav5
Behav6	Rsist Change	3,30	3,09	1,15	1,07	0,68	47,24	0,502	1.744	2	0,418	Behav6
Behav7	Fear	2,81	2,94	1,23	1,25	-0,34	34,06	0,733	0,277	2	0,871	Behav7
Behav8	Day-to-Day	3,43	2,89	0,96	1,41	1,44	29,17	0,161	6,679	2	0,035	Behav8
Behav9	Department	3,03	3,14	1,26	1,21	-0,31	46,54	0,755	0,017	2	0,991	Behav9
Behav10	Expectation	3.03	3,23	1,11	0,92	-0,70	49,64	0,489	1,515	2	0,469	Behav10
Behav11	Compliance	2,96	2,90	1,09	0,97	0,21	43,47	0,836	1,303	2	0,521	Behav11
Behav12	File	3,19	3,16	1,20	1,26	0,09	37,84	0,927	6,003	2	0,998	Behav12
Behav13	Bored	2,93	2,67	1,13	1,59	-0.57	21,57	0,572	5,503	2	0,063	Behav13
Behav14	Credibility	3,16	2,95	1,03	1,31	0,58	33,29	0,563	1,012	2	0,603	Behav14

Appendix 2: Ten-Country Group Test Statistics

ANOVA Variable	Label	u AUT	u FRA	u GBR	u ITA	u SPA	u AUL	u JAP	u Lat1	u Lat2	u CON	F Ratio	F Prob.	K-W X2	Alpha n-par	Variable
LPY	LPYears	7,2	5,3	6,4	6,2	4,6	5,6	3,9	5,2	5,8	6,4	2,47	0,013	29,56	0,000	LPY
MPY	MPYears	3,9	3,2	3,0	4,2	2,7	3,4	2,6	2,5	3,0	3,2	4,55	0,000	35,85	0,000	MPY
Reas1	Problems	3,6	3,9	3,6	4,3	4,1	3,7	4,4	4,2	4,2	3,6	2,97	0,002	24,56	0,004	Reas1
Reas2	Learn f Past	2,9	3,8	3,5	3,0	3,4	3,1	4,3	3,4	3,8	2,9	3,92	0,000	32,85	0,000	Reas2
Reas3	Decide	3,0	3,9	3,0	3,2	3,8	2,6	4,0	3,0	3,4	4,0	4,25	0,000	33,92	0,000	Reas3
Reas4	Act early	4,0	3,6	3,8	4,0	4,0	3,9	3,3	3,6	4,4	3,8	2,48	0,010	22,72	0,007	Reas4
Reas5	Antple Chage	4,5	4,2	4,5	3,8	4,5	4,3	4,3	4,2	4,0	4,1	1,75	0,079	18,61	0,029	Reas5
Reas9	Have Guide	3,9	3,5	4,3	4,1	4,2	4,0	4,6	4,4	4,3	4,3	2,87	0,003	28,04	0,000	Reas9
Reas14	Rsurce Allct	3,0	4,2	4,4	4,5	3,6	4,0	3,9	4,0	4,0	3,7	4,55	0,000	35,10	0,000	Reas14

Variable	Label	u AUT	u FRA	u GBR	u ITA	u SPA	u AUL	u JAP	u Lat1	u Lat2	u CON	F Ratio	F Prob.	K-W X2	Alpha n-par	Variable
Char3	Quantitative	2,7	2,7	2,9	3,4	2,2	2,7	3,7	3,2	3,3	2,7	3,86	0,000	31,59	0,000	Char3
Char5	Action Ortd	3,5	4,0	3,6	4,2	3,3	3,5	4,3	3,6	4,0	4,1	2,95	0,002	22,20	0,008	Char5
Char6	Change Ortd	3,8	4,3	3,5	3,3	2,5	3,4	3,5	3,3	3,1	3,4	4,04	0,000	31,40	0,000	Char6
Char11	Bonus Plan	2,6	3,5	3,5	3,2	2,7	3,1	2,5	3,3	2,7	3,2	2,00	0,040	17,85	0,040	Char11
Char13	Annual Cycle	4,2	3,9	4,4	4,6	3,8	4,4	1,5	3,7	4,4	4,2	13,94	0,000	60,54	0,000	Char13
Char14	Staff Plans	2,7	3,1	2,6	3,6	3,3	2,4	4,3	3,2	4,0	2,5	5,19	0,000	39,93	0,000	Char14
Char15	Line Plans	3,0	3,6	3,7	3,5	3,2	3,8	2,0	3,0	3,2	3,1	2,94	0,003	24,00	0,004	Char15
Char16	Intuition	2,2	2,5	1,9	2,6	2,3	2,1	2,6	2,8	2,8	2,5	1,28	0,249	9,92	0,357	Char16

Variable	Label	u AUT	u FRA	u GBR	u ITA	u SPA	u AUL	u JAP	u Lat1	u Lat2	u CON	F Ratio	F Prob.	K-W X2	Alpha n-par	Variable
Act3	Extrapolate	3,8	3,9	4,3	3,1	3,7	4,4	3,9	3,5	4,1	3,6	1,64	0,102	12,57	0,180	Act3
Act6	M&R's	2,0	3,3	3,8	3,2	2,1	3,9	3,2	2,0	2,2	2,6	6,75	0,000	50,00	0,000	Act6
Act11	Perfmce Revs	4,0	3,7	3,5	4,2	3,5	3,6	4,4	4,1	4,2	3,5	2,33	0,016	20,20	0,017	Act11

Variable	Label	u AUT	u FRA	u GBR	u ITA	u SPA	u AUL	u JAP	u Lat1	u Lat2	u CON	F Ratio	F Prob.	K-W X2	Alpha n-par	Variable
Behav3	Padding	3,5	3,4	3,1	3,8	3,1	3,3	4,2	3,9	3,4	3,4	1,94	0,051	16,30	0,061	Behav3
Behav4	Plan = End	3,2	3,1	2,3	3,4	3,3	3,6	2,9	3,5	3,4	2,7	1,25	0,267	13,09	0,159	Behav4
Behav8	Day-to-Day	3,5	3,4	3,3	4,1	4,0	3,7	4,5	4,0	3,4	3,8	2,01	0,041	19,89	0,019	Behav8
Behav13	Bored	1,7	2,9	3,2	4,0	3,7	3,4	3,7	3,7	3,8	3,3	3,46	0,000	24,23	0,004	Behav13

GPSR Compliance

The European Union's (EU) General Product Safety Regulation (GPSR) is a set of rules that requires consumer products to be safe and our obligations to ensure this.

If you have any concerns about our products, you can contact us on ProductSafety@springernature.com

In case Publisher is established outside the EU, the EU authorized representative is:

Springer Nature Customer Service Center GmbH
Europaplatz 3
69115 Heidelberg, Germany

Batch number: 10732714

Printed by Printforce, the Netherlands